Treasures

A Reading/Language Arts Program

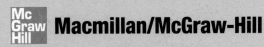

Macmillan/McGraw-Hill

Contributors

Time Magazine

RFB&D 🎧
learning through listening

Students with print disabilities may be eligible to obtain an accessible, audio version of the pupil edition of this textbook. Please call Recording for the Blind & Dyslexic at 1-800-221-4792 for complete information.

A

The McGraw·Hill Companies

Macmillan/McGraw-Hill

Published by Macmillan/McGraw-Hill, of McGraw-Hill Education, a division of The McGraw-Hill Companies, Inc., Two Penn Plaza, New York, New York 10121.

Printed in the United States of America

1 2 3 4 5 6 7 8 9 006/055 13 12 11 10 09

Treasures

A Reading/Language Arts Program

Program Authors

Dr. Diane August
Senior Research Scientist, Center for
  Applied Linguistics
Washington, D.C.

Dr. Donald R. Bear
University of Nevada, Reno
Reno, Nevada

Dr. Janice A. Dole
University of Utah
Salt Lake City, Utah

Dr. Jana Echevarria
California State University, Long Beach
Long Beach, California

Dr. Douglas Fisher
San Diego State University
San Diego, California

Dr. David J. Francis
University of Houston
Houston, Texas

Dr. Vicki L. Gibson
Educational Consultant, Gibson Hasbrouck
  and Associates, Massachusetts

Dr. Jan E. Hasbrouck
Educational Consultant – J.H. Consulting
Los Angeles, California

Dr. Scott G. Paris
Center for Research and Practice,
National Institute of Education
Singapore

Dr. Timothy Shanahan
University of Illinois at Chicago
Chicago, Illinois

Dr. Josefina V. Tinajero
University of Texas at El Paso
El Paso, Texas

Macmillan/McGraw-Hill

Program Authors

Dr. Diane August

Center for Applied Linguistics, Washington, D.C.

- Principal Investigator, Developing Literacy in Second-Language Learners: Report of the National Literacy Panel on Language-Minority Children and Youth
- Member of the New Standards Literacy Project, Grades 4–5

Dr. Donald R. Bear

University of Nevada, Reno

- Author of *Words Their Way* and *Words Their Way with English Learners*
- Director, E.L. Cord Foundation Center for Learning and Literacy

Dr. Janice A. Dole

University of Utah

- Investigator, IES Study on Reading Interventions
- National Academy of Sciences, Committee Member: Teacher Preparation Programs, 2005–2007

Dr. Jana Echevarria

California State University, Long Beach

- Author of *Making Content Comprehensible for English Learners: The SIOP Model*
- Principal Researcher, Center for Research on the Educational Achievement and Teaching of English Language Learners

Dr. Douglas Fisher

San Diego State University

- Co-Director, Center for the Advancement of Reading, California State University
- Author of *Language Arts Workshop: Purposeful Reading and Writing Instruction* and *Reading for Information in Elementary School*

Dr. David J. Francis

University of Houston

- Director of the Center for Research on Educational Achievement and Teaching of English Language Learners (CREATE)
- Director, Texas Institute for Measurement, Evaluation, and Statistics

Dr. Vicki Gibson

Educational Consultant Gibson Hasbrouck and Associates, Massachusetts

- Author of *Differentiated Instruction: Grouping for Success*

Dr. Jan E. Hasbrouck

Educational Consultant JH Consulting, Los Angeles

- Developed Oral Reading Fluency Norms for Grades 1–8
- Author of *The Reading Coach: A How-to Manual for Success*

Dr. Scott G. Paris

Center for Research and Practice, National Institute of Education, Singapore

- Principal Investigator, CIERA, 1997–2004

Dr. Timothy Shanahan

University of Illinois at Chicago

- Member, National Reading Panel
- President, International Reading Association, 2006
- Chair, National Literacy Panel and National Early Literacy Panel

Dr. Josefina V. Tinajero

University of Texas at El Paso

- Past President, NABE and TABE
- Co-Editor of *Teaching All the Children: Strategies for Developing Literacy in an Urban Setting* and *Literacy Assessment of Second Language Learners*

Consulting and Contributing Authors

Dr. Adria F. Klein
Professor Emeritus,
California State University,
San Bernardino

• President, California
  Reading Association, 1995
• Co-Author of *Interactive
  Writing* and *Interactive
  Editing*

Dolores B. Malcolm
St. Louis Public Schools
St. Louis, MO

• Past President, International
  Reading Association
• Member, IRA Urban
  Diversity Initiatives
  Commission
• Member, RIF Advisory
  Board

Dr. Doris Walker-Dalhouse
Minnesota State University,
Moorhead

• Author of articles on
  multicultural literature and
  reading instruction in urban
  schools
• Co-Chair of the Ethnicity, Race,
  and Multilingualism Committee,
  NRC

Dinah Zike
Educational Consultant

• Dinah-Might Activities, Inc.
  San Antonio, TX

Program Consultants

Kathy R. Bumgardner
Language Arts Instructional
Specialist
Gaston County Schools, NC

Elizabeth Jimenez
CEO, GEMAS Consulting
Pomona, CA

Dr. Sharon F. O'Neal
Associate Professor
College of Education
Texas State University
San Marcos, TX

Program Reviewers

Mable Alfred
Reading/Language Arts Administrator
Chicago Public Schools, IL

Suzie Bean
Teacher, Kindergarten
Mary W. French Academy
Decatur, IL

Linda Burch
Teacher, Kindergarten
Public School 184
Brooklyn, NY

Robert J. Dandorph
Principal
John F. Kennedy Elementary School
North Bergen, NJ

Suzanne Delacruz
Principal, Washington Elementary
Evanston, IL

Carol Dockery
Teacher, Grade 3
Mulberry Elementary
Milford, OH

Karryl Ellis
Teacher, Grade 1
Durfee School, Decatur, IL

Christina Fong
Teacher, Grade 3
William Moore Elementary School
Las Vegas, NV

Lenore Furman
Teacher, Kindergarten
Abington Avenue School
Newark, NJ

Sister Miriam Kaeser
Assistant Superintendent
Archdiocese of Cincinnati
Cincinnati, OH

LaVonne Lee
Principal, Rozet Elementary School
Gillette, WY

SuEllen Mackey
Teacher, Grade 5
Washington Elementary School
Decatur, IL

Jan Mayes
Curriculum Coordinator
Kent School District
Kent, WA

Bonnie Nelson
Teacher, Grade 1
Solano School, Phoenix, AZ

Cyndi Nichols
Teacher, Grade K/1
North Ridge Elementary School
Commack, NY

Sharron Norman
Curriculum Director
Lansing School District
Lansing, MI

Renee Ottinger
Literacy Leader, Grades K–5
Coronado Hills Elementary School
Denver, CO

Michael Pragman
Principal, Woodland Elementary School
Lee's Summit, MO

Carol Rose
Teacher, Grade 2
Churchill Elementary School
Muskegon, MI

Laura R. Schmidt-Watson
Director of Academic Services
Parma City School District, OH

Dianne L. Skoy
Literacy Coordinator, Grades K–5
Minneapolis Public Schools
Minneapolis, MN

Charles Staszewski
ESL Teacher, Grades 3–5
John H. William School, No. 5
Rochester, NY

Patricia Synan
New York City Department
of Education

Stephanie Yearian
Teacher, Grade 2
W. J. Zahnow Elementary
Waterloo, IL

Unit 6   The Big Question

What is your neighborhood like?

Enduring Understanding and Essential Questions

In this unit, children will read and write about their neighborhood. As they progress through the unit, they will also develop and apply key comprehension skills that good readers use as they read.

Big Idea	Enduring Understanding	Essential Questions
Theme: Neighborhood	Many different people live and work in our neighborhood.	What is your neighborhood like?

Comprehension	Enduring Understanding	Essential Questions
Identify Main Idea and Details Week 1 Week 2	Good readers identify the main idea of what they read and the details that support it.	What is the main idea and the details that support it?
Retell Week 3	Good readers can retell the important parts of a story in order.	How can you retell the story using the important parts from the beginning, middle, and end of the story?

Theme: Neighborhood

Planning the Unit

Teaching the Unit

Literature Selections

Wrapping Up the Unit

Additional Resources

Unit Assessment

Unit 6 Contents

Theme: **Neighborhood**

Unit Theme Opener, page xvi

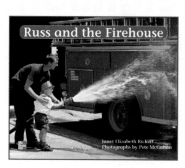

Big Book

Big Book

	WEEK 1	**WEEK 2**
ORAL LANGUAGE		
• **Oral Vocabulary**	**Theme** Our Neighborhood	**Theme** People and Places
• **Phonemic Awareness**	**Phonemic Awareness** Phoneme Isolation Phoneme Blending Phoneme Segmentation	**Phonemic Awareness** Phoneme Isolation Phoneme Segmentation Phoneme Blending
WORD STUDY		
• **Phonics**	**Phonics** Introduce /h/h (Initial)	**Phonics** Introduce /d/d (Initial and Final), /r/r (Initial)
• **High-Frequency Words**	**High-Frequency Word** *are*	**High-Frequency Words** *for*, *you*
READING		
• **Listening Comprehension**	**Comprehension** **Strategy:** Summarize **Skill:** Identify Main Idea and Details	**Comprehension** **Strategy:** Summarize **Skill:** Identify Main Idea and Details
• **Fluency**	**Fluency** Build Fluency: Word Automaticity Echo-Read, Read for Fluency	**Fluency** Build Fluency: Word Automaticity Echo-Read, Choral-Read, Read for Fluency
• **Leveled Readers**	**Approaching** *In My Neighbohood* **On Level** *Where Are We?* **Beyond** *Places in the Neighborhood* **ELL** *We Are Here*	**Approaching** *People Who Help* **On Level** *This Is for You* **Beyond** *The Good Idea* **ELL** *For You*
LANGUAGE ARTS		
• **Grammar**	**Grammar** Sentences	**Grammar** Sentences
• **Writing**	**Writing** Dialogue	**Writing** Directions

Read-Aloud Trade Book

WEEK 3

Theme
Neighborhood Workers

Phonemic Awareness
Phoneme Categorization
Phoneme Segmentation
Phoneme Blending

Phonics
Review Initial: /h/h, /d/d, /r/r; Final /d/d;
-ad, -at, -an, -ap, -am; Word Families

High-Frequency Words
are, for, you

Comprehension
Strategy: Summarize
Skill: Retell

Fluency
Build Fluency: Word Automaticity
Echo-Read, Choral-Read, Read for Fluency

Approaching *We Work for You*

On Level *Panda House*

Beyond *Bunny Town Helpers*

ELL *A House for You*

Grammar and Writing
Naming Words, Sentences

Half-Day Kindergarten

Use the chart below to help plan your half-day kindergarten schedule. Choose Small Group and Workstation Activities as your time allows during the day.

ORAL LANGUAGE

- **Phonemic Awareness**
- **Build Background**
- **Oral Vocabulary**

WORD STUDY

- **Phonics:** /d/d, /h/h, /r/r
- **High-Frequency Words:** *are, for, you*

READING

- **Share the Big Books:** *Russ and the Firehouse; Bus Stops*
- **Read-Aloud Trade Book:** *Alicia's Happy Day*
- **Read-Aloud Anthology**
- **Big Book of Explorations**
- **Fluency Practice**

LANGUAGE ARTS

- **Shared Writing**
- **Interactive Writing**
- **Independent Writing**

INDEPENDENT PRACTICE

- **Activity Book Pages**
- **Practice Book Pages**
- **Handwriting Practice**

Unit 6 Resources

Theme: Neighborhood

Literature

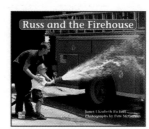

Big Book

Big Book

Read-Aloud Trade Book

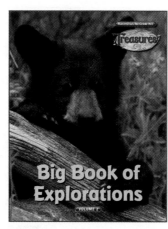

Big Book of Explorations (2)

Decodable Readers

Approaching Level	On Level	Beyond Level	ELL

Leveled Readers

Read-Aloud Anthology
Includes Plays for Readers Theater

Oral Vocabulary Cards
(30 sets)

Retelling Cards

Teaching Support

Teacher's Edition

Teacher's Resource Book

Home-School Connection

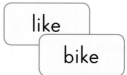

High-Frequency Word Cards

Word-Building Cards

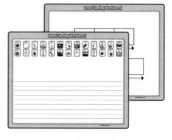

Sound-Spelling WorkBoards

Puppet

Sound-Spelling Cards

Photo Cards

Student Practice

Activity Book

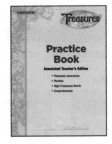

Practice Book

Handwriting
- Ball and Stick
- Slant

Literacy Workstation Flip Charts

Teaching Chart

Differentiated Resources

English Language Learners

ELL Resource and Practice Books

Visual Vocabulary Resources

Response to Intervention

Tier 2
- Phonemic Awareness
- Phonics
- Vocabulary
- Comprehension
- Fluency

Tier 3

Class Management Tools

How-to Guide

Rotation Chart

Weekly Contracts

Assessment

Unit Assessment

Assess Unit Skills
- Phonemic Awareness
- Phonics
- High-Frequency Words
- Listening Comprehension

Unit 6 Resources

Digital Solutions

Go to **ConnectED** http://connected.mcgraw-hill.com
Online Center

☑ Prepare/Plan

ONLINE www.macmillanmh.com

Teacher's Edition Online

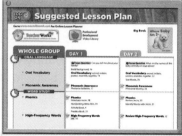

TeacherWorks™ Plus
All-In-One Planner and Resource Center

Available on CD-ROM
• Interactive Teacher's Edition
• Printable Weekly Resources

Implementation Modules

• Support on how to implement the reading program

Balanced Literacy Planner

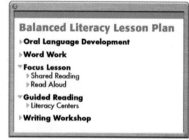

Balanced Literacy Lesson Plan
▸ **Oral Language Development**
▸ **Word Work**
▾ **Focus Lesson**
  ▸ Shared Reading
  ▸ Read Aloud
▾ **Guided Reading**
  ▸ Literacy Centers
▸ **Writing Workshop**

• Create customized weekly balanced literacy planners

ELL Strategies

• Teaching strategies for English Language Learners

Reading Video Library

• Video clips of instructional routines

Leadership Handbook

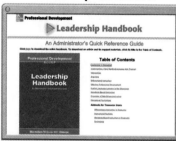

• Professional development for school principals

☑ Teach/Learn

ONLINE www.macmillanmh.com

Animated Activities

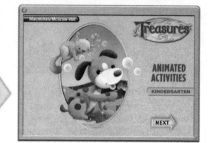

• Animated comprehension activities

Classroom Presentation Toolkit

• Weekly transparencies, graphic organizers, and guided instruction and practice

---

Additional Professional Development

• **Instructional Routine Handbook**
• **Writing Professional Development Guide**
• **Managing Small Groups**
• **Leadership Handbook:**
  An Administrator's Quick Reference Guide

Also available
Reading Yes!
Video Workshops on CD-ROM

Unit 6 Resources

☑ **Assess**

ONLINE www.macmillanmh.com

Leveled Reader Database

- Search and print Leveled Reader titles

Weekly Activities

- Oral Language
- Research Roadmap
- Research and Inquiry
- Vocabulary and Spelling
- Author and Illustrator

Progress Monitoring

Unit 1 Reteaching and Intervention Opportunities

- Prescriptions for Reteaching
- Student Profile System

Online and
CD-ROM materials are
Interactive White Board Ready!

IWB

Available on CD

- **Listening Library**
- **Sound Pronunciation**

- **New Adventures with Buggles and Beezy**

Diagnostic Assessment

Screening, Diagnosis, and Placement

Use your state or district screener to identify children at risk. In addition, see tests in the **Diagnostic Assessment** book for information on determining the proficiency of children according to specific skills. Use the results to place children in the program.

■ Diagnostics should be given at the beginning of the school year after you have had time to observe children and they become familiar with classroom routines. Use the diagnostics to determine children in need of intervention or to identify specific prerequisite skill deficiencies that you need to teach during Small Group differentiated instruction time.

Progress Monitoring Assessment

Meeting Grade-Level Expectations

Use these tests at the end of each unit (every 3 weeks). Multiple questions and next-steps information are provided.

Ongoing Informal Assessments

■ Daily Quick Check Observations

Formal Assessments

■ **Unit Assessment**

Benchmark Assessment

Give once a year to determine whether children have mastered the grade-level content standards and to document long-term academic growth.

Test Alignment

GRADE K UNIT 6 ASSESSED SKILLS	TerraNova/ CAT 6	SESAT	TPRI	DIBELS*
COMPREHENSION STRATEGIES AND SKILLS				
• Strategy: Summarize	◆	◆	◆	◆
• Skills: Identify main idea and details, Retell	◆	◆	◆	◆
VOCABULARY/HIGH-FREQUENCY WORDS				
• Words that compare, Sequence words				
• *are, for, you*	◆	◆	◆	◆
PHONEMIC AWARENESS				
• Phoneme isolation (initial /h/, initial and final /d/, initial /r/)	◆	◆	◆	◆
• Phoneme blending	◆	◆	◆	◆
• Phoneme segmentation	◆	◆	◆	◆
PHONICS				
• *Hh, Dd, Rr*	◆	◆	◆	◆
TEXT FEATURES				
• Maps, Captions				
GRAMMAR				
• Sentences				

*Data from DIBELS serve as indicators of overall reading comprehension performance, not specific skills.

KEY

TerraNova/CAT 6	TerraNova, The Second Edition
SESAT	Stanford Early School Achievement Test
TPRI	Texas Primary Reading Inventory
DIBELS*	Dynamics Indicators of Basic Early Literacy Skills

Theme Project: Neighborhoods Near and Far

Introduce the Theme

Sing the theme song. Then guide children to generate questions related to the theme and topic of class-wide interest. For example: *What is your neighborhood like? How are neighborhoods the same? How are they different?*

Won't You Be My Neighbor?

It's a beautiful day in this neighborhood,

A beautiful day for a neighbor.

Would you be mine?

Song on Listening Library Audio CD

Research and Inquiry
Self-Selected Theme Project

Step 1 Planning a Project

What do I want to learn about neighborhoods?

- Use the **Big Books, Teaching Chart,** and **Photo Cards** to show different kinds of neighbors and neighborhoods.
- Have children ask themselves: *What do I want to learn about neighborhoods?*
- Help children decide what people or sources can help answer their research questions.

Step 2 Doing the Project

- Guide children to use text sources found at the library or media center to answer their neighborhood questions.

Research Strategy

Maps can help us find our way around a neighborhood or school. Maps are helpful when we go to a new place, so we won't get lost.

Step 3 Document and Evaluate Research

How can I share what I have learned?

You might suggest:

- making a map of the school playground
- painting a picture of neighborhoods in different countries
- performing a skit about the neighborhood and community

Encourage children to use writing in conjunction with their visuals.

Help children decide what materials they will need for their presentation. See the Unit Closer on pages 1550–1551.

Unit 6
Neighborhood

The **Big** Question

What is your
neighborhood like?

38A

Teaching Chart 38A

Introduce Theme Project

NEIGHBORHOOD

Let's look at this photo. It is of children playing ball on the grass. It shows lots of homes and buildings in the background. Point to the children, ball, and houses and buildings in the background. *What neighborhood activity do you enjoy doing with your friends? What kind of neighborhood is this?*

- Ask: *How would you describe this neighborhood?*

- Ask: *Where do you think this neighborhood is located?*

- *Throughout this unit we will be learning about our neighborhood, people and places, and neighborhood workers.*

Connect to Content

Mapping Your School

Discuss how maps help people identify where they are and get around a new place. For example, a visitor to our school might use a map of our school to find his or her way to our classroom. We might also give a visitor directions using terms such as *left*, *right*, *behind*, or *next to*.

Social Studies

Connect to Content

Activity: Puzzle Maps

Ask: *How would a new student find the library?*

■ Have small groups of children create classroom maps, cut each map into five large pieces, and place their pieces in labeled, zippered plastic bags.

■ Ask children to switch maps with other groups and assemble them. Have children ask each other questions, such as: *What is next to the classroom library?*

Character Building: Citizenship

Explain that being a good citizen means doing your part to make your community better. Taking pride in where you live, work, and go to school can make you feel good inside.

Minilesson

Exploring Advertisements

Explain Have you ever seen a television commercial for your favorite food or toy? What about a billboard along the side of the road? These are examples of **advertisements**. An advertisement is a public notice. It gives you information about a product or event and encourages you to try it.

Discuss Ask: *What are some things you have seen advertised?* (food, toys, store sales, cleaning products)

Apply Have children create an advertisement announcing a friend's act of kindness. They may use words, pictures, or act out a skit. They should include the child's name and what he or she did that was so kind.

Favorite Books and Stories

Discuss favorite books and stories that children have read so far during the year. Tell children to name their favorite stories and then participate in shared oral readings with classmates.

Connect to Content

Activity: When I'm All Grown Up

Ask: *What do you want to be when you grow up?*

- Have children cut out pictures of community workers from magazines. Then paste them horizontally across the top of chart paper.

- Ask children to discuss the workers' jobs and their responsibilities. Have them predict which jobs will be most and least popular.

- Then invite each child to put a sticker below the picture that shows what he or she wants to be when he or she grows up.

- Have children count the votes and record the results on a graph.

Listening and Speaking

Guide children to
- participate in a conversation on a specific topic with you;
- describe people, places, things, and locations;
- respect the age, gender, and interests of the listener.

Community Workers

Doctor   Firefighter   Crossing Guard   Carpenter

Minilesson

Using Direction and Location Words

Explain **Direction** and **location words** tell us where things are. For example: The plate is *on top of* the table; the shoes are *under* the bed; the dog is *in front of* the house. Direction and location words are found in recipes, driving directions, and step-by-step instructions.

Discuss Ask: *What are some other examples of direction words?* (left, right, above, below, next to, behind, over)

Apply With children, play a game of "Simon Says." For example: Say "Simon Says put your hands on top of your head." Emphasize location and direction words in your intonation.

LOG ON ▶ **FIND OUT**

Research For technology research and presentation strategies, see the Computer Literacy lesson on pages 1548–1549. For additional research and inquiry, go to **www.macmillanmh.com**.

Week 1 ★ At a Glance

Priority Skills and Concepts

 Comprehension
- **Genre:** Folktale, Expository
- **Strategy:** Summarize
- **Skill:** Identify Main Ideas and Details
- **Skill:** Classify and Categorize

 High-Frequency Word
- *are*

Oral Vocabulary
- Build Robust Vocabulary: *borrow*, *equipment*, *frequently*, *neighborhood*, *organize*

Fluency
- Echo-Read
- Word Automaticity

 Phonemic Awareness
- Phoneme Isolation
- Phoneme Blending
- Phoneme Segmentation

 Phonics
- *Hh*

Grammar
- Sentences

Writing
- Dialogue

Key    Tested in Program   Review Skill

Digital Learning

Digital solutions to help plan and implement instruction

☑ **Teacher Resources**

LOG ON ▶

ONLINE www.macmillanmh.com

▶ **Teacher's Edition**
  - Lesson Planner and Resources also on CD-ROM

*Teacher*Works™ *Plus*

▶ **Professional Development**
  - Video Library

Professional Development

☑ **Student Resources**

LOG ON ▶

ONLINE www.macmillanmh.com

▶ **Leveled Reader Database**

▶ **Activities**
  - Oral Language Activities
  - Phonics Activities
  - Vocabulary/Spelling Activities

Listening Library
  - Recordings of Literature Big Books, Read-Aloud Trade Books, and Leveled Readers

Weekly Literature

Theme: Our Neighborhood

Student Literature

A mix of fiction and nonfiction

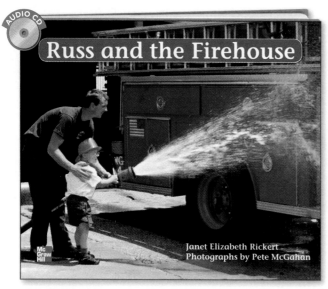

Big Book

Genre Expository

Big Book of Explorations

Genre Expository

Support Literature

Interactive Read-Aloud Anthology

Genre Folktale

Oral Vocabulary Cards
- Listening Comprehension
- Build Robust Vocabulary

Decodable Reader

Resources for Differentiated Instruction

Leveled Readers: Social Studies

GR Levels Rebus–F

Genre	Expository

- Same Theme
- Same Vocabulary/Phonics
- Same Comprehension Skills

Approaching Level

On Level

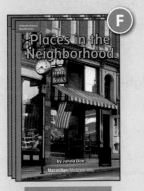

Beyond Level

ELL

LOG ON **Leveled Reader Database**
Go to www.macmillanmh.com.

Practice

Activity Book

Practice Book

ELL Practice Book

Response to Intervention

Tier 2
Tier 3

- Phonemic Awareness
- Phonics
- Vocabulary
- Comprehension
- Fluency

Unit Assessment

Assess Unit Skills

- Phonemic Awareness
- Phonics
- High-Frequency Words
- Listening Comprehension

HOME-SCHOOL CONNECTION

- Family letters in English and Spanish
- Take-home stories and activities

Go to **www.macmillanmh.com** for Online Lesson Planner

 **TeacherWorks** *Plus*
All-In-One Planner and Resource Center

Professional Development
Video Library

Big Book
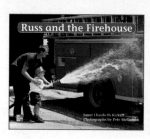
Russ and the Firehouse

WHOLE GROUP

ORAL LANGUAGE

	DAY 1	DAY 2
• Oral Vocabulary	**? Focus Question** Who is a neighbor? Build Background, 1306 **Oral Vocabulary** *borrow, equipment, frequently, neighborhood, organize*, 1306	**? Focus Question** What are some jobs people do at the firehouse? **Oral Vocabulary** *borrow, equipment, frequently, neighborhood, organize*, 1314 Sequence Words, 1321
• Phonemic Awareness	**Phonemic Awareness** Phoneme Isolation, 1309	**Phonemic Awareness** Phoneme Blending, 1322

WORD STUDY

• Phonics	**Phonics** Introduce /h/h, 1310 Handwriting: Write *Hh*, 1311 Activity Book, 4 Practice Book, 121	**Phonics** Review /h/h, /p/p, /o/o, 1322 Blend with /h/h, 1323
• High-Frequency Words	**High-Frequency Word** *are*, 1308	**Review High-Frequency Words**, 1324

READING

• Listening Comprehension • Apply Phonics and High-Frequency Words • Fluency	**Share the Big Book** *Russ and the Firehouse* **Strategy:** Summarize, 1307 **Skill:** Identify Main Idea and Details, 1307 Big Book	**Reread the Big Book** *Russ and the Firehouse* **Strategy:** Summarize, 1316 **Skill:** Identify Main Idea and Details, 1316 Retell, 1320 **Decodable Reader:** *Are Caps Hats?* 1324 Activity Book, 5–6 Practice Book, 122 **Fluency** Echo-Read, 1320

LANGUAGE ARTS

• Writing • Grammar	**Shared Writing** Dialogue, 1313 **Grammar** Sentences, 1312	**Interactive Writing** Dialogue, 1325

ASSESSMENT

• Informal/Formal	**Quick Check** Phonemic Awareness, 1309	**Quick Check** Comprehension, 1320

 **SMALL GROUP Lesson Plan** **Differentiated Instruction 1300–1301**

Priority Skills

Phonemic Awareness/Phonics /h/h	High-Frequency Words *are*	Oral Vocabulary Sequence Words	Comprehension Strategy: Summarize Skill: Identify Main Idea and Details

Half-Day Kindergarten

Teach Core Skills
Focus on tested skill lessons, other lessons, and small group options as your time allows.

DAY 3

? Focus Question What are some special places in your neighborhood?

Oral Vocabulary *borrow, equipment, frequently, neighborhood, organize,* 1326

Oral Vocabulary Cards: "In Our Neighborhood"

Phonemic Awareness
Phoneme Blending, 1331

Phonics
Review /h/h, /f/f, /k/c, /t/t, 1332
Blend with /h/h, 1333
Read Words, 1333

High-Frequency Word
are, 1330
Activity Book: "We Are," 7–8
Practice Book, 123–124
Read for Fluency, 1330

Read the Big Book of Explorations
"Let's Look at Maps," 2–7
Text Feature: Use Maps, 1328

Big Book of Explorations

Independent Writing
Prewrite and Draft Dialogue, 1335

Grammar
Sentences, 1334

`Quick Check` High-Frequency Words, 1330

DAY 4

? Focus Question What are ways you and your family can help find a lost pet?

Oral Vocabulary *borrow, equipment, frequently, neighborhood, organize,* 1336

Sequence Words, 1339

Phonemic Awareness
Phoneme Segmentation, 1340

Phonics
Picture Sort, 1340
Blend with /h/h, /f/f, /o/o, 1341
Activity Book, 9–10
Practice Book, 125–126

Review High-Frequency Words, 1342

Interactive Read Aloud
Listening Comprehension, 1338
Read Aloud: "The Black Cat,"
Decodable Reader:
Are Caps Hats? 1342

Read Aloud

Independent Writing
Revise and Edit Dialogue, 1343

`Quick Check` Phonics, 1341

DAY 5
Review and Assess

? Focus Question What are some things you learned about living in a neighborhood?

Oral Vocabulary *borrow, equipment, frequently, neighborhood, organize,* 1344

Sequence Words, 1346

Phonemic Awareness
Phoneme Segmentation, 1347

Phonics
Read Words, 1348
Dictation, 1348
Activity Book, 12

High-Frequency Words
are, to, have, is, play, 1348

Read Across Texts
Strategy: Summarize, 1345
Skill: Identify Main Idea and Details, 1345
Activity Book, 11

Fluency Word Automaticity, 1346

Independent Writing
Publish and Present Dialogue, 1349

Weekly Assessment, 1376–1377

Differentiated Instruction

What do I do in small groups?

Teacher-Led Small Groups

Independent Activities

IF... children need additional instruction, practice, or extension based on your  Quick Check observations for the following priority skills

- **Phonemic Awareness**
  Phoneme Isolation, Blending, Segmentation

- **Phonics**
  Hh

- **High-Frequency Word**
  are

- **Comprehension**
  Strategy: Summarize
  Skill: Identify Main Idea and Details

THEN...

Approaching	Preteach and
ELL	Reteach Skills
On Level	Practice
Beyond	Enrich and Accelerate Learning

 Suggested Small Group Lesson Plan

	DAY 1	DAY 2
Approaching Level **Tier 2** • Preteach/Reteach Tier 2 Instruction	• Oral Language, 1350 • High-Frequency Words, 1350 ELL High-Frequency Words Review, 1350 • Phonemic Awareness, 1351 • Phonics, 1351 ELL Sound-Spellings Review, 1351	• Oral Language, 1356 • High-Frequency Words, 1356 ELL • Phonemic Awareness, 1357 • Phonics, 1357
On Level • Practice	• High-Frequency Words, 1352 • Phonemic Awareness/Phonics, 1352 ELL	• Phonics, 1358
Beyond Level • Extend/Accelerate Gifted and Talented	• High-Frequency Words/Vocabulary, 1353 ELL Expand Oral Vocabulary, 1353 • Phonics, 1353	• Phonics, 1358
ELL • Build English Language Proficiency • See ELL in other levels.	• Oral Language Warm-Up, 1354 • Academic Language, 1354 • Vocabulary, 1355	• Access to Core Content, 1359

Small Group

Focus on Leveled Readers

Levels Rebus–F

Approaching

On Level

Beyond

ELL

Additional Leveled Readers

LOG ON ▶ **Leveled Reader Database**
www.macmillanmh.com

Search by

- Comprehension Skill
- Content Area
- Genre
- Text Feature

- Guided Reading Level
- Reading Recovery Level
- Lexile Score
- Benchmark Level

Subscription also available

Manipulatives

Sound-Spelling WorkBoards

Sound-Spelling Cards

Photo Cards

High-Frequency Word Cards

Visual Vocabulary Resources

DAY 3

- High-Frequency Words, 1360 **ELL**
- Phonemic Awareness, 1360
- Decodable Reader, 1361
- Phonics, 1361

- Decodable Reader, 1362

- Decodable Reader, 1362

- Access to Core Content, 1363
- Grammar, 1363

DAY 4

- Phonemic Awareness, 1364
- Phonics, 1364 **ELL**
- Leveled Reader Lesson 1, 1365

- Leveled Reader Lesson 1, 1366 **ELL**

- Leveled Reader Lesson 1, 1367
  Synthesize, 1367

- Leveled Reader, 1368–1369

DAY 5

- Phonemic Awareness, 1370
- Phonics, 1370 **ELL**
- Leveled Reader Lesson 2, 1371
- High-Frequency Words, 1371

- Leveled Reader Lesson 2, 1372

- Leveled Reader Lesson 2, 1373 **ELL**
- Expand Vocabulary, 1373

- Fluency, 1374
- High-Frequency Words, 1375
- Writing, 1375

What do I do with the rest of my class?

Teacher-Led Small Groups

Independent Activities

- Activity Book
- Practice Book
- ELL Practice Book
- Leveled Reader Activities
- Literacy Workstations
- Online Activities
- Buggles and Beezy

Classroom Management Tools

Weekly Contract

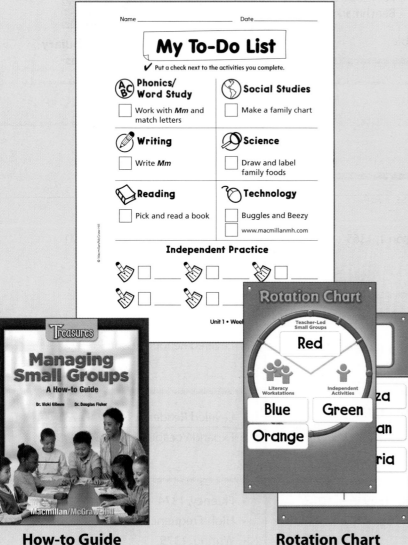

Name _____ Date _____

My To-Do List

✔ Put a check next to the activities you complete.

Phonics/ Word Study
- Work with *Mm* and match letters

Social Studies
- Make a family chart

Writing
- Write *Mm*

Science
- Draw and label family foods

Reading
- Pick and read a book

Technology
- Buggles and Beezy
- www.macmillanmh.com

Independent Practice

Unit 1 • Week

Treasures
Managing Small Groups
A How-to Guide
Dr. Vicki Gibson   Dr. Douglas Fisher
Macmillan/McGraw-Hill

How-to Guide

Rotation Chart

Teacher-Led Small Groups

Red

Literacy Workstations   Independent Activities

Blue   Green

Orange

za
an
ria

Rotation Chart

Phonics Activities

- Match Letters
- Match Letters to Sounds
- Blend Words

Meet the Author/Illustrator

Print   Close Window

Taro Gomi
- Taro was born in Tokyo, Japan, in 1945.
- He has published over 300 books!
- He also designs stationery and clothes, and makes animated videos for children.

Other books by Taro Gomi
- Gomi, Taro. *Spring Is Here*. New York: Macmillan/McGraw-Hill, 1993.
- Gomi, Taro. *My Friends*. New York: Macmillan/McGraw-Hill, 1997.

- Read Other Books by the Author or Illustrator

Practice

Activity Book

Practice Book

ELL Practice Book

Independent Activities

ONLINE INSTRUCTION www.macmillanmh.com

Available on CD

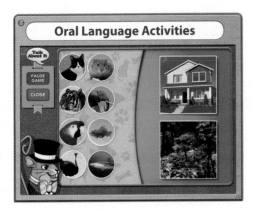

- Focus on Unit Vocabulary and Concepts
- English Language Learner Support

- Leveled Reader Database
- Search titles by level, skill, content area, and more

LISTENING LIBRARY
Recordings of selections
- Literature Big Books
- Read-Aloud Trade Books
- Leveled Readers
- ELL Readers

NEW ADVENTURES WITH BUGGLES AND BEEZY
Phonemic awareness and phonics activities

- Differentiated Lists and Activities

Leveled Reader Activities

Approaching

On Level

Beyond

ELL

See inside cover of all Leveled Readers.

Literacy Workstations

See lessons on pages 1304–1305.

Managing the Class

What do I do with the rest of my class?

Reading

Objectives

- Read and discuss a book with a group
- Read a nonfiction book aloud

Phonics/Word Study

Objectives

- Match words that begin with the same letter and sound; write the words
- Use Word-Building Cards to form words

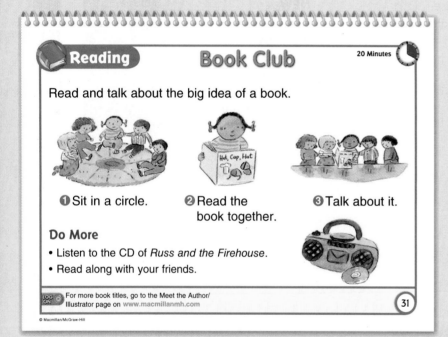

Reading — Book Club — 20 Minutes

Read and talk about the big idea of a book.

❶ Sit in a circle. ❷ Read the book together. ❸ Talk about it.

Do More
- Listen to the CD of *Russ and the Firehouse*.
- Read along with your friends.

For more book titles, go to the Meet the Author/Illustrator page on www.macmillanmh.com

31

© Macmillan/McGraw-Hill

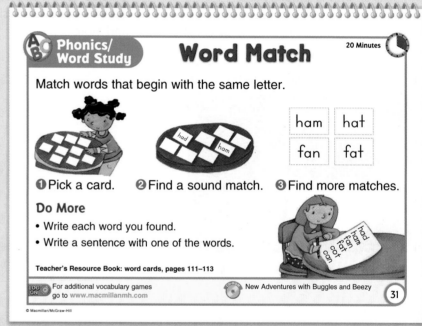

Phonics/Word Study — Word Match — 20 Minutes

Match words that begin with the same letter.

ham hat
fan fat

❶ Pick a card. ❷ Find a sound match. ❸ Find more matches.

Do More
- Write each word you found.
- Write a sentence with one of the words.

Teacher's Resource Book: word cards, pages 111–113

For additional vocabulary games go to www.macmillanmh.com

New Adventures with Buggles and Beezy

31

© Macmillan/McGraw-Hill

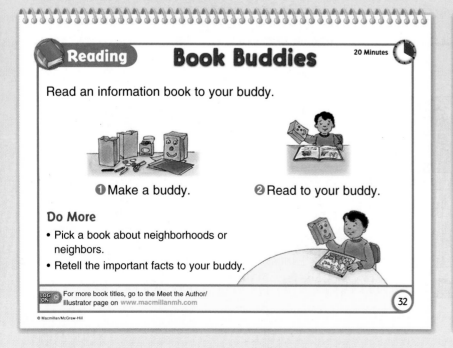

Reading — Book Buddies — 20 Minutes

Read an information book to your buddy.

❶ Make a buddy. ❷ Read to your buddy.

Do More
- Pick a book about neighborhoods or neighbors.
- Retell the important facts to your buddy.

For more book titles, go to the Meet the Author/Illustrator page on www.macmillanmh.com

32

© Macmillan/McGraw-Hill

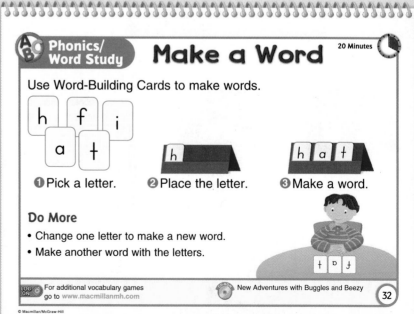

Phonics/Word Study — Make a Word — 20 Minutes

Use Word-Building Cards to make words.

h f i
a t

❶ Pick a letter. ❷ Place the letter. ❸ Make a word.

Do More
- Change one letter to make a new word.
- Make another word with the letters.

For additional vocabulary games go to www.macmillanmh.com

New Adventures with Buggles and Beezy

32

© Macmillan/McGraw-Hill

Literacy Workstations

 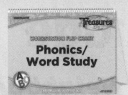  

Literacy Workstation Flip Charts

Writing

Objectives

- Write words that begin with *Hh*
- Write and illustrate a sentence about a neighborhood place

Content Literacy

Objectives

- Sort tools by their use; draw and label a picture of someone who uses tools
- Draw a picture of a neighborhood place and write about it

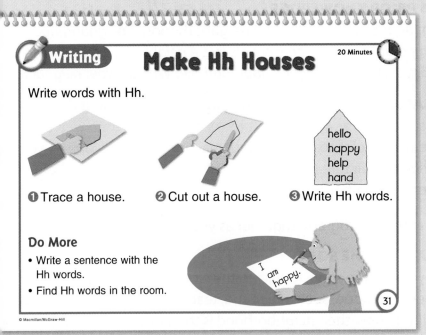

Writing — **Make Hh Houses** — 20 Minutes

Write words with Hh.

❶ Trace a house.   ❷ Cut out a house.   ❸ Write Hh words.

hello
happy
help
hand

Do More
- Write a sentence with the Hh words.
- Find Hh words in the room.

I am happy.

31

© Macmillan/McGraw-Hill

Science — **Tool Talk** — 20 Minutes

Sort tools by how they are used.

❶ Look at tools.   ❷ Think about tools.   ❸ Sort tools.

Do More
- Draw a picture of someone in the neighborhood who uses tools.
- Label your drawing.

Builders use hammers.

Internet Research and Inquiry Activity
www.macmillanmh.com

32

© Macmillan/McGraw-Hill

Writing — **In the Neighborhood** — 20 Minutes

Write about neighborhood places.

I go to the _____.   I go to the school.   I go to the school.

❶ Write the sentence.   ❷ Finish the sentence.   ❸ Draw a picture.

Do More
- Draw and label other places in the neighborhood.

school   firehouse   post office

32

© Macmillan/McGraw-Hill

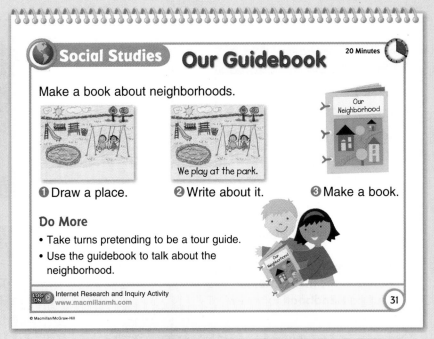

Social Studies — **Our Guidebook** — 20 Minutes

Make a book about neighborhoods.

We play at the park.   Our Neighborhood

❶ Draw a place.   ❷ Write about it.   ❸ Make a book.

Do More
- Take turns pretending to be a tour guide.
- Use the guidebook to talk about the neighborhood.

Internet Research and Inquiry Activity
www.macmillanmh.com

31

© Macmillan/McGraw-Hill

WHOLE GROUP

Oral Language
- Build Background

✓ **Comprehension**
- Read *Russ and the Firehouse*
- Strategy: Summarize
- Skill: Identify Main Idea and Details

✓ **High-Frequency Words**
- Introduce *are*

✓ **Phonemic Awareness**
- Phoneme Isolation

✓ **Phonics**
- Introduce /h/*h*
- Handwriting: Write *Hh*

Grammar
- Sentences

Writing
- Shared Writing: Dialogue

SMALL GROUP

- Differentiated Instruction, pages 1350–1375

Oral Vocabulary

Week 1

borrow	equipment
frequently	neighborhood
organize	

Review

beneath	enter	habitat
raise	responsibility	

Use the **Define/Example/Ask** routine in the **Instructional Routine Handbook** to review the words.

Oral Language

 Build Background: *Neighborhood*

INTRODUCE THE THEME

Tell children that this week they will be talking and reading about the **neighborhood**, or the place where you live.

Write the following question on the board: *Who is a neighbor?* Guide children to repeat the question and to identify syllables in words. Say the word *is* and clap the beat. *How many beats did you hear?* (1) Then have children segment *neigh-bor* and clap. *How many beats did you hear?* (2) Prompt children to answer the question on the board.

ACCESS PRIOR KNOWLEDGE

Have children describe their own neighborhoods. *A neighborhood is an area of a city or town where people live. A neighbor is a person who lives near you. What is your neighborhood like? Who are your neighbors?*

Think Aloud Let's look at this picture. I see a girl and a dog. She is standing at a mailbox. It looks like she got an envelope in the mail. **(Point to the girl, dog, mailbox, and envelope as you describe the picture.)** I think the mail carrier is a worker who delivers mail in her neighborhood.

■ Look at the photograph together as you sing the song.

 INNOVATE ON THE SONG

Create lyrics for the song, replacing the word *neighbor* with a person in the neighborhood, such as a friend, teacher, or mail carrier. Discuss with children how their neighborhood is the same as or different from the one shown in the photo. Have children take turns and speak one at a time as they discuss the neighborhood.

It's a beautiful day
in this neighborhood,
a beautiful day for a neighbor.
Would you be mine?
Could you be mine?

Oral Language · Neighborhood Week 1 38

Teaching Chart 38

Share the Big Book
Listening Comprehension

PREVIEW AND PREDICT Display the cover. Have children identify the front cover. *Let's read about a boy at the firehouse.* Read aloud the title and the names of the author and the photographer. *What can you see at the firehouse in your* **neighborhood**?

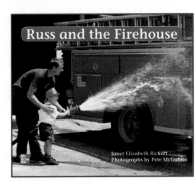

Big Book

GENRE: INFORMATIONAL TEXT/ EXPOSITORY Tell children that this book is an **expository** text. It tells facts about real people and places.

STRATEGY **Summarize**

EXPLAIN/MODEL Remind children that retelling a story's main idea and other important events can help you understand a story.

Think Aloud I will stop at the beginning, middle, and end to remind myself of the main story events that have happened.

SKILL **Identify Main Idea and Details**

EXPLAIN/MODEL Tell children that figuring out a story's main idea, or what a story is mostly about, is important to understanding a story. Explain that a book's details tell more about its main idea.

Think Aloud As I read the story, I will look for the main idea and details. I will be a good reader by reminding myself of the main events in the book.

Read the Big Book

SET PURPOSE Have children think about the purpose of listening to the book to find out what Russ does at the firehouse and to become involved in real and imagined events. Use the **Define/Example/Ask** routine to teach the story words on the inside cover of the **Big Book**.

Respond to Literature

MAKE CONNECTIONS Have children sequence story events by writing or drawing what happens. Have them write or dictate another activity that they would add to the story and then read it aloud.

Objectives

- Discuss the theme
- Use oral vocabulary words *neighborhood* and *equipment*
- Innovate on song lyrics
- Listen and respond to a story
- Summarize/identify main idea and details

Materials

- Teaching Chart 38
- Big Book: *Russ and the Firehouse*

ELL

Use the Interactive Question-Response Guide for *Russ and the Firehouse*, **ELL Resource Book** pages 154–159, to guide children through a reading of the book. As you read *Russ and the Firehouse*, make meaning clear by pointing to pictures, demonstrating word meanings, paraphrasing text, and asking children questions.

Digital Learning

Story and song on **Listening Library Audio CD**

Objectives

- Read the high-frequency word *are*
- Review the high-frequency words *have, to, is, play*
- Identify the word *are* in speech and text

Materials

- High-Frequency Word Cards: *are, have, to, is, play*
- Teaching Chart 39

ELL

Reinforce Vocabulary
Display the High-Frequency Word Cards *are, have, to, is, play*. Gesture to include everybody as you say: *We are in class.* Then point to individual children and say, for example: *Mario is in class. Lucy is in class. Mario and Lucy are in class.* Hold up a book and say: *We have a book to read.* Then hold up a board game and say: *We have a game to play.* Continue pointing to other children and holding other objects.

High-Frequency Words

 **are**

are

INTRODUCE Display the **High-Frequency Word Card** for **are**. Use the **Read/Spell/Write** routine to teach the word.

- **Read** Point to and say the word *are*. *We* are *in school today.*
- **Spell** *The word* are *is spelled* a-r-e. *Let's read and spell* are *together.*
- **Write** *Now let's write the word* are *on our papers. Let's spell aloud the word as we write it:* are, a-r-e.

SPIRAL REVIEW

REVIEW *have, to, is, play*
Display each card and have children read it.

have	to
is	play

READ THE RHYME AND CHIME
Have children point to *are* each time they see it in the Rhyme and Chime. Repeat the rhyme together for fluency. Then add *are* to the class Word Wall.

Hippos Are Happy

Hippos are happy.
Hippos are hip.
Hippos are huge.
Hippos are heavy.

High-Frequency Word: are
Phonics: /h/h

Neighborhood Week 1 39

Unit 6
Rhyme and Chime

Teaching Chart 39

TIME TO MOVE!

Play "Follow the Leader." Ask children to copy what you are doing and saying. Lead them in stretching in place and saying: *We are reaching to the ceiling.* Next, lead them in nodding their heads and saying: *We are nodding.* Last, lead them in jumping and saying: *We are jumping.*

Phonemic Awareness

 ## Phoneme Isolation

Model

Display the **Photo Card** for *hat*.

Repeat with the Photo Card for *horse*.

Today we are going to learn a new sound. Listen for the sound at the beginning of *hat*: /h/. *Hat* has /h/ at the beginning. Say the sound with me: /h/. What is the sound? Let's give ourselves a *hug* when we hear /h/ at the beginning of a word.

Read the "Hippos Are Happy" Rhyme and Chime again. Have children give themselves a hug every time they hear /h/.

Hippos are happy.
Hippos are hip.
Hippos are huge.
Hippos are heavy.

 ### Review /f/, /o/

Display the Photo Card for *fan*.

Repeat with *ostrich*.

This is a *fan*. The beginning sound in *fan* is /f/. What is the sound?

Guided Practice/Practice

Display and name the Photo Cards. Children identify words that begin with /h/. Guide practice with the first card. Continue orally with the words *ham, hit, fan, hunt, on, happy*.

Say the name of the picture with me. Tell me the sound you hear at the beginning of the word.

Quick Check

Can children identify initial /h/ sound?

During **Small Group Instruction**

If No → **Approaching Level** Provide additional practice, page 1351.

If Yes → **On Level** Children blend sounds in words with /h/, page 1352.

Beyond Level Children read words with *h*, page 1353.

Objectives

- Identify initial /h/ sound
- Review initial /o/ and /f/

Materials

- Photo Cards: *fan, farm, feet, hammer, hand, hat, horse, October, ostrich, otter*

ELL

Pronunciation Display and have children name Photo Cards from this and prior lessons to reinforce phonemic awareness and word meanings. Point to a card and ask: *What do you see?* (a hat) *What is the sound at the beginning of the word* hat? (/h/). Repeat using Photo Cards with words that begin with the /f/ and /o/ sounds.

Objectives

- Match the letter *h* to the /h/ sound
- Recognize the difference between a letter and a word
- Handwriting: Write *Hh*

Materials

- Sound-Spelling Card: *Hippo*
- Teaching Chart 39
- Handwriting
- Handwriting Teacher's Edition
- Activity Book, p. 4
- Practice Book, p. 121

ELL

Variations in Languages
Some children, particularly those whose first language is Spanish, may need extra practice identifying the /h/ sound, as the *h* in Spanish is silent. Use the Approaching Level Phonics lessons for additional pronunciation and decoding practice.

 Sound Pronunciation

See **Sound Pronunciation CD** for a model of the /h/ sound. Play this for the children needing additional models.

Phonics

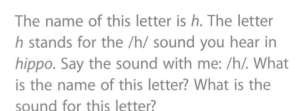

✓ Introduce /h/*h*

Model

Display the *Hippo* **Sound-Spelling Card**.

The name of this letter is *h*. The letter *h* stands for the /h/ sound you hear in *hippo*. Say the sound with me: /h/. What is the name of this letter? What is the sound for this letter?

Read the "Hippos Are Happy" Rhyme and Chime. Reread the title. Point out that the word *Hippos* in the title begins with the letter *H*. *This is the word* Hippos. *It begins with the letter* H. Model placing a self-stick note below the letter *H* in *Hippos*. Repeat with *Happy*.

Teaching Chart 39

Guided Practice/Practice

Reread the Rhyme and Chime. Stop after each line. Children place self-stick notes below the letter *h* in words that begin with *h*. Guide practice with *Hippos* in line 1.

Let's place a sticky-note below the letter *h* at the beginning of a word. Yes, the words *Hippos* and *happy* begin with the letter *h*.

Corrective Feedback

If children need help with /h/, review the word *hip*. *This is the /h/ sound at the beginning of* hip: /h/ /i/ /p/, hip. *Let's blend* hip *together:* /hhhiiip/, hip. *Now it's your turn. Blend* hip. *Repeat with* ham *and* hat.

Build Fluency: Sound-Spellings

SPIRAL REVIEW Display the following **Word-Building Cards**: *a, c, f, h, i, m, n, o, p, r, s, t.* Have children chorally say each sound. Repeat and vary the pace.

Handwriting: Write *Hh*

MODEL Model holding up your writing hand. Say the handwriting cues as you write the uppercase and lowercase forms of *Hh* on the board. Then trace the letters on the board and in the air as you say /h/.

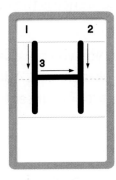

Straight down. Go back to the top. Straight down. Straight across the dotted line.

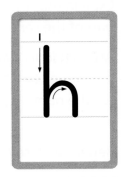

Straight down. Go to the dotted line. Around and down.

PRACTICE Ask children to hold up their writing hand.

- Say the cues together as children trace with their index finger the letters you wrote on the board.

- Have children write *H* and *h* in the air as they say /h/.

- Distribute handwriting practice pages. Observe children's pencil grip and paper position, and correct as necessary. Have children say /h/ each time they write *h*.

For Tier 2 instruction, see page 1351.

Daily Handwriting
Check that children form letters starting at the top and moving to the bottom. See **Handwriting Teacher's Edition** for ball-and-stick and slant models.

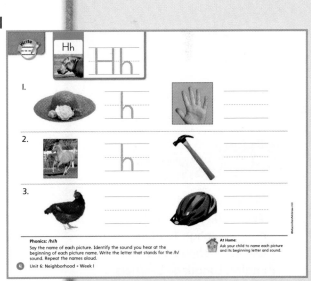

Activity Book, page 4
Practice Book, page 121

Objectives

- Use complete simple sentences
- Understand and use prepositions and prepositional phrases

Materials

- Big Book: *Russ and the Firehouse*

ELL

Basic and Academic Vocabulary Display the photo on page 16 of *Russ and the Firehouse* and pair English Language Learners with fluent speakers. Have partners make up sentences about the photo. Write their sentences, read them chorally, and ask: *What is the naming part of your sentence? What is the telling part of your sentence?*

Grammar

Sentences

MODEL Remind children that a sentence tells a complete thought. Explain that a sentence has to have a naming part and a telling part. *The naming part tells who or what the sentence is about. The telling part tells what happens.*

- Tell children that you will say a sentence. Say: *The dog ran fast.* Explain that the naming part of the sentence is the *dog*; the telling part of the sentence is *ran fast*.

- Ask a child to stand. Tell children that you will say a sentence about him or her. Say, for example: *Juanita likes pretzels.* Ask children to tell the naming part and the telling part of your sentence. (Juanita/likes pretzels)

- Repeat with several more children.

PRACTICE Show children the photo on page 8 of *Russ and the Firehouse*.

- Model saying sentences about the picture. For example:

> *Russ holds the hose.*
>
> *The firefighter helps.*
>
> *Uncle Jerry and Russ clean the **equipment**.*

- After each sentence, ask children to identify the naming part and the telling part. Then show children the photo on page 16. Have children make up their own sentences about the photo.

- Then discuss parts of a sentence. Explain to children that sometimes a sentence contains certain words, such as *for, on, at,* and *in.* Say sentences using these simple prepositions. *I will say a sentence; when I say one of those words, I will raise my hand:* This flower is *for* you. (for) The gift is *on* the table. (on) My baby brother is *at* home. (at) The girl is *in* school. (in)

- Say more sentences using these prepositions. *I will say a sentence, when I say one of those words, you raise your hand:* This gift is *for* you. (for) The book is *on* the table. (on) My friend is *at* the park. (at) The bird is *in* the tree. (in) After each sentence, help children to identify the preposition.

Writing

Shared Writing: Dialogue

BRAINSTORM

- Read and display page 4 of the **Big Book** *Russ and the Firehouse* and point to the speech balloon. *Russ comes into the firehouse and says, "Hi, I'm Russ." What else might he say?* Explain that words that a character says are called dialogue.

WRITE
Draw three speech balloons on chart paper.

- Tell children that they will write complete sentences for new speech balloons for the book. Display and read page 5.

    Uncle Jerry might greet Russ by saying, "Welcome to the firehouse!"

- Write the sentence in a speech balloon. Cut out the balloon and tape it to the Big Book page. Read the sentence with children.

- Continue by reading pages 16 and 27. After you read each page, have children tell you what Russ could say. Guide them to include sensory details. Write their suggestions in the speech balloons.

- Cut out the speech balloons and tape them to the correct pages. Read the completed sentences with children. Have children check that the sentences make sense and are in the correct order.

- Leave the speech balloons in the Big Book to refer to later.

Write About It
Have children draw a picture of a place they would like to visit in their **neighborhood**.

Objective
- Write dialogue

Materials
- **Big Book:** *Russ and the Firehouse*

5-Day Writing

	Dialogue
DAY 1	Shared: Dialogue
DAY 2	Interactive: Dialogue
DAY 3	Independent: Prewrite and Draft Dialogue
DAY 4	Independent: Revise and Edit Dialogue
DAY 5	Independent: Publish and Present

ELL

Prewriting Planning
How do you think the principal greets a visitor to our school? (Welcome to our school.) *Now tell me how you would introduce yourself to a visitor.* Model an example: *Hello, I am _____.*

Transitions That Teach

While children wait in line, have them describe their **neighborhood**.

WHOLE GROUP

Oral Language
• Build Robust Vocabulary

✓ **Comprehension**
• Reread *Russ and the Firehouse*
• Strategy: Summarize
• Skill: Identify Main Idea and Details
• Fluency: Echo-Read

Vocabulary
• Sequence Words
• Story Words: *flashlight, helmet*

✓ **Phonemic Awareness**
• Phoneme Blending

✓ **Phonics**
• Review
• Blend with /h/*h*
• Decodable Reader: *Are Caps Hats?*

Writing
• Interactive Writing: Dialogue

SMALL GROUP

• Differentiated Instruction, pages 1350–1375

Oral Vocabulary

Week 1

borrow	equipment
frequently	neighborhood
organize	

Review

beneath	enter	habitat
raise	responsibility	

Use the **Define/Example/Ask** routine in the **Instructional Routine Handbook** to review the words.

Oral Language

 Talk About It

Build Robust Vocabulary

INTRODUCE WORDS

Tell children that they are going to talk about two of the jobs Russ did in the **Big Book** *Russ and the Firehouse*. Read pages 7–20 aloud. *Many neighborhoods have firehouses. Firefighters help keep our neighborhoods safe. Firefighters use equipment to help them do their jobs. In the book, Uncle Jerry and Russ checked the equipment to make sure it worked.*

Vocabulary Routine

Use the routine below to discuss the meaning of each word.

Define: A **neighborhood** is a small section of a town or city where people live. Say the word with me.
Example: Many of us live in the neighborhood near our school.
Ask: What other places are in the same neighborhood as our school?

Define: The tools or machines you use to do something are called **equipment**. Say the word with me.
Example: The equipment in the school office includes telephones, computers, printers, and copy machines.
Ask: What equipment does a firefighter use?

CREATE A CHART

Use **Teaching Chart G3** to create a two-column chart. Add heads as shown. Guide children to use complete sentences when speaking. Have children name the equipment that must be cleaned or inspected. Then read the completed chart together.

Jobs at a Firehouse

Inspect the Equipment	Clean the Equipment
ax	boots
fire hydrant	ladders
flashlight	fire truck
helmet	tires

Listen for Rhyme

IDENTIFY RHYME

Tell children that words rhyme when they have the same ending sounds. *The word* still *rhymes with* hill. Tell children *still* and *hill* end with the /iiilll/ sounds. Recite the rhyme. Point out the words that rhyme. Have children generate more rhymes using the words.

RHYME ABOUT OUR NEIGHBORHOOD

Play the fingerplay "Five Brave Firefighters," using the **Listening Library Audio CD**. Then teach children the words and recite the song together. Discuss with children how firefighters do an important job in the neighborhood.

Five Brave Firefighters

Five brave firefighters sit very still

Until they see a fire on top of the hill.

Use fingers to number firefighters, then pantomime the actions.

One rings the bell, ding-dong;

Two pulls his big boots on;

Three jumps in the fire engine red;

Four pops a fire hat on her head;

Five drives the truck to the spot,

As the big yellow flames get very hot.

Shh! goes the water from the spout,

And quick as a wink, the fire is out.

Clap hands.

Objectives

- Discuss the theme
- Categorize story details that support the main idea
- Use oral vocabulary words *neighborhood* and *equipment*
- Generate rhyme

Materials

- Big Book: *Russ and the Firehouse*
- Graphic Organizer; Teaching Chart G3
- Listening Library Audio CD

Digital Learning

Fingerplay on Listening Library Audio CD

ELL
ENGLISH LANGUAGE LEARNERS

Beginning	**Intermediate**	**Advanced**
Confirm Understanding Review oral vocabulary using the **Big Book** *Russ and the Firehouse.* For example, display page 12. Say: *This is a fire hydrant. What is this?* (a fire hydrant) Repeat with other pages.	**Enhance Understanding** Display the same page of the Big Book and ask: *What are Russ and Uncle Jerry checking?* (They are checking a fire hydrant.) *Who uses this equipment?* Guide children to answer in complete sentences.	**Share Information** Form pairs and have partners describe to each other a piece of fire-fighting equipment Russ checks, or inspects, in the book. Guide pairs to describe in detail.

Objectives

- Summarize
- Identify main idea and details
- Respond to a story
- Develop fluency

Materials

- Big Book: *Russ and the Firehouse*
- Retelling Cards
- Activity Book, pp. 5–6
- Practice Book, p. 122

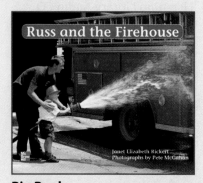

Big Book

Digital Learning

Story on **Listening Library Audio CD**

ELL

Gesture and Talk
Use gestures, talking, and other strategies to help make the text comprehensible.

p. 4
firehouse: Point to the firefighter on page 4. Say: *He works in a* firehouse.

p. 6
firefighter: Draw flames. Point to the firefighter. Pretend to be a firefighter using an imaginary hose.

Reread the Big Book
Listening Comprehension

CONCEPTS ABOUT PRINT Display the cover and read the title aloud with children as you track the print. Have children tell what they remember about the story.

 STRATEGY Summarize

Remind children that thinking about the important events and details in a book can help them to understand it. Guide children to name some of the key events in sequence in the book.

 SKILL Identify Main Idea and Details

Remind children that yesterday they learned that books have big ideas. *Let's reread* Russ and the Firehouse *and decide what the big idea is.*

Think Aloud This book is about a boy working at a **neighborhood** firehouse. I think the big idea of the book is about the jobs firefighters do at the firehouse and the **equipment** they use.

Read the **Big Book** and use the prompts on the inside back cover.

pages 4–5

AUTHOR'S CRAFT
- Once upon a time *is a phrase that we usually see in fairy tales. Is this a fairy tale? How do you know?*

Once upon a time, not too long ago, there was a little boy named Russ who got a job at a firehouse.

His mom took him there to see his Uncle Jerry, who is a fireman.

pages 6–7

MAIN IDEA AND DETAILS
Think Aloud We said the big idea might be about the different types of work at the firehouse. I think this is true, since Russ gets a job there.

Uncle Jerry asked Russ if he would like to stay and help around the firehouse. Russ said, "Yes!"

Russ got to meet everyone…

Develop Comprehension

page 9

CONCEPTS ABOUT PRINT

- *Can you find the word that starts with a capital H?* (*Hey*)

...and do all sorts of neat things.

pages 10–11

CONCEPT WORDS: SEQUENCE WORDS

- *What do Russ and Uncle Jerry check first?* (They check the ax first.)

Uncle Jerry told Russ that a very important part of being a fireman is cleaning all the equipment and making sure it works.

Uncle Jerry and Russ inspected the equipment. First an ax,...

page 12

PHONEMIC AWARENESS

- *Listen to the words on this page. Raise your hand when you hear a word that starts with the /h/ sound.* (*hydrant*)

...then a fire hydrant, ...

...then a flashlight,...

page 14

SUMMARIZE

Think Aloud What important things have happened? Russ came to the firehouse, and his uncle asked him to help. Russ met the other firefighters and worked around the firehouse.

...and finally a helmet.

Uncle Jerry asked Russ to help him clean the fire boots.

Comprehension

Main Idea and Details
- (pages 6–7) I think the big idea of the book might be about working at a firehouse, since Russ gets a job at the firehouse.

Summarize
- (pages 8–14) What important things have happened? Russ came to the firehouse and his uncle asked him to help. Russ used the hose and then inspected the ax, the hydrant, the flashlight, and a helmet.

Story Words
(page 13) flashlight   (page 14) helmet

About the Author: Janet Elizabeth Rickert
Janet Elizabeth Rickert has been writing stories about her son Russ, who has Down Syndrome, since he was a toddler. Janet is a registered nurse and is a member of the National Association for Down Syndrome.

Big Book Inside Back Cover

ELL

pp. 10–11
clean, inspect: Act out scrubbing something. Say *clean*. Have children act out cleaning classroom objects and use the word. *Do you clean your hands before eating?* Say the word *inspect as you* look over something carefully. Have children repeat as they imitate your actions.

ax: Point to the picture of an *ax*. Tell children to join you in acting out chopping with an ax while they say *ax*.

pp. 12–13
fire hydrant: Point to the fire hydrant. Point to the water coming out and make a sound of gushing water. Say: *Water comes out of the fire hydrant.* Have children point to the fire hydrant and name it.

flashlight: Show children an actual flashlight. Have them operate or pretend to operate one as they say *flashlight*.

pp. 14–15
boots: Point to the boots. Run your hands over your shoe and up your leg, imitating something on the foot. Have children repeat.

Text Evidence

Main Idea and Details

Explain Remind children that when they answer a question, they must support their answer with text evidence.

Discuss Have children look at and listen to pages 16-21. Ask them to recall main events that happened in the story. Have children talk about it by looking at and pointing out the illustrations.

ELL

pp. 16–17
ladder: Point to the ladder. Have children climb imaginary ladders with you and say the word *ladder*.

p. 22
tires: Point to the tires on the picture of the fire truck. Then point to the tires on a toy truck. Say *wheels, tires*. Have children repeat and point to other toys that have tires. *Does a bicycle have tires?*

p. 23
hose: Point to the picture of the *hose*. Pretend to use a hose, imitating the sound of spraying water. Have children pretend to use a hose and say the word with you.

Develop Comprehension

pages 16–17

 MAIN IDEA AND DETAILS

- *What kind of work is Russ doing at the firehouse?* (He is helping to inspect and clean the firefighters' tools and equipment.)

Then, Russ helped Uncle Jerry clean the fire ladders.

pages 18–19

SPIRAL REVIEW **CLASSIFY AND CATEGORIZE**

- *What equipment does Russ inspect and clean here?* (ladder)
- *What other equipment did Russ inspect and clean?*

Russ scrubbed and rinsed them until they sparkled in the sun.

Next, Uncle Jerry and Russ gave Sparky, the firehouse dog, a bath.

pages 20–21

 SUMMARIZE

- *What important things have happened so far?*

When Russ was done, Sparky shook all the water off ... and Russ got wet too!

Then, Uncle Jerry and Russ cleaned the fire truck ...

pages 22–23

CONCEPTS ABOUT PRINT

Think Aloud I see an exclamation mark. I will read these words with lots of expression.

... and the tires!

Uncle Jerry helped Russ spray all the soap off with a big fire hose.

pages 24–25

✔ **MAIN IDEA AND DETAILS**

■ *What is the big idea of these pages?* (Russ is being thanked for helping out at the firehouse.)

But now it was getting late and Russ had done a lot of work, so his mom came to take him home. ㉔

The firemen said, "Thank you, Russ," and asked if Russ could come back soon. Russ was excited, and said, "Yes!" Everybody waved good-bye . . . ㉕

pages 26–27

✔ **SUMMARIZE**

■ *What did Russ do at the firehouse?* (He helped to clean the firefighters' tools and equipment.)

And that is how Russ got a job at the firehouse. ㉖

The End! ㉗

Respond to Literature

TALK ABOUT IT Have children talk about the words and photographs and refer to the book as they answer the questions. Have them retell a main event from the selection.

■ *What were some ways Russ helped at the firehouse?* (He helped check axes, helmets, and other equipment. He helped clean ladders, trucks, and the dog.) **LOCATE**

■ *What could Russ do the next time he goes to the firehouse?* (He could help check the hoses, slide down the pole, or wear the firefighters' boots.) **COMBINE**

■ *What is the big idea of the book?* (The big idea of the book is that firefighters do many things at the neighborhood firehouse.) **CONNECT**

Retell

Retelling Cards

GUIDED RETELLING

Tell children that now they will use the pictures on the cards to retell *Russ and the Firehouse.*

- Display **Retelling Card 1**. Based on children's needs, use either the Modeled, Guided, or ELL prompts. The ELL prompts contain support for English Language Learners based on levels of language acquisition.

- Repeat the procedure with the rest of the Retelling Cards, using the prompts to guide children's retelling.

- Discuss the story. *What did Russ learn about firehouses? What* **equipment** *did he see?*

- Have children sequence the main events of the story by writing or drawing descriptions of *Russ and the Firehouse.* Have children use their work to retell the main events to the class or a partner.

Fluency: Echo-Read

MODEL Reread page 25, using an emphatic tone as you read the dialogue. Reread the page and have children echo-read as you track the print.

Quick Check

Can children identify main idea and details to help understand a story?
Can children retell the main events of a story?

Retelling Rubric

 Excellent **4**

Retells the selection without prompting, using detailed information, and referring to text structure and features. Clearly describes the main idea.

3 **Good**

Retells the selection with little guidance, using some details, and occasionally referring to text structure and features. Generally describes the main idea.

2 **Fair**

Retells the selection with some guidance, using limited details. Partially describes the main idea.

 Unsatisfactory **1**

Retells the selection only when prompted, using limited details. Does not describe the main idea.

Vocabulary

Sequence Words

Say the following and dramatize each action:

First, we cook.

Next, we eat.

Last, we wash the dishes.

- Repeat each line and point out the word that tells the order in which things happen. Have children repeat the sentences.

- Play a modified version of "Simon Says" with children. First, *Simon says clap.* Next, *Simon says stand up.* Last, *touch your toes.* Repeat this sequence a few times with different directions.

NAME SEQUENCE WORDS Have children follow directions such as: First, *get a book.* Next, *open the book.* Last, *point to a picture.*

Story Words: *flashlight, helmet*

Display page 13 of *Russ and the Firehouse* and point out the picture of the flashlight. Then point to the written word on that page.

Explain that the word *flashlight* is made up of two words, *flash* and *light. A flashlight is a small lamp that you hold in your hand.* Show children a real one. Have them take turns shining it on something.

Display page 14 of *Russ and the Firehouse* and point out the picture and the word *helmet. What kind of helmets have you seen? Who else wears helmets? A helmet and flashlight are pieces of* **equipment** *that firefighters need to be safe.*

COMPOUND WORDS Remind children that compound words are made up of two smaller words. Flashlight *is made up of the two smaller words* flash *and* light. Ask children to identify other compound words.

  TIME TO MOVE!

Have children make pretend flashlights with their hands. Show them actions such as turning on, using, and turning off their imaginary flashlights. Have them follow actions in sequence.

Objectives

- Use sequence words
- Learn the story words *flashlight, helmet*
- Recognize compound words

Materials

- Big Book: *Russ and the Firehouse*
- flashlight
- Activity Book, p. 6

Digital Learning

LOG ON ▶ For children who need additional language support and oral vocabulary development, use the activities found at **www.macmillanmh.com**.

ELL

Reinforce Meaning Draw a smiley face on the board. As you draw each part, say: *First, we draw a circle. Next, we draw eyes inside the circle. Last, we draw a smile inside the circle.* Repeat the steps. Have children say the sentences as they gesture making smiley faces in the air.

Activity Book, page 6

Objectives
- Orally blend sounds to form words
- Identify letters for initial /h/, /o/, /p/ sounds
- Blend with initial /h/h

Materials
- Puppet
- Word-Building Cards
- pocket chart

Phonemic Awareness

✓ Phoneme Blending

Model

Use the **Puppet** to model how to blend the sounds in the word *hop*.

Repeat the routine with *had*.

Happy is going to say the sounds in a word. Listen to Happy as he says each sound: /h/ /o/ /p/. Happy can blend these sounds to say the word: *hop*. Say the sounds with Happy: /h/ /o/ /p/, /hooop/, *hop*. What is the word? (*hop*)

Guided Practice/Practice

Say the sounds. Children blend the sounds to form the words. Guide practice with the first word.

Happy is going to say the sounds in a word. Listen to Happy as he says each sound. Blend the sounds to say the word.

/h/ /a/ /d/   /h/ /a/ /m/   /h/ /ī/ /k/

/h/ /i/ /t/   /h/ /o/ /t/   /h/ /i/ /p/

Phonics

✓ Review

h	p	o

Model

Hold up **Word-Building Card** *h*.

Repeat the routine for the letters *p* and *o*.

This is the letter *h*. The letter *h* stands for /h/. You hear /h/ at the beginning of *house*.

Say the word. Write the letter *h*. Repeat with *pot*.

The beginning sound in the word *house* is /h/. The letter *h* stands for the /h/ sound. I'll write *h*.

Guided Practice/Practice

Say each word. Children write the letter that stands for the initial sound. Guide practice with the first word.

Listen as I say each word. Write the letter that stands for the beginning sound.

hand   pull   on   help

ox   hip   pin   otter

Build Fluency: Sound-Spellings

 Display the following **Word-Building Cards**: *a, c, f, h, i, m, n, o, p, r, s, t.*
Have children chorally say each sound. Repeat and vary the pace.

 ## Blend with /h/*h*

Model

Place Word-Building Card *h* in the pocket chart.

This letter is *h*. It stands for the /h/ sound. Say /h/.

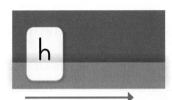

Place Word-Building Card *o* next to *h*. Move your hand from left to right.

This is the letter *o*. It stands for /o/. Listen as I blend the two sounds together: /hooo/. Now you say it. (/hooo/)

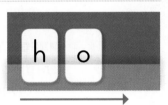

Place Word-Building Card *p* next to *ho*. Move your hand from left to right.

Repeat the routine with *hat*.

This is the letter *p*. It stands for /p/. Listen as I blend the three sounds together: /hooop/. Now you say it. (/hooop/, *hop*)

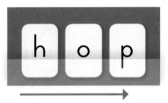

Guided Practice/Practice

Children blend the sounds to form words. Guide practice with the first word.

hip	ham	him	hit	mad
hot	had	hid	hop	had

ELL

Reinforce Meaning Review the meaning of the words in the Guided Practice. First, model saying each word for children to repeat. Then prompt them to demonstrate the meaning of words they know by pointing to examples or pictures, acting out, using antonyms, and paraphrasing.

Objectives

- Read decodable words with /h/h
- Read the high-frequency words *a, are, I, is, see*

Materials

- Decodable Reader: *Are Caps Hats?*
- High-Frequency Word Cards: *a, are, I, is, see*

Decodable Text

For additional decodable passages, see pages 19–20 of the **Teacher's Resource Book**.

Decodable Reader

Read *Are Caps Hats?*

Are Caps Hats?

 REVIEW HIGH-FREQUENCY WORDS Display the **High-Frequency Word Cards** for **a**, **are**, **I**, **is**, and **see**. Review the words using the **Read/Spell/Write** routine.

MODEL CONCEPTS ABOUT PRINT *I hold the book so the words on the cover are right side up. I read each sentence from left to right. I turn each page after I read it.*

PREDICT Ask children to say the title and describe the cover. *What are the children wearing on their heads? Do you think the story will be real or made up? Why?*

FIRST READ Have children point to each word, sounding out the decodable words and saying the sight words quickly. Children should chorally read the story the first time through.

DEVELOP COMPREHENSION Ask the following: *What are Nat and Tom doing? What does Min do while wearing his hat? Is Tim wearing a hat or cap?*

 SECOND READ Have partners reread the book together. Circulate, listen in, and provide corrective feedback.

A hat is on Nat.
Nat can sit on top.

2

A cap is on Tom.
Tom can fit him in.

3

A hat is on Min.
Min can sip, sip, sip.

4

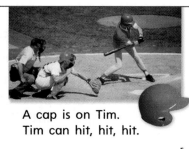

A cap is on Tim.
Tim can hit, hit, hit.

5

A hat is on Pam.
Pam can tap it.

6

A hat is on Sam.
Sam can tip it!

7

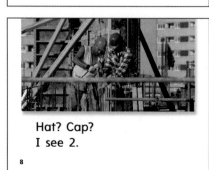

Hat? Cap?
I see 2.

8

Decodable Reader

Writing

Interactive Writing: Dialogue

REVIEW
Display and read aloud the pages in the **Big Book** *Russ and the Firehouse* with the speech balloons that you created in the Day 1 Shared Writing activity.

WRITE
Today we are going to write more sentences for pictures. Display a photo from **Teaching Chart 2, 8,** or **12** that shows a **neighborhood** setting. Collaborate with children to write the sentence frames in speech balloons on chart paper.

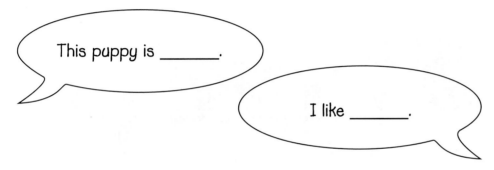

This puppy is _____.

I like _____.

- Explain that the sentences should tell what children in the picture might say. Have children suggest words for each sentence. Write their ideas in the frames to complete the sentences. Ask children to help by writing all of the letters they know.

- Read the completed sentences together as you track the print. Cut out the speech balloons and attach them to the pictures.

- Save the pictures and speech balloons to use in other writing activities.

- Then work with children to dictate additional sentences and to add details to what one of the children might say. Check with children that writing is in proper sequence.

Write About It

Ask children to draw in their Writer's Notebook. Ask them to draw an animal they've seen around their neighborhood or in a book, such as Sparky, the neighborhood firehouse dog. Ask them to write a caption or label for their drawing using the high-frequency word *is* or *play*.

Objectives

- Write dialogue
- Use letter knowledge to write letters in a word
- Develop draft by adding and sequencing detail

Materials

- Big Book: *Russ and the Firehouse*
- Shared Writing from Day 1
- Teaching Chart 2, 8, or 12

5-Day Writing	
Dialogue	
DAY 1	Shared: Dialogue
DAY 2	Interactive: Dialogue
DAY 3	Independent: Prewrite and Draft Dialogue
DAY 4	Independent: Revise and Edit Dialogue
DAY 5	Independent: Publish and Present

ELL

Prewriting Planning
Remind children that words inside speech balloons are the actual words that people or animals might speak. Have children dictate a sentence for you to write inside a speech balloon.

Transitions That Teach

While children line up for lunch, name activities and have children name the **equipment** needed to do each activity.

WHOLE GROUP

Oral Language
- Build Robust Vocabulary
- Oral Vocabulary Cards: "In Our Neighborhood"

✔ **Comprehension**
- Read "Let's Look at Maps"
- Text Feature: Use Maps

✔ **High-Frequency Words**
- Review *are*

✔ **Phonemic Awareness**
- Phoneme Blending

✔ **Phonics**
- Review /h/h, /f/f, /t/t, /k/c
- Blend with /h/h

Grammar
- Sentences

Writing
- Independent Writing: Dialogue

SMALL GROUP

- Differentiated Instruction, pages 1350–1375

Additional Vocabulary

To provide 15–20 minutes of additional vocabulary instruction, see Oral Vocabulary Cards 5-Day Plan. The pre- and posttests can be found in the **Teacher's Resource Book**, pages 224–225.

Oral Language

 Talk About It

Build Robust Vocabulary

BUILD BACKGROUND
Display **Oral Vocabulary Card 1** for "In Our Neighborhood" and read the title aloud. *There are many different places in neighborhoods that are there to help people. What kinds of places have you seen in your neighborhood?* Ask children to tell what they think is happening in the picture and predict what this selection will be about.

- Read the selection on the back of the cards. Check children's understanding using the Discuss, Compare and Contrast, and Main Idea and Details prompts. Pause at each oral vocabulary word and read the definition.

Oral Vocabulary Cards

Vocabulary Routine

Use the routine below to discuss the meaning of each word.

Define: When you **borrow** something, you use it for a short time and then return it. Say the word with me.
Example: We don't have enough markers, so we will borrow some from the other class.
Ask: What kinds of books would you like to borrow from the library?

Define: To **organize** means "to arrange things in a neat and orderly way." Say the word with me.
Example: The librarian organizes the books according to what they are about.
Ask: What things are organized in our classroom? How are they organized?

Define: **Frequently** means "often." Say the word with me.
Example: We sing songs during class frequently.
Ask: What activities do you and your family do frequently?

- Use the routine on Cards 1 and 2 to review the words **neighborhood** and **equipment**.

 SPIRAL REVIEW

- Review last week's words: *beneath, enter, habitat, raise, responsibility.*

Listen for Rhyme

IDENTIFY RHYME

Tell children that they will sing another song about the neighborhood. Play the rhyme and have children join in. Explain that the word *play* rhymes with *day* because they both end in /ā/. Guide children to name which two other words rhyme. (*call/all*) Then have children tell which of the following pairs of words rhyme: *street/hand, sleep/night, day/say, bright/light*.

TALK ABOUT THE NEIGHBORHOOD

Talk about the song and how it relates to the theme. Ask children to tell what they think is happening in the song. *What do the boys and girls do in their neighborhood?* Guide children to use complete sentences. For example, recast children's responses using complete sentences.

Come Out to Play

Girls and boys, come out to play,

The moon doth shine as bright as day;

Leave your supper, and leave your sleep,

And come with your playfellows into the street.

Come with a whoop, come with a call,

Come with a good will, or not at all.

Objectives

- Discuss the theme
- Use oral vocabulary words *borrow, equipment, frequently, neighborhood,* and *organize*
- Recognize rhyming words

Materials

- Oral Vocabulary Cards: "In Our Neighborhood"

Digital Learning

Song on **Listening Library Audio CD**

Objectives

- Retell important facts
- Interpret maps to find information
- Identify the topic and details in expository text
- Create a map

Material

- Big Book of Explorations, Vol. 2: "Let's Look at Maps," pp. 2–7
- poster board or butcher paper

Content Vocabulary

map a drawing of a place as it looks from above

symbol a picture that stands for a real thing

map key a list of the symbols used on a map

 Social Studies # Informational Text

Genre

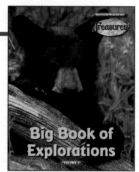

Big Book of Explorations

INFORMATIONAL TEXT: EXPOSITORY Tell children that this selection is **expository** text, a text that explains or gives information. Some expository text gives information using words and drawings. Tell children that some drawings give more information than words do.

READ "LET'S LOOK AT MAPS"

- **Preview and Predict** Display the first page and read the title as you track the print. To build background, point to the map on page 2. *This type of drawing is called a map.* Turn the pages and point out that there are different kinds of maps. *What will this selection be about?*

- **Content Vocabulary** Introduce and discuss the vocabulary words.

- **Text Feature: Maps** *A map is a drawing that shows where places are located. We can use a map to learn how to get somewhere.* Point to the map on page 2. *This map shows where different places in a neighborhood are located. What places do you see on this map?*

CONTENT FOCUS

As you read page 3, point out that the map shows different symbols. Then point to the Key. Explain that a Key shows what each symbol on a map stands for. Point to the symbol for the library on the Key and then to the library on the map. Repeat for the remaining symbols.

Ask children what they see on the map on pages 4–5. Explain the words such as *left/right, in front of/behind,* and *next to* tell about where things are located. Have children use these words in complete sentences to answer the questions on these pages. Then ask: *Where is the house on this map?* (It is to the right of the bakery.) *What is behind the library?* (The park is behind the library.) *Where is the police station?* (It is to the left of the fire station.)

Read aloud page 6. Point to Alaska and Hawaii, and explain why these states are shown as insets on the United States map. After reading page 7, ask children to discuss similarities and differences among the maps in the selection.

pages 2–3

pages 4–5

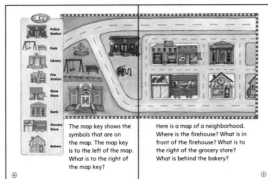

pages 6–7

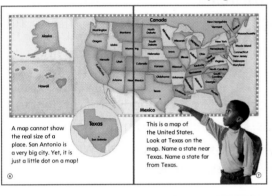

Retell and Respond

- *What are maps used for?*

- *What places did the maps in this selection show?*

- *Why is a bookshelf a good symbol for a library?*

- *What is the topic, or main idea, of this selection?*

Connect to Content

Social Studies: Map the Classroom

- You will need a large poster board or sheet of butcher paper.

- Review that a map is a drawing that shows where places are located. Tell children that they will create a map of their classroom.

- Ask children to describe the location of things in the classroom using location words. For example: *The easels are behind the reading corner.*

- Have children suggest and draw symbols on the map to stand for areas and items in the classroom.

ELL

Beginning

Confirm Understanding
Point to the library on page 3 and say: *This must be the library. I see a bookshelf. It's a good symbol for the library. What is the symbol for the library?* (a bookshelf) Continue with the other rooms.

Intermediate

Enhance Understanding
As you read each page, ask questions such as these: *Do you think a bookshelf is a good symbol for a library? Why?* Guide children to answer in complete sentences.

Advanced

Map Study Ask children to look at the map on pages 6–7. *Let's look for the state we live in. Which states are next to our state? Show and tell me. Which states are near the ocean? Show me. Which states are near Canada? Show me. Where is Mexico? Show me.*

Objectives

- Read the high-frequency word *are*
- Review the high-frequency word *we*

Materials

- High-Frequency Word Cards: *We, are*
- Big Book of Explorations, Vol. 2: "Let's Look at Maps"
- pocket chart
- Picture Cards; Teacher's Resource Book, pp. 92–94
- index card with: period mark
- Activity Book, pp. 7–8
- Practice Book, pp. 123–124

High-Frequency Words

 are

 are

SPIRAL REVIEW **REVIEW** Display the **High-Frequency Word Card** for **are**. Review the word using the **Read/Spell/Write** routine.

Repeat the routine for the word **we**.

MODEL *I am going to read a sentence from "Let's Look at Maps."* Read the sentence on page 2, *A map is a drawing that shows where places are,* and hold up the card when you say the word *are*.

PRACTICE Read pages 3–4 of the selection. Tell children to nod when you say the word *are*.

APPLY Build sentences in the pocket chart using High-Frequency Word Cards and **Picture Cards**. Have children point to the high-frequency words. Use the sentence below and the following: *We are [jumping]. We are [hopping]. We are [swimming].*

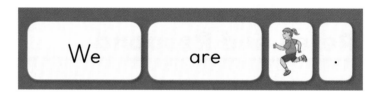

| We | | are | | . |

READ FOR FLUENCY Have children use the Take-Home Book to review high-frequency words and practice fluency. Guide children to use fluent phrasing as they read.

Quick Check

Can children read the word *are*?

During **Small Group Instruction**

If No → **Approaching Level** Provide additional practice with high-frequency words, page 1360.

If Yes → **On Level** Children are ready to read the Take-Home Book.

Beyond Level Children are ready to read the Take-Home Book.

TIME TO MOVE!

Tell children to act out various actions, such as riding a bike, as they respond: *We are riding bikes.*

Activity Book, pages 7–8
Practice Book, pages 123–124

Phonemic Awareness

✓ Phoneme Blending

Model

Use the Puppet to say the sounds.

Listen as Happy says the sounds in a word: /h/ /i/ /p/. Happy can blend the sounds together: *hip*. Say the sounds with Happy: /h/ /i/ /p/. Now say the word: *hip*.

Repeat the routine with *hop*.

Guided Practice/Practice

Say the sounds. Children blend the sounds to say the words. Do the first word together.

Happy is going to say the sounds in words. Listen to Happy as he says each sound. Blend the sounds to say the word.

/h/ /a/ /d/	/h/ /i/ /m/	/h/ /ō/ /m/
/h/ /i/ /l/	/h/ /ō/ /l/	/h/ /ē/

Objective
- Blend sounds to form words

Materials
- Puppet

Objectives

- Review sound-spellings for /h/h, /f/f, /k/c, /t/t
- Blend sounds in words with /h/h

Materials

- Word-Building Cards
- pocket chart

Phonics

 ## Review

Model

Display **Word-Building Card** *h*.

Repeat for *c, f, t.*

This letter is *h*. The letter *h* stands for /h/. *House* has /h/ at the beginning. Say /h/ with me. What's the sound? What's the name of the letter?

Point to the initial letter.

Repeat with *fast*.

I will write a word. I'll point to the letter that stands for the beginning sound: *happy*. *Happy* begins with /h/, so I'll point to the letter *h*.

Guided Practice/Practice

Children point to the letter that stands for the initial sound.

Guide practice with the first word.

I'm going to say more words. You will point to the letter that stands for the beginning sound.

| help | cap | fun | tiger | cot | ten |
| here | tail | find | car | hot | fork |

Build Fluency: Sound-Spellings

SPIRAL REVIEW Display the following Word-Building Cards: *a, c, f, h, i, m, n, o, p, r, s, t.* Have children chorally say each sound. Repeat and vary the pace.

Blend with /h/h

Model

Place **Word-Building Card** *h* in the pocket chart.

This letter is *h*. The letter *h* stands for the /h/ sound. Say /h/.

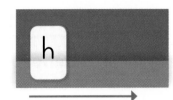

Place Word-Building Card *i* next to *h*. Move your hand from left to right.

This letter is *i*. The letter *i* stands for the /i/ sound. Listen as I blend the two sounds together: /hiii/. Now you say it. (/hiii/)

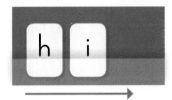

Place Word-Building Card *t* next to *hi*. Move your hand from left to right.

This letter is *t*. The letter *t* stands for the /t/ sound. Listen as I blend the three sounds: /hiiit/. Now you say it. (/hiiit/)

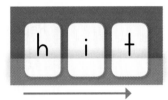

Repeat the routine with *hid*.

Guided Practice/Practice

Children blend the sounds to form words. Guide practice with the first word.

hat	fin	hip	hit	pop
hop	pot	cap	can	hot

 Read Words

Apply

Write the words and sentences. Guide practice with the word *hit*, using the **Sound-by-Sound Blending Routine**. Read the sentences with children.

> hit hip
> I can hit.
> Are you hip?

ELL

Pronunciation The /i/ sound does not have an exact equivalent in some languages, including Spanish. Help children pronounce /i/ correctly by modeling the pronunciation of words with medial /i/ and having them repeat the words after you. Display the small **Sound-Spelling Cards** with articulation photos to guide children.

ELL

Basic and Academic Vocabulary Display animal Photo Cards from this and prior lessons. Pair English Language Learners with fluent speakers and have partners make up sentences that name a Photo Card animal and tell whether it lives on land or in water. Write partners' sentences, read them chorally, and ask: *What animal is your sentence about? Where does the animal in your sentence live?*

Grammar

Sentences

MODEL Remind children that a sentence tells a complete thought. Explain that a sentence has to have a naming part and a telling part. *The naming part tells who or what the sentence is about. The telling part tells what happens.*

- Tell children that you will say a complete sentence. Say: *The girl ate breakfast.* Explain that the naming part of the sentence is the *girl*; the telling part of the sentence is *ate breakfast.*

- Ask a child to stand. Tell children that you will say a sentence about him or her. Say, for example: *Joey likes baseball.* Ask children to tell the naming part and the telling part of your sentence. (Joey/likes baseball)

- Repeat with other children.

PRACTICE Show children the **Photo Cards**. Model saying complete sentences about the photos. For example:

- *The dolphin swims in the sea.*

- *The deer leaps over the log.*

- *The umpire wears a mask.*

After each sentence, ask children to identify the naming part and the telling part. Have children make up their own complete sentences with a naming part and telling part about the Photo Cards.

Then remind children about sentences that use the words *in, on, at,* and *for.* Model saying sentences using the prepositions.

- *The fish swims* in *the lake.*

- *The frog leaps* on *the rock.*

- *The man sits* at *the table.*

- *The grandmother waits* for *the bus.*

After each sentence, guide children to identify the proposition.

Writing

Independent Writing: Dialogue

Display the speech balloons from the Shared and Interactive Writing activities.

BRAINSTORM

WRITING TRAIT: IDEAS Tell children that they will draw a picture of themselves doing an activity and write a sentence about what they might say. First they must choose an idea to write about.

Think Aloud Let me think of something I like to do. I like to go to the library. When I'm reading, I might say, "This is a good book!"

PREWRITE

Ask children to think of something they enjoy. Ask them what they might say as they do it. List their ideas on the board as a reference.

> Things We Like to Do
> go to the library
> play games
> go swimming

- Draw a picture of yourself smiling as you read a book. Draw a speech balloon and write the sentence *This is a good book!* inside. Read the sentence aloud as you track the print.

- Have children select an activity from the list to write about.

DRAFT

- Have children draw a picture of themselves doing the activity they chose. Ask them to draw a speech balloon and to write a sentence that tells what they might say as they do the activity.

- Collect and save children's work to use tomorrow.

Write About It
Have children draw in their Writer's Notebook. Have them draw themselves at a **neighborhood** playground and label the **equipment**.

Objectives
- Write dialogue
- Plan a draft
- Use writing trait: ideas
- Use letter knowledge to write words and sentences

Materials
- Interactive Writing from Day 2

5-Day Writing
Dialogue	
DAY 1	Shared: Dialogue
DAY 2	Interactive: Dialogue
DAY 3	Independent: Prewrite and Draft Dialogue
DAY 4	Independent: Revise and Edit Dialogue
DAY 5	Independent: Publish and Present

ELL

Prewriting Planning
Before children begin working on their Writer's Notebooks, ask them to name and describe playground equipment they like. List equipment children mention and help them label the equipment they draw.

Transitions That Teach

As children line up, have them name things they sometimes **borrow** and why they borrow them.

WHOLE GROUP

Oral Language
- Build Robust Vocabulary

✔ **Comprehension**
- Read Aloud: "The Black Cat"

Vocabulary
- Sequence Words
- Story Words: *flashlight, helmet*

✔ **Phonemic Awareness**
- Phoneme Segmentation

✔ **Phonics**
- Picture Sort
- Blend with /h/h, /f/f, /o/o
- Decodable Reader:
  Are Caps Hats?

Writing
- Independent Writing: Revise and Edit Dialogue

Oral Language

 Talk About It

Build Robust Vocabulary

THINGS TO DO WHEN A PET IS LOST

Display page 19 of *Russ and the Firehouse* and discuss what the firefighters would do if Sparky the dog was lost.

- *How could the firefighters let the people in the* **neighborhood** *know that Sparky was lost? How could they* **organize** *a plan to find Sparky? What* **equipment** *might they use to help them find Sparky?*

CREATE A POSTER

Draw a lost-pet poster with the heading as shown below. Ask children what other information they would include about the pet.

Think Aloud Making posters is one way to tell people in the neighborhood about a lost dog. I'll write *Lost Pet* on the poster. Sparky is white with black spots. So let's add the words *white dog with black spots.*

Guide children to suggest additional details, such as the name of the dog, special traits, and an address or phone number to contact. Read the poster with children as you track the print.

Post the posters in the classroom so children can read them on their own for enjoyment.

Lost Pet

White dog with black spots
Red collar
Dog's name: Sparky
Likes to ride in trucks
Call the firehouse: 555-1234

ELL
ENGLISH LANGUAGE LEARNERS

Beginning	Intermediate	Advanced
Confirm Understanding Read the description of Sparky on the poster, one detail at a time. Then turn to pages 19–20 of the **Big Book** *Russ and the Firehouse* and ask children to find each detail in the photographs of the dog.	**Add Details** Have children look at the photographs of Sparky in the Big Book and prompt them to add details to the description of the dog on the poster. For example, ask: *What size is Sparky? What do you remember about him?*	**Extend Ideas** Have children suggest places they would put the posters and think of other ways to inform people about a lost pet. *Where would you put the posters in your neighborhood? Why? What other things can you do?*

Listen for Alliteration

IDENTIFY ALLITERATION

Remind children that sometimes, a group of words begin with the same sound. For example, in *Baby boy bounces the ball*, most of the words in the group begin with the same sound, /b/.

NEIGHBORHOOD RHYME

Tell children that they will recite "Five Brave Firefighters" that they learned earlier in the week. Play the rhyme and have children join in. Ask: *Where do you see firefighters in your **neighborhood**? What type of **equipment** do they use?*

Discuss other types of community helpers in the neighborhood that they have talked about, such as police and paramedics. *What do they do?*

Ask: *Which words in "Five Brave Firefighters" begin with the same sound?* (*five, firefighters, fire, flames*) *Let's think of more words that begin with the /f/ sound to add. For example,* Five firefighters fight the flames. Have children repeat the line, emphasizing the /f/ sound.

Five Brave Firefighters

Five brave firefighters sit very still

Until they see a fire on top of the hill.

Use fingers to number firefighters, then pantomime the actions.

One rings the bell, ding-dong;

Two pulls his big boots on;

Three jumps in the fire engine red;

Four pops a fire hat on her head;

Five drives the truck to the spot,

As the big yellow flames get very hot.

Shh! goes the water from the spout,

And quick as a wink, the fire is out.

Clap hands.

Objectives

- Listen for and recognize alliteration
- Contribute ideas for a poster
- Use oral vocabulary words *borrow, equipment, frequently, neighborhood,* and *organize*

Materials

- Big Book: *Russ and the Firehouse*

Oral Vocabulary

Have children use each word in a sentence about this week's stories.

borrow	equipment
frequently	neighborhood
organize	

Review Work with children to review last week's words. Ask questions, such as: *What do you raise when you need to ask a question?*

beneath	enter
habitat	raise
responsibility	

Digital Learning

Fingerplay on **Listening Library Audio CD**

Objectives

- Listen and respond to a folktale
- Recognize recurring phrases and the big idea of a folktale

Materials

- Read-Aloud Anthology: "The Black Cat," pp. 81–87

ELL

Build Understanding

Explain to children what picture-drawing stories are. Read a portion of the story and have children make a drawing that reflects story details in the part you read. For example, children can trace the capital letter *T* for *Tommy* and the capital letter *S* for *Sally*.

Readers Theater

BUILDING LISTENING AND SPEAKING SKILLS

Distribute copies of "The Three Little Pigs," Read-Aloud Anthology pages 169–184. Have children practice performing the play throughout the unit. Assign parts and have children present the play or perform it as a dramatic reading at the end of the unit.

Interactive
Read Aloud

Listening Comprehension

Read Aloud

GENRE: LITERARY TEXT/FOLKTALE

Tell children that you will be drawing as you tell the folktale. Ask them to watch and listen carefully. Tell children that many stories begin the same way. Point out that this one begins with the words, "Once upon a time…"

CULTURAL PERSPECTIVES

"The Black Cat" is an American picture-drawing folktale. Telling picture-drawing stories is a tradition that can be found in many cultures around the world, including that of the Japanese and the Inuit. Australian Aborigines are known for drawing story-pictures in the sand with fingers or sticks as their **equipment**.

READ "THE BLACK CAT"

- **MODEL ASKING QUESTIONS ABOUT SUMMARIZING** Use the Think Alouds provided at point of use in the folktale for the strategy.

- **MODEL FLUENT READING** Read aloud the folktale with fluent expression. Stop occasionally so that children can predict what will happen next.

- **EXPAND VOCABULARY** See page 81 of the **Read-Aloud Anthology** to teach new words using the **Define/Example/Ask** routine.

Respond to Literature

TALK ABOUT IT Ask children to tell the big idea of the story. Ask them to trace their fingers over the outline of the cat.

- *Where did you think Tommy and Sally might find the mother cat?*

- *What main parts of the story can you recall by looking at the cat?*

Write About It

Tell children to draw a picture of a black cat. Ask them to write a label or sentence about where it might go.

Vocabulary

Sequence Words

REVIEW SEQUENCE WORDS
Each time I say a sequence word, tap the table. Read the following story:

> Todd wants to make a birthday card for his grandma. First, he gets a yellow piece of paper. Yellow is Grandma's favorite color. Next, he draws big red flowers on the front of the card. Todd writes "Happy Birthday. Love, Todd" inside the card. Last, Todd asks Dad to help him mail the card. "Grandma will like this card," says Dad.

Story Words: *flashlight, helmet*

Display page 13 of *Russ and the Firehouse.* Explain that a *flashlight* is a type of tool. Ask children for examples of other types of tools or **equipment** people use.

Display page 14. Talk about people who wear *helmets* and the jobs they do.

To extend the lesson, take the class to the school library. Assist children in finding and checking out books about materials people use in their jobs.

REVIEW COMPOUND WORDS
Remind children that compound words are made up of shorter words. Have them identify the two shorter words in the word *flashlight.*

TIME TO MOVE!

Direct groups of three children to different parts of the classroom. *Go to the bookshelf. Mina, go first. Ben, go next. Lee, go last. Go to the sink. Sara, go first. Matt, go next. Dee, go last.* Continue until each child has had a chance to follow directions to three different areas of the classroom.

Objectives
- Use sequence words
- Review story words *flashlight, helmet*
- Review compound words
- Follow directions in sequence

Materials
- Big Book: *Russ and the Firehouse*

ELL

Reinforce Vocabulary
Divide the board into thirds and number the parts *1, 2, 3.* Call children to the board and group them evenly under each part. Then tell the groups to perform certain actions, such as: *First, I want group one to look up. Next, I want group two to look down. Last, I want group three to wave.* Have the groups trade positions and repeat with other actions.

Objectives

- Segment sounds in words
- Sort words by initial sound/letter /h/h, /f/f, /o/o
- Blend sounds in words with /h/h, /f/f, /o/o

Materials

- Sound Box
- WorkBoard Sound Boxes; Teacher's Resource Book, p. 136
- markers
- Word-Building Cards
- pocket chart
- Photo Cards: *farm, feather, feet, fire, fish, five, football, fork, fox, hair, hammer, hand, hat, hay, helicopter, hippo, hook, horse, house, October, octopus, olive, ostrich, otter, owl, ox*
- Activity Book, pp. 9–10
- Practice Book, pp. 125–126

ELL

Pronunciation Display and have children name **Photo Cards** from this and prior lessons to reinforce sound-letter relationships and word meanings. Point to a card and ask: *What do you see?* (a hammer) *What is the sound at the beginning of the word* hammer? (/h/) *What is the letter?* (h) Repeat with other cards.

Phonemic Awareness

 ## Phoneme Segmentation

Model

Use the **Sound Boxes**.

Place a marker in each box as you say the sounds.

Repeat with *hop*.

Listen as I say the sounds in the word *hit*: /h/ /i/ /t/.

I will place a marker in a box as I say each sound: /h/ /i/ /t/. There are three sounds in *hit,* so I placed a marker in three boxes. Say the sounds in *hit* with me: /h/ /i/ /t/. What is the word? What are the sounds in *hit*?

Guided Practice/Practice

Children segment the sounds and say the word. Guide practice with the first row.

hip, /h/ /i/ /p/	*hot,* /h/ /o/ /t/
had, /h/ /a/ /d/	*ham,* /h/ /a/ /m/
hat, /h/ /a/ /t/	*him,* /h/ /i/ /m/

Phonics

 ## Picture Sort

Model

Place **Word-Building Card** *h* in the pocket chart.

Repeat with *f* and *o*.

This is the letter *h*. The letter *h* stands for the /h/ sound.

Hold up the **Photo Card** for *hammer*.

Repeat with *feather*.

Here is a picture of a hammer. *Hammer* begins with /h/. I will place *hammer* under the letter *h*.

Children continue to sort the Photo Cards. Guide practice with the next card.

Build Fluency: Sound-Spellings

  Display the following **Word-Building Cards**: *a, c, f, h, i, m, n, o, p, s, t.* Have children chorally say each sound. Repeat and vary the pace.

✦ Blend with /h/h, /f/f, /o/o

Model

Place Word-Building Card *h* in the pocket chart.

This is the letter *h*. The letter *h* stands for the /h/ sound. Say /h/.

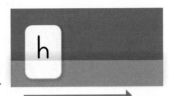

Place Word-Building Card *a* next to *h*. Move your hand from left to right.

This is the letter *a*. The letter *a* stands for the /a/ sound.

Let's blend these two sounds together: /haaa/. Say it again. (/haaa/)

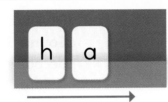

Place Word-Building Card *t* next to *ha*. Move your hand from left to right.

Repeat the routine for *fat* and *ham*.

This is the letter *t*. The letter *t* stands for the /t/ sound. Now let's blend all three sounds together: /haaat/. Let's say it again. (/haaat/, *hat*)

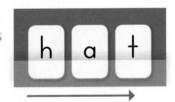

Guided Practice/Practice

Children blend the sounds to form words. Guide practice with the first word.

| fin | pot | hat | not | hip | can |
| hot | hop | fan | him | cap | pin |

Corrective Feedback

Blending: Sound Error Model the sound that children missed, then have them repeat the sound. For example, for the word *hat*, say: *My turn.* Tap under the letter *h* in the word *hat* and say: *Sound? What's the sound?* Then return to the beginning of the word. Say: *Let's start over.* Blend the word with children again.

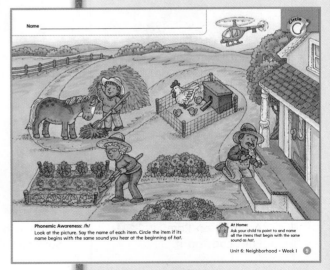

Activity Book, pages 9–10
Practice Book, pages 125–126

Objectives

- Read decodable words with /h/h
- Read the high-frequency word *are*
- Review the high-frequency words *for, you, is, play, see, the, to*
- Reread for fluency

Materials

- Decodable Reader: *Are Caps Hats?*
- High-Frequency Word Cards: *for, you, is, play, see, the, to*
- Sound-Spelling Cards: *Dolphin, Rose*

Decodable Text

For additional decodable passages, see pages 19–20 of the **Teacher's Resource Book**.

Decodable Reader

Read *Are Caps Hats?*

Are Caps Hats?

 REVIEW Review this week's high-frequency words and phonics skills using the word lists on the inside back cover of *Are Caps Hats?*

Review the high-frequency words **for**, **you**, **is**, **play**, **see**, **the**, and **to** using the **Read/Spell/Write** routine. Then have children chorally read the high-frequency word list.

Review the phonics skills /d/d and /r/r using the *Dolphin* and *Rose* **Sound-Spelling Cards**. Then have children chorally read the decodable word list. Model blending as needed and take note of children who struggle while reading these words. Provide additional instruction and practice during Small Group time.

MODEL CONCEPTS ABOUT PRINT

Demonstrate book handling. *I hold the book so that the cover is on the front and the words are not upside down. I open the book by turning the cover. Then I turn each page as I read it.*

 SECOND READ Have children reread the book with a partner. Have partners turn to each other to ask and answer questions about the text. Circulate and listen in, providing corrective feedback as needed. Then have children reread the book independently.

A hat is on Nat.
Nat can sit on top.

2

A cap is on Tom.
Tom can fit him in.

3

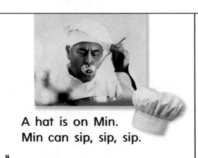

A hat is on Min.
Min can sip, sip, sip.

4

A cap is on Tim.
Tim can hit, hit, hit.

5

A hat is on Pam.
Pam can tap it.

6

A hat is on Sam.
Sam can tip it!

7

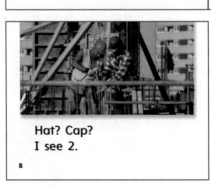

Hat? Cap?
I see 2.

8

Decodable Reader

Writing

Independent Writing: Dialogue

REVISE AND EDIT

Distribute children's drawings and speech balloons from Day 3. Have them reread their speech balloons and check for the following:

- Did I write a sentence for my speech balloon?

- Does the sentence begin with a capital letter?

- Does the sentence express what I want it to in the picture? Can I add more detail?

- Did I draw a picture of someone or something in my neighborhood?

Circulate and help children as they review and revise their sentences by adding details. Tell them to write their name at the top of the paper. Have children share their sentences with a partner.

Write About It

Ask children to draw a picture of where they like to go in their **neighborhood** to spend time indoors. Have them label the drawing.

WHOLE GROUP

Oral Language
- Build Robust Vocabulary

✔ **Comprehension**
- Strategy: Summarize
- Skill: Identify Main Idea and Details
- Read Across Texts

✔ **Vocabulary**
- Review High-Frequency Words
- Build Fluency
- Review Sequence Words

✔ **Phonemic Awareness**
- Phoneme Segmentation

✔ **Phonics**
- Read Words
- Dictation

Writing
- Independent Writing: Publish and Present

SMALL GROUP

- Differentiated Instruction, pages 1350–1375

Review and Assess
Oral Language
Build Robust Vocabulary

REVIEW WORDS

Review this week's oral vocabulary words with children. Explain that all of the words will be used to discuss moving to a new home. Talk about what it means to move to a new home. *Sometimes we need to move away from our old neighborhood and move into a new one.*

Use the following questions to check children's understanding:

- What might a new **neighborhood** have if you were to move to a new home?

- What kind of **equipment** would a moving company need to help you move to a new home?

- What could you ask to **borrow** from a new neighbor if you were to move to a new home?

- How would you help **organize** the kitchen in a new home?

- Would you **frequently** like to move to a new home? Why or why not?

REVIEW SONGS AND RHYMES ABOUT THE NEIGHBORHOOD

Recite the rhyme "Five Brave Firefighters" and ask children to sing along. Have children describe what firefighters do in the neighborhood. Then sing the song "Come Out to Play" with children. Have children name the words that begin with the same sound.

Review and Assess
Comprehension

STRATEGY Summarize

REFLECT ON THE STRATEGY Tell children that good readers remind themselves of the important things that have happened in a story as they read it.

Think Aloud Thinking about the main events helps me understand the big idea of the story.

SKILL Identify Main Ideas and Details

Lead children in reviewing how they used the skill of recognizing main idea and details in *Russ and the Firehouse* and "The Black Cat."

- *What jobs did Russ do at the firehouse? What **equipment** did he clean and inspect?*

- *What was the big idea of the book?*

- *What happened after Tommy and Sally decided to search for the cat?*

- *What was the story mostly about?*

Reading Across Texts

Create a chart like the one shown to compare and contrast the nonfiction book *Russ and the Firehouse* and the nonfiction article "Let's Look at Maps." Talk together about the people and places shown in the **neighborhoods**. You may wish to add another column for "The Black Cat."

Russ and the Firehouse	Let's Look at Maps
nonfiction	nonfiction
photographs	photographs and illustrations
about real things	about real things
how a boy helps out in a firehouse	how maps show us places

Objectives

- Review summarizing
- Review main idea and details
- Compare and contrast genres
- Listen and share information

Materials

- Big Book: *Russ and the Firehouse*
- Big Book of Explorations, Vol. 2: "Let's Look at Maps"
- Read-Aloud Anthology: "The Black Cat," pp. 81–87
- Activity Book, p. 11

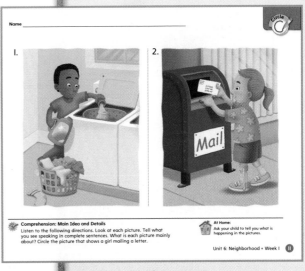

Activity Book, page 11

Objectives
- Review high-frequency words *are, to, have, is, play*
- Build fluency
- Review sequence words

Materials
- High-Frequency Word Cards: *are, to, have, is, play*

Fluency

Connected Text Have children reread this week's **Decodable Reader** with a partner. Circulate, listen in, and note those children who need additional instruction and practice reading this week's decodable and sight words.

Review and Assess

Vocabulary

 ## High-Frequency Words

Distribute one of the following **High-Frequency Word Cards** to children: **are**, **to**, **have**, **is**, and **play**. Say: *When you hear the word that is on your card, stand and hold up your card.*

- *We like* to *play.*
- *Boots and axes* are *firefighters'* **equipment**.
- *I* have *a toy boat.*
- *My sweater* is *blue.*
- *Let's walk* to *the library.*

Build Fluency: Word Automaticity

Rapid Naming Display the High-Frequency Word Cards *are, to, have, is,* and *play*. Point quickly to each card, at random, and have children read the word as quickly as they can.

are	to	have	is	play

Sequence Words

Display High-Frequency Word Cards *are, to,* and *have* in a row. Ask a child to move the cards so that *are* is the *first* card. Ask another child to move the cards so that *to* is the *next* card. Ask a third child to move the cards so that *have* is the *last* card. Repeat with other children. Have children repeat the sequence words as quickly as they can.

TIME TO MOVE!

Ask children to listen to three-part directions, then do what you have requested. *The first step is to raise your hand. The next step is to wave at me. The last step is to put your hand down.*

Review and Assess
Phonemic Awareness

Phoneme Segmentation

Guided Practice

Use the **Sound Box** to segment the sounds in the word *hop*.

Repeat with *hide*.

Let's say the sounds in the word *hop*: /h/ /o/ /p/. We'll place a marker in a box as we say each sound in *hop*. There are three sounds in *hop*: /h/ /o/ /p/. Say the sounds again with me: /h/ /o/ /p/.

Practice

Distribute Sound Boxes and markers.

Say each word. Children say each sound as they place a marker in a box.

I will say a word. You say each sound in the word as you place a marker in a box.

hat, /h/ /a/ /t/	*it*, /i/ /t/
hip, /h/ /i/ /p/	*hid*, /h/ /i/ /d/
him, /h/ /i/ /m/	*hot*, /h/ /o/ /t/
ham, /h/ /a/ /m/	*fat*, /f/ /a/ t/

Objective

- Segment words into phonemes

Materials

- Sound Box
- WorkBoard Sound Boxes; Teacher's Resource Book, p. 136
- markers

Objectives

- Review sound-spellings /f/f, /h/h, /o/o
- Read and write simple one-syllable words

Materials

- Word-Building Cards
- pocket chart
- 4 index cards with: *We, can, hop,* period mark
- 4 index cards with: *We, are, hot,* period mark
- Sound Box
- WorkBoard Sound Boxes; Teacher's Resource Book, p. 136
- markers
- Activity Book, p. 12

Phonics: /h/h
Say the name of each picture. Identify the sound that you hear at the beginning of each picture name. Write the letter below the picture if its name begins with the /h/ sound.

At Home: Ask your child to say the name of each picture that begins with the same sound as house.

⑫ Unit 6: Neighborhood • Week 1

Activity Book, page 12

Review and Assess
Phonics
Build Fluency: Sound-Spellings

Rapid Naming Display the following **Word-Building Cards**: *a, c, f, h, i, m, n, o, p, s, t.* Have children chorally say each sound as quickly as they can.

✓ Read Words

Apply

Distribute the first set of cards. Have children stand in sequence.	Let's read the sentence together. *We can hop.*
Repeat, using the other set of cards.	Let's read this sentence together. *We are hot.*

✓ Dictation

Dictate sounds for children to spell.

Listen as I say a sound. Repeat the sound, then write the letter that stands for the sound.

/a/   /t/   /s/   /f/   /m/

/k/   /o/   /h/   /n/   /i/

Then dictate words for children to spell. Model for children how to use the **Sound Boxes** to segment the sounds in the words. Have them repeat.

Write the letters and words on the board for children to self-correct.

Now let's write some words. I will say a word. I want you to repeat the word, then think about how many sounds are in the word. Use your Sound Boxes to count the sounds. Then write one letter for each sound you hear.

dad	hop	mad	him
dot	Ron	tap	hat
ram	mat	fan	mop

Review and Assess
Writing

Independent Writing: Dialogue

PUBLISH

Explain to children that you will gather their pictures and speech balloons to make a class book.

- Brainstorm ideas for a title, such as "What We Say."

- Have a few children work on a cover for the book. Write the title on the cover.

- Make holes along the edges of the cover and each page.

- Bind the pages together with yarn.

PRESENT

Have children take turns reading their speech balloons and telling what the pictures show.

LISTENING, SPEAKING, AND VIEWING

- Remind children to speak clearly and to be good listeners when a classmate is speaking.

- Praise children for their hard work and place the finished book in the Reading Workstation. Children may wish to add a copy of their work to their Writing Portfolios.

Write About It
Have children draw a picture of a person from their **neighborhood** who uses special **equipment**, such as a helmet. Ask them to label their drawing.

Objective
- Publish and present writing

Materials
- children's writing from Day 4

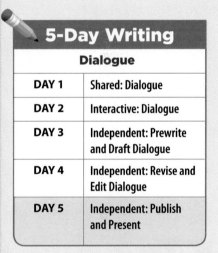

5-Day Writing
	Dialogue
DAY 1	Shared: Dialogue
DAY 2	Interactive: Dialogue
DAY 3	Independent: Prewrite and Draft Dialogue
DAY 4	Independent: Revise and Edit Dialogue
DAY 5	Independent: Publish and Present

Transitions That Teach
While children pack up, have them talk about ways they can **organize** their book bags or the classroom.

Approaching Level

Oral Language

Objective Preteach oral vocabulary: *neighborhood, equipment*
Materials • none

THEME WORDS: *neighborhood, equipment*

- Tell children the meanings for **neighborhood** and **equipment**. A neighborhood *consists of people who live close to one another. There is a firehouse in my* neighborhood. Equipment *refers to tools or supplies that are needed. A firefighter needs special* equipment *to do his job.*

- Discuss the words with children. *What is your* neighborhood *like? What* equipment *do we use in school?*

- Have children use the following sentence frames to generate complete oral sentences using the words: *Many of us live in the neighborhood near* _____. *A firefighter uses all kinds of equipment, such as* _____.

High-Frequency Words

Objective Preteach high-frequency words
Materials • **High-Frequency Word Card:** *are*

PRETEACH WORD: *are*

- Display the **High-Frequency Word Card** for **are**.

- **Read** Point to and say the word *are. This is the word* are. *We use it to say:* You are, we are, they are. *You are my friend.*

- **Spell** *The word* are *is spelled* a-r-e. Have children read and spell *are*.

- **Write** Finally, have children write the word *are*.

- Have children work with a partner to make up sentences using the word *are*. Ask them to talk about what the other is like: *You are funny; you are quiet;* etc.

HIGH-FREQUENCY WORDS REVIEW

Display the High-Frequency Word Cards for words previously taught, one card at a time, and have children chorally read and spell the word. Mix and repeat. Note words children need to review.

Tier 2

ELL

Partners When pairing children to make up sentences, pair English Language Learners with children who are more proficient. Write their sentences, read them together, and point out the high-frequency word *are*.

Approaching Level

Phonemic Awareness

Objective   Identify initial /h/ sound

Materials   • **Photo Cards:** *hair, hammer, hand, hat, helicopter, hippo, horse, house*
                 • **Sound-Spelling Card:** *Hippo*

PHONEME ISOLATION

Model

■ Display the **Photo Card** for *hat. This is a hat. Listen for the beginning sound in* hat: */haaat/.* Hat *begins with /h/. Repeat for the other words.*

■ Distribute the small **Sound-Spelling Cards**. Point out the articulation picture. *When I say the sound, I can feel air come out of my mouth.*

Guided Practice/Practice

■ Have children select a Photo Card, name it, and say the initial sound: *This is a _____. _____ begins with /h/.*

Phonics

Objective   Recognize words that begin with /h/*h*

Materials   • **Photo Cards:** *hammer, hand, hat, horse, house*
                 • **Word-Building Cards**

PRETEACH: RECOGNIZE /h/*h*

Model

■ Display the Photo Cards for *hat* and *hand* and **Word-Building Card** *h. The name of this letter is* h. H *stands for the sound that you hear at the beginning of* hat. *Let's place the* h *card on the picture of the* hat *because* hat *begins with /h/. Repeat with* hand.

■ *Say /h/. Trace the* h *on your Word-Building Card as you say /h/.*

Guided Practice/Practice

■ Display the Photo Cards. *This is a horse. What sound do you hear at the beginning of* horse? *What letter stands for /h/? Let's place an* h *on the* horse *because* horse *begins with /h/. Repeat with the remaining Photo Cards for /h/*h.

■ Guide children to trace the letter *h* on their Word-Building Cards.

■ Point out objects in the classroom with names that begin with /h/. Hold the *h* card next to each as children say /h/ chorally.

SOUND-SPELLINGS REVIEW

Tier 2

Display Word-Building Cards *m, a, s, p, t, i, n, c, o, f, h*, one at a time. Have children chorally say the sound. Repeat and vary the pace.

ELL

Sound-Letter Relationships Provide additional practice in pronouncing the /h/ sound and naming the corresponding letter *h*, as children point to it.

On Level

High-Frequency Words

Objective Review high-frequency words *are, play, is, have, to*

Materials • **High-Frequency Word Cards:** *are, play, is, have, to*

REVIEW

- Display the **High-Frequency Word Card** for **are**.

- **Read** Point to and say the word *are. This is the word* are. *We can say:* You are, We are, *and* They are. *He is playing. We are playing.*

- **Spell** *The word* are *is spelled* a-r-e. Have children read and spell *are*.

- **Write** Finally, have children write the word *are*.

- Repeat with **play**, **is**, **have**, and **to**. Then have partners make up sentences using the words: *I have two sisters. They are older than me.*

Phonemic Awareness/Phonics

Objective Review recognizing and blending initial /f/f, /h/h, /n/n, /o/o, and /t/t

Materials • **Puppet** • pocket chart

PHONEME BLENDING

Model

- Hold up the **Puppet**. Say the sounds /h/ /o/ /p/. *Let's help Happy blend these sounds into a word:* /h/ /o/ /p/, /hooop/, hop. Repeat the routine with *hat*, /haaat/, /h/ /a/ /t/.

Practice

- Say: *Happy is going to say the sounds in a word. Listen as he says each sound.* Then have children blend the sounds to form words: /p/ /o/ /p/, /p/ /o/ /t/, /p/ /i/ /t/, /f/ /a/ /t/, /h/ /a/ /t/, /h/ /o/ /t/.

REVIEW /h/h, /o/o

Model

- Display **Word-Building Card** h. *The name of this letter is* h. H *stands for the sound we hear at the beginning of* hat. Hat *begins with* /h/. *What is the sound? I'll hold up the* h *card because* hat *begins with* h. Repeat with *o* and *on*.

- Say: *hammer, happy, fish, happy, ox, otter, pumpkin, hat, cat, octopus.* Children hold up their Word-Building Cards and say /h/ and hold up letter *h* for words that begin with /h/ and say /o/ and hold up letter *o* for words that begin with /o/. Guide practice with the first two words.

Puppet

ELL

Minimal Contrasts Provide additional practice in pronouncing and blending vowel sounds that do not transfer directly to the native language of children using minimal-contrast word pairs such as *hat/hot* and *pat/pot*.

Beyond Level

High-Frequency Words/Vocabulary

Objective Review high-frequency words
Materials • none

✔ ACCELERATE

- Write *what* and *there* on the board.

- **Read** Point to and say the word *what*. *This is the word* what. *It is sometimes used to ask a question: What stores are in your neighborhood?*

- **Spell** *The word* what *is spelled* w-h-a-t. Have children read and spell *what*.

- **Write** Have children write the word *what*. Repeat with *there*.

- Have children work with a partner to make up questions and answers using the words *what* and *there*.

EXPAND ORAL VOCABULARY

- **Antonyms** Review the meaning of the oral vocabulary word *frequently* with children. Then explain that an *antonym* is a word that means the opposite of another word.

- Say: *An* antonym *for the word* frequently *is* rarely. *If something* rarely *happens, it does not happen often. I* rarely *get up early on Saturday because I like to sleep.*

- Have children take turns using the new word *rarely* in a sentence. Then tell children that they will work with a partner to discuss things they rarely do or things that rarely happen.

Phonics

Objective Read words with initial /h/*h*
Materials • **Sound-Spelling Card:** *Hippo* • **Word-Building Cards**

✔ ENRICH

- Display the *Hippo* **Sound-Spelling Card**. Remind children that the /h/ sound is spelled with the letter *h*. Hammer *begins with the /h/ sound. What other words begin with /h/?*

- Write each word below on the board for children to read. Model blending the sounds in each word. Use the following words: *hill, hiss, hint, hugs, help, hand, hits, hush, hunt, hash, hub.*

- Display **Word-Building Cards** *a, e, i, o, u, b, l, m, n, p, h, d, s,* and *t.* Have partners make as many words as they can. Ask them to list their words, and then share their lists.

ELL ENGLISH LANGUAGE LEARNERS

Oral Language Warm-Up

Content Objective Learn theme vocabulary
Language Objective Repeat and act out a fingerplay to demonstrate understanding
Materials • **Listening Library Audio CD**

BUILD BACKGROUND KNOWLEDGE

All Language Levels

- Introduce the unit theme "Neighborhood" using the rhyme "Five Brave Firefighters." Display a picture of a firefighter. Teach the word *firefighter* as you point to the picture. Have children repeat the word.

- Play "Five Brave Firefighters" on the **Listening Library Audio CD**. Act out each line as you chant the rhyme.

- Explain that firefighters help keep our neighborhoods safe. Emphasize key words such as *fire engine*.

- Play the rhyme several times until children begin to correctly repeat the rhyme and can act out the motions.

- Ask children to tell what they know about firefighters. Build on their responses to model speaking in complete sentences. For example: *A firefighter uses lots of equipment.*

> **Five Brave Firefighters**
> *Five brave firefighters sit very still*
> *Until they see a fire on top of the hill.*
> Use fingers to number firefighters, then pantomime the actions.
> *One rings the bell, ding-dong;*
> *Two pulls his big boots on;*
> *Three jumps in the fire engine red;*
> *Four pops a fire hat on her head;*
> *Five drives the truck to the spot,*
> *As the big yellow flames get very hot.*
> *Shh! Goes the water from the spout,*
> *And quick as a wink, the fire is out.*
> Clap hands.

Academic Language

Language Objective Use academic language in classroom conversations

All Language Levels

- This week's academic words are **boldfaced** throughout the lesson. Define the word in context and provide a clear example from the selection. Then ask children to generate an example or a word with a similar meaning.

Cognates

Help children identify similarities and differences in pronunciation and spelling between English and Spanish cognates:

Cognates

organize	*organizar*
idea	*idea*
details	*detalles*
dialogue	*diálogo*

Academic Language Used in Whole Group Instruction

Oral Vocabulary Words	Vocabulary and Grammar Concepts	Strategy and Skill Words
borrow **equipment** **frequently** **neighborhood** **organize**	**sequence words** **sentences**	**main idea** **details** **summarize** **dialogue**

ELL ENGLISH LANGUAGE LEARNERS

Vocabulary

Language Objective Demonstrate understanding and use of key words by discussing a neighborhood

Materials • **Visual Vocabulary Resources**

PRETEACH KEY VOCABULARY

All Language Levels

Use the **Visual Vocabulary Resources** to preteach the weekly oral vocabulary words *borrow, equipment, frequently, neighborhood,* and *organize.* Focus on one or two words per day. Use the following routine that appears in detail on the cards.

- Define the word in English and provide the example given.

- Define the word in Spanish, if appropriate, and indicate if the word is a cognate.

- Display the picture and explain how it illustrates or demonstrates the word.

- Then engage children in structured partner-talk about the image, using the key word.

- Ask children to chorally say the word three times.

- Point out any known sound-spellings or focus on a key aspect of phonemic awareness related to the word.

PRETEACH FUNCTION WORDS AND PHRASES

All Language Levels

Use the Visual Vocabulary Resources to preteach the function words *first* (as an adverb) and *finally.* Focus on one word per day. Use the detailed routine on the cards.

- Define the word in English and, if appropriate, in Spanish. Point out if the word is a cognate.

- Refer to the picture and engage children in talk about the word. For example, children will partner-talk using sentence frames, or they will listen to sentences and replace a word or phrase with the new function word.

- Ask children to chorally repeat the word three times.

TEACH BASIC WORDS

Beginning/Intermediate

Use the Visual Vocabulary Resources to teach the basic words *wash, scrub, rinse, spray, bathe,* and *brush.* Teach these "cleaning words" using the routine provided on the card.

Visual Vocabulary Resources

Approaching Level

Oral Language

Objective Reinforce oral vocabulary
Materials • none

THEME WORDS: *neighborhood, equipment*

- Say: *We've talked about* **neighborhoods** *and how many neighborhoods have firehouses. Firefighters help keep our neighborhoods safe. Firefighters use* **equipment** *to help them do their jobs.*

- *What other places are in the same neighborhood as our school?* Have children speak in complete sentences to answer the questions.

- *Have you seen a firehouse in a neighborhood? What does it look like?*

- *Some of the equipment we have at school includes telephones, computers, printers, and copy machines. What equipment does a firefighter use?*

High-Frequency Words

Objective Reteach high-frequency words
Materials • **High-Frequency Word Card:** *are* • **Sound-Spelling WorkBoards**

RETEACH WORD: *are*

Tier 2

- Distribute a **WorkBoard** to each child. Then display the **High-Frequency Word Card** for **are**.

- Use the **Read/Spell/Write** routine to reteach the word. Point to and say the word. *This is the word* are. *We say: You* are, *we* are, *they* are. *We are a big class.* Are *is spelled* a-r-e. Have children read and spell *are*. Then have them write the word on their WorkBoards.

- Have children work with a partner to make up sentences using the word *are*. Ask them to talk about their class as a whole.

CUMULATIVE REVIEW

Display the High-Frequency Word Cards for words previously taught, one card at a time, and have children chorally read and spell the word. Mix and repeat. Note words children need to review.

ELL

Partners When pairing children to make up sentences, pair English Language Learners with children who are more proficient. Write their sentences, read them together, and point out the high-frequency word *are*.

Approaching Level

Phonemic Awareness

Objective   Identify and blend initial sounds
Materials   • **Puppet**

✔ **PHONEME BLENDING**   *Tier 2*

Model

■ Hold up the **Puppet**. *Happy is going to say the sounds in a word:
/h/ /o/ /p/. Happy can blend these sounds together: /hooop/. Now you
can say the sounds: /h/ /o/ /p/. Say the word with Happy:* hop.

Guided Practice/Practice

■ Have the Puppet say /m/ /o/ /p/. *Now you blend the sounds and
say the words with Happy:* /mmmooop/, mop. *Repeat with the
following:*

/p/ /o/ /p/	/p/ /o/ /t/	/h/ /o/ /t/	/n/ /o/ /d/
/h/ /a/ /t/	/h/ /i/ /t/	/f/ /a/ t/	/h/ /a/ /m/
/f/ /i/ /t/	/h/ /i/ /p/	/h/ /a/ /z/	/f/ /a/ /n/

Phonics

Objective   Reinforce letter-sound correspondence for /h/*h*
Materials   • **Sound-Spelling Card:** *Hippo*   • **Word-Building Cards**
                  • **Sound-Spelling WorkBoards**

✔ **RETEACH /h/*h***

Model

■ Display the *Hippo* **Sound-Spelling Card**. *The letter* h *stands for
the /h/ sound as in* hat. *What is this letter? What sound does it
stand for? Repeat with* horse.

■ Trace *h* on a small **Word-Building Card**. *I will say a sentence. We
will trace* h *on the cards when we hear /h/. Say:* Hilary has many
healthy habits.

Guided Practice/Practice

■ Distribute a **WorkBoard** to each child. *Say:* hot, ham, has, map,
hill, horse, dog, tree, hippo. *Children write* h *on their WorkBoard
when they hear /h/. Guide them with the first two words.*

■ **Read the Decodable Reader**   Read *Are Caps Hats?* with children.
Have them echo-read each page. Chorally reread the story.

CUMULATIVE REVIEW

Display Word-Building Cards *m, a, s, p, t, i, n, c, o, f,* and *h,* one at a
time. Point to the letters in a random order. Have children chorally
say the sound. Repeat and vary the pace.

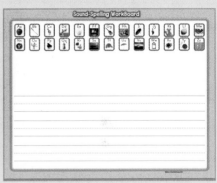

Puppet

Sound-Spelling WorkBoard

Decodable Reader

Corrective Feedback

Association Error If
children have difficulty
identifying initial /h/, say:
My turn: /haaat/, hat. *I
hear the /h/ sound at the
beginning of* hat: /haaat/.
*What is the sound? What is
the letter? Let's start over.*
Repeat the word *hat* for
children to identify the
position of /h/.

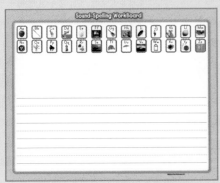

Sound-Spelling WorkBoard

On Level

Phonics

Objective Review recognizing and blending initial /f/f, /h/h, /n/n, /o/o, and /t/t

Materials • **Word Building Cards** • pocket chart • **Sound-Spelling WorkBoards**

REVIEW /f/f, /h/h, /n/n, /o/o, /t/t

Model

- Display **Word-Building Card** f. *The name of this letter is* f. *F stands for the sound we hear at the beginning of* fan. Fan *begins with* /f/. *What is the sound? I'll hold up the* f *card because* fan *begins with* f. Repeat with *h* and *hand*, *n* and *nose*, *o* and *ox*, and *t* and *turtle*.

- Distribute Word-Building Cards to children. Say: *fish, happy, table, hill, new, fork, fin, top, ham, next, on, nut, teeth, otter,* and *ox.* Children hold up their Word-Building Cards and say the initial sound of each word. Guide practice with the first two words.

- **Blend Words** Place Word-Building Cards *o* and *n* in the pocket chart. Move your hand from left to right below the letters as you blend the word. Repeat with *hot* and *not*.

- Have children write the words several times on their **WorkBoards** as they say /o/ /n/; /h/ /o/ /t/; /n/ /o/ /t/.

Beyond Level

Phonics

Objective Read words with initial /h/h

Materials • **Sound-Spelling Card:** *Hippo* • **Word-Building Cards**
• pocket chart

ACCELERATE

- Display the *Hippo* **Sound-Spelling Card**. Tell children that the /h/ sound is spelled with the letter *h*. Hippo *begins with* /h/. *What words do you know that have* /h/?

- **Review Short *i*** Display the Word-Building Cards *s, l, i, p* in the pocket chart. Point to the letters as you say each sound. *The word* slip *has four sounds:* /s/ /l/ /i/ /p/. *Let's say the sounds together:* /s/ /l/ /i/ /p/. *Listen as I blend the sounds:* /sssllliiip/. Guide children in blending the sounds and reading *slip*. Help children read words with short *i*. Write these words on the board for children to blend and read: *habit, snip, chin, hilltop, skin, still, swim, stick, spin, himself, spill.*

Corrective Feedback

If children have difficulty blending words with /h/, demonstrate the /h/ sound while modeling the correct mouth position. *This is the /h/ sound at the beginning of* hand. *Let's blend* hand *together:* /haaannnd/, hand. Repeat with *hat, had.*

ELL ENGLISH LANGUAGE LEARNERS

Access to Core Content

Content Objective Develop listening comprehension
Language Objective Discuss text using key words and sentence frames
Materials • **ELL Resource Book,** pp. 154–159

✔ PRETEACH BIG BOOK

ELL Resource Book

| All Language Levels |

Use the Interactive Question-Response Guide on **ELL Resource Book** pages 154–159 to introduce children to *Russ and the Firehouse*. Preteach half of the selection on Day 1 and half on Day 2.

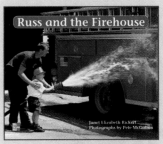

Big Book

■ Use the prompts provided in the guide to develop meaning and vocabulary. Use the partner-talk and whole-class responses to engage children and increase student talk. Remind children to listen attentively and face the child speaking.

■ When completed, revisit the selection and prompt children to talk about the photographs. Provide sentence starters as needed and build on children's responses to develop language.

Beginning	Intermediate	Advanced
Use Visuals During the Interactive Reading, select several pictures. Describe them and have children summarize what you said.	**Summarize** During the Interactive Reading, select a few lines of text. After you read them and explain them, have children summarize the text.	**Expand** During the Interactive Reading, select a larger portion of text. After you read it and explain it, have children summarize the text.

Approaching Level

High-Frequency Words

Objective Recognize high-frequency words *are, play, is, have, to*

Materials
- **High-Frequency Word Cards:** *are, play, is, have, to*
- **Word-Building Cards**

✔ **REVIEW WORDS:** *are, play, is, have, to*

- Display the **High-Frequency Word Card** for **are**. Say the word and have children repeat it. Point to each letter and have children name it.

- Distribute **Word-Building Cards** *a, r, e*. Model putting the letters together to form *are*. Then have children form *are*.

- Repeat the above routines with the words **play**, **is**, **have**, and **to**.

- Ask a question with the word *are*: *Where are we?* Have children use *are* to answer the question. Continue with the other words.

CUMULATIVE REVIEW

Display the High-Frequency Word Cards for words previously taught, one card at a time. Have children chorally read and spell the word. Mix and repeat. Note words children need to review.

ELL

Extra Practice During the Cumulative Review, pair children at different levels of proficiency and have partners take turns reading and spelling the high-frequency words to each other.

Phonemic Awareness

Objective Blend phonemes to form words

Materials
- **Puppet**

✔ **PHONEME BLENDING**

Tier 2

Model
- *Listen as Happy says the sounds for* hip: /h/ /i/ /p/. *Now Happy will blend the sounds:* /hiiip/, /hip/, hip. *Happy put the sounds together to say the word:* /hiiip/, hip. *Now listen again, I'll do another word.* Repeat blending with the word *hit*: /hiiit/, /h/ /i/ /t/, hit.

Guided Practice/Practice
- Guide children in blending by having them sit in a circle on the floor. Select three who are sitting side by side. Ask the first child to say the /h/ sound. Have the next child say /i/, /iii/. Have the third child say /l/. Have them blend the sounds, /hiiilll/, hill. Then have them say the word together.

- Follow the routine to say the following words:

/h/ /i/ /d/	/s/ /i/ /p/	/t/ /i/ /p/	/h/ /i/ /l/
/n/ /i/ /p/	/h/ /i/ /t/	/s/ /i/ /t/	/t/ /i/ /n/
/f/ /i/ /t/	/h/ /i/ /m/	/t/ /i/ /m/	/h/ /a/ /m/

Approaching Level

Phonics

Objectives Review blending /h/h, /f/f, /o/o, /p/p, /i/i, /n/n, and /s/s to form words; build fluency

Materials • **Word-Building Cards** • pocket chart

REVIEW /h/h, /f/f, /o/o, /p/p, /i/i, /n/n, /s/s

Tier 2

Model

■ Place **Word-Building Card** h in the pocket chart. *The name of this letter is* h. *The letter* h *stands for the /h/ sound. Say /h/. What is the letter? What is the sound?*

■ Place o next to h. *The name of this letter is* o. *The letter* o *stands for the /o/ sound. Say /o/. What is the letter? What is the sound? Repeat with the letter* p.

■ Move your hand from left to right below the letters. *Listen as I blend the sounds together: /h/ /o/ /p/, /hooop/, hop. What's the word? Let's blend the sounds together to say the word: /h/ /o/ /p/, /hooop/, hop.*

Guided Practice/Practice

■ Give the f, i, n cards to children. Each child says the sound for the letter on his or her card: /f/ /i/ /n/. Have children blend the sounds to say the word *fin*. Repeat with *sip* and *pin*.

Build Fluency

■ Have children blend *hop, fin, sip,* and *pin* as quickly as they can.

Decodable Reader

Objective Preteach Decodable Reader *Are Caps Hats?*

Materials • **Decodable Reader:** *Are Caps Hats?*

PRETEACH *Are Caps Hats?*

■ Display the cover of the book and read the title. Open to the title page and point out the title. *Let's read the title together.* Have children sound out each word as you run your finger under it. Point out the word *are*. *Look at the picture. What do you think we will read about in this book?*

■ Page through the book. Ask children what they see in each picture. Ask them to find the word *are*.

■ Read the book chorally with children. Have them point to each word as they read it. Provide corrective feedback as needed.

■ Ask children to use *are* to talk about the pictures. For example: *The workers are on top.* After reading, ask children to recall things they read about.

Decodable Reader

ON YOUR OWN

Make a Hat

Have children revisit the hats in *Are Caps Hats?* Then have them use craft supplies to make hats.

On Level

Decodable Reader

Objective   Reread *Are Caps Hats?* to develop fluency
Materials   • **Decodable Reader:** *Are Caps Hats?*

REREAD FOR FLUENCY

- Ask children to page through the illustrations in *Are Caps Hats?* Have children use their own words to retell what the book was about.

- Have children reread a page or two of *Are Caps Hats?* Work with them to read with accuracy and expression. Model reading a page. Point out how you read the exclamation with expression. Guide children and review sounds as necessary if they have difficulty blending sounds in words.

- Provide time to listen as children read their page(s). Comment on their accuracy and expression and provide corrective feedback by modeling proper fluency.

Decodable Reader

Beyond Level

Decodable Reader

Objective   Reread *Are Caps Hats?* to reinforce fluency and phonics
Materials   • **Decodable Reader:** *Are Caps Hats?*

REREAD FOR FLUENCY

- Have partners reread *Are Caps Hats?*

- As you listen to children read, comment on their accuracy and expression. Provide corrective feedback by modeling fluency. Guide children and review sounds as necessary if they have difficulty blending sounds in words.

INNOVATE

- Have children draw pictures of a hat decorated with an object whose name begins with /h/. Help them write a caption for their drawings. For example: *A hat with a ham.*

Beyond Level

Leveled Reader Lesson 1

Objective   Read *Places in the Neighborhood* to apply skills and strategies
Materials   • **Leveled Reader:** *Places in the Neighborhood*

BEFORE READING

- **Preview and Predict** Read the title and the name of the author. *What do you see on the cover? What do you think the book is about? What might happen?* Turn to the title page and point out that it also has the title and the name of the author. Page through the book with children and pause to name unfamiliar items. Have children predict what might happen based upon what they see.

- **Introduce Story Words** Point to the words *apartment buildings* on page 4. Read the sentence. Have children use the picture to explain what *apartment buildings* are. Repeat with *office buildings* on page 8.

- **Set a Purpose for Reading** *Let's find out what places are in a neighborhood.*

DURING READING

- Remind children that when they come to an unfamiliar word, they can look for familiar chunks in the word, break the word into syllables and sound out each part, or think about what the word might mean. If the word does not sound right or make sense in the sentence, children can self-correct.

- Monitor children's reading and provide help as needed.

AFTER READING

- Ask children to point out words they had trouble reading and to share the strategies they used.

- Have children retell the story and share personal responses. *Which place in this neighborhood would you like to visit? Why?*

- **Synthesize** *The map on page 15 includes roads, houses, and trees. What other places and things could be added to the map?*

- Have children work in pairs to list places that could be shown on a neighborhood map, such as a school, a fire department, stores, and a playground.

- **Model** Draw a made-up neighborhood map on a large sheet of paper. Use simple shapes to represent various buildings, and label them. Discuss the map. Then tell children that they will draw and label a map of their own neighborhood or of an imaginary neighborhood. Remind them to include places they listed with their partners.

Leveled Reader

Draw a Map

Point out the map on page 15 of *Places in the Neighborhood*. Discuss the streets and buildings in the neighborhood. Ask children to draw and label their own map.

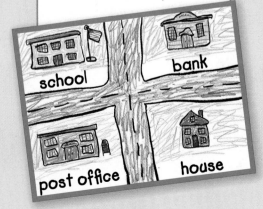

Leveled Reader

Vocabulary

Preteach Vocabulary Use the routine in the **Visual Vocabulary Resources**, pages 331–332, to preteach the ELL Vocabulary listed on the inside front cover of the Leveled Reader.

ELL ENGLISH LANGUAGE LEARNERS

Leveled Reader

Content Objective Read to apply skills and strategies

Language Objective Retell information using complete sentences

Materials • **Leveled Reader:** *We Are Here*

BEFORE READING

All Language Levels

- **Preview** Read the title *We Are Here*. Ask: *What's the title? Say it again.* Repeat with the author's name. Point to the cover photo and say: *I see two firefighters and a boy.* Point to the firefighters and the boy as you name them. *They are at a firehouse. Now turn to a partner and tell about this picture.*

- **Page Through the Book** Use simple language to tell about the photo on each page. Immediately follow up with questions such as: *Are they at the school? Do you see the school?*

- **Review Skills** Use the inside front cover to review the phonics skill and high-frequency words.

- **Set a Purpose** Say: *Let's read to find out about places in the neighborhood.*

DURING READING

All Language Levels

- Have children whisper-read each page, or use the differentiated suggestions below. Circulate, listen in, and provide feedback.

- **Retell** Stop after every two pages and ask children to state what they have learned so far. Reinforce language by restating children's comments when they have difficulty using story-specific words. Provide differentiated sentence frames to support children's responses and engage children in partner-talk where appropriate.

Beginning	Intermediate	Advanced
Echo-Read Have children echo-read after you.	**Choral-Read** Have children choral-read with you.	**Choral-Read** Have children choral-read.
Check Comprehension Point to pictures and ask questions such as: *Are they at a market? Point to some food.*	**Check Comprehension** Ask questions/prompts such as: *Describe what you see in this photo. What did the author tell us about places in a neighborhood?*	**Check Comprehension** Ask: *What did you learn about a neighborhood?* Read sentences that name places in the neighborhood.

ENGLISH LANGUAGE LEARNERS

AFTER READING

All Language Levels

Book Talk Children will work with peers of varying language abilities to discuss their books for this week. Display the four **Leveled Readers** read this week: *Places in the Neighborhood* (Beyond Level), *Where Are We?* (On Level), *In My Neighborhood* (Approaching Level), and *We Are Here* (English Language Learners).

Ask the questions and provide the prompts below. Call on children who read each book to answer the questions or respond to the prompt. If appropriate, ask children to find the pages in the book that illustrate their answers.

- What neighborhood places did your book show?
- Name the places in the book.
- What did you learn about places to buy things?
- What places have you visited? What do you do there?
- What is your favorite place to visit from the book? Tell about it.

Develop Listening and Speaking Skills Tell children to remember the following:

■ Share information in cooperative learning interactions. Remind children to work with their partners to retell the story and complete any activities. Ask: *What happened next in the story?*

■ Employ self-corrective techniques and monitor their own and other children's language production. Children should ask themselves: *What parts of this passage were confusing to me? Can my classmates help me clarify a word or sentence that I don't understand?*

■ Use high-frequency English words to describe people, places, and objects.

■ Narrate, describe, and explain with specificity and detail. Ask: *Where did the story take place? Can you describe the setting? What else did you notice?*

■ Express opinions, ideas, and feelings on a variety of social and academic topics. Ask: *What do you think about the characters in the story?*

Puppet

Approaching Level

Phonemic Awareness

Objective   Segment sounds in words

Materials
- **Sound Boxes**   • markers
- **WorkBoard Sound Boxes; Teacher's Resource Book,** p. 136

PHONEME SEGMENTATION

Tier 2

Model
- Use the **Sound Boxes** to segment the sounds in the word *hop. I am going to say the sounds in* hop. *Listen:* /h/ /o/ /p/, hop. *I will place a marker in a box as I say each sound in* hop. *There are three sounds in* hop: /h/ /o/ /p/. Repeat with *hip.*

Guided Practice/Practice
- Distribute Sound Boxes and markers. *I will say a word. Say each sound in the word as you place a marker in a box. Then tell me the sounds.* Say these words and have children say each sound as they place a marker in a box: *hat,* /h/ /a/ /t/; *hid,* /h/ /i/ /d/; *him,* /h/ /i/ /m/; *hip,* /h/ /i/ /p/; *hot,* /h/ /o/ /t/; *hit,* /h/ /i/ /t/.

ELL

Sound-Letter Relationships Provide additional practice in pronouncing the sounds /h/, /f/, /o/, /i/ and naming the corresponding letters, as children point to them.

Phonics

Objective   Identify initial sounds /h/h, /f/f, /o/o, /i/i, and build fluency

Materials
- **Photo Cards:** *fan, farm, feather, feet, fire, fork, hammer, hand, hat, helicopter, hippo, horse, inch, inchworm, ink, insect, invitation, octopus, olive, ostrich, otter, ox*   • **Word-Building Cards** • pocket chart
- **Sound-Spelling WorkBoards**

BUILD FLUENCY: LETTER-SOUND CORRESPONDENCE

Tier 2

Model
- Place **Word-Building Cards** *h, f, o, i* in the pocket chart. Place the **Photo Cards** facedown in a stack. Pick the first card, name the picture, and identify its initial sound. Place the Photo Card under the letter that stands for the beginning sound.

Guided Practice/Practice
- Have each child choose a Photo Card, say the name of the picture, identify its initial sound, and place it in the pocket chart under the proper letter. Guide practice with the first Photo Card.

Build Fluency
- Display the Word-Building Cards. Have children name each letter as quickly as they can. Then ask them to write the letters on their **WorkBoards** several times as they say the sounds.

Approaching Level

Leveled Reader Lesson 2

Objective Reread *In My Neighborhood* to reinforce fluency, phonics, and identifying main idea and details

Materials • **Leveled Reader:** *In My Neighborhood*

FOCUS ON FLUENCY

- Tell children that you will read one page of the book, and they should read that page right after you. They should follow along in their books and try to read at the same speed and with the same expression that you use.

SKILL IDENTIFY MAIN IDEA AND DETAILS

- *What is this book all about? What are some things in the neighborhood?*

REREAD PREVIOUSLY READ BOOKS

- Distribute copies of the past six **Leveled Readers**. Tell children that rereading the books will help them develop their skills and enjoy language.

- Circulate and listen in as children read. Stop them periodically and ask them how they are figuring out words or checking their understanding. Tell children to read other previously read Leveled Readers during independent reading time.

High-Frequency Words

Objective Review high-frequency words *are, play, is,* and *have*

Materials • **High-Frequency Word Cards:** *are, play, is, have*

BUILD WORD AUTOMATICITY: *are, play, is, have*

- Distribute copies of the **High-Frequency Word Card** for **are**. Say the word and have children repeat it. Have children name the letters in the word. Repeat with the words **play**, **is**, and **have**.

- **Build Fluency** Use the High-Frequency Word Cards to review previously taught words. Repeat, guiding children to read more rapidly.

Leveled Reader

Meet Grade-Level Expectations

As an alternative to this day's lesson, guide children through a reading of the On Level Leveled Reader. See page 1366. Because both books contain the same vocabulary, phonics, and comprehension skills, the scaffolding you provided will help most children gain access to this more challenging text.

Corrective Feedback

Throughout the lessons, provide feedback based on children's responses. If the answer is correct, ask another question. If the answer is tentative, restate key information to assist the child. If the answer is wrong, provide corrective feedback such as hints or clues, refer to a visual such as a **Sound-Spelling Card** or story illustration, or probe with questions to help the child clarify any misunderstanding.

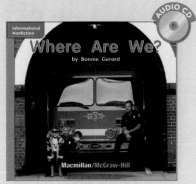

Leveled Reader

Make a Collage

Have children select a page from the book and draw or cut out magazine pictures of things that might be found at the place on that page. Children can paste the pictures on paper to make a collage. Have children label their collage to tell where the items would be found.

On Level

Leveled Reader Lesson 2

Objective	Reread to apply skills and strategies to retell a story
Materials	• **Leveled Reader:** *Where Are We?*

BEFORE READING

■ Ask children to page through *Where Are We?* and recall what the book is about. Reinforce vocabulary by repeating children's sentences using more sophisticated language. For example: *Yes, the children are at the school. They are starting their school day.*

DURING READING

■ Have children join you in a choral-reading of the story. Model reading with expression. *When I read page 2, I emphasized where they were by saying the word* school *a little stronger. I used the same strong emphasis when I read* market *on page 3. I wanted to emphasize that we are seeing a new place.* Ask children to use the same kind of expression when they read. Have children practice rereading a few lines with expression. Discuss how reading a variety of texts with expression can help them enjoy the language.

■ Assign each child a page. Have children practice by whisper-reading. *Follow along as other children read, and be ready to come in when it is your turn. Remember, use lots of expression.*

AFTER READING

■ Have children retell the selection in their own words.

■ *What is the book all about? What are some places where the children and parents are? Could this story really happen? Why or why not?*

Leveled Reader Library

Beyond Level

Leveled Reader Lesson 2

Objective   Reread to apply skills and strategies to retell a story
Materials   • **Leveled Reader:** *Places in the Neighborhood*

BEFORE READING

- Ask children to look back at *Places in the Neighborhood.* Tell them that the main idea of the story is "A neighborhood has many places." Ask: *What are some of the places in this neighborhood?*

DURING READING

- Assign a child a page of the book to read aloud. Have children practice by whisper-reading. *Follow along as each child reads, and be ready to come in when it is your turn. Remember, use lots of expression.* Have children ask questions about the text.

AFTER READING

- Explain that summarizing is telling the most important ideas in the story. Model the strategy: *The story is about places we see in a neighborhood, such as homes, stores, and places where people work and learn.* Guide children to write their own summaries of the story.

Expand Vocabulary

Objective   Learn and apply the meaning of the new words *store, office buildings,* and *factories* and brainstorm words for buildings
Materials   • **Leveled Reader:** *Places in the Neighborhood*

ENRICH: *store, office buildings, factories*

Gifted Talented

- Write the words *store, office buildings,* and *factories* on cards. Display *store* and read aloud the sentence *We shop at a store.* Have children point to *store* in the **Leveled Reader**. Ask questions: *At what stores do you shop?*

- Ask children to use the picture to tell what a *store* is. (a place that sells things)

- Ask children to use *store* in sentences. Then repeat with *office buildings* and *factories.*

- Ask: *What other kinds of buildings are in a neighborhood or town?* Have children brainstorm other kinds of buildings. Record their responses in a web with "Neighborhood Buildings" in the center oval. Have children use the words speaking in complete sentences.

Leveled Reader

ON YOUR OWN

Write a Story

Have children write a story about taking a walk in the neighborhood.

ELL

Partners When children write a story about taking a walk in the neighborhood, pair English Language Learners with children who are more proficient. Prompt pairs to talk to each other about places in the neighborhood.

ELL ENGLISH LANGUAGE LEARNERS

Fluency

Content Objectives Reread the Decodable Reader to develop fluency; develop speaking skills

Language Objective Tell a partner what a selection is about

Materials • **Decodable Reader:** *Are Caps Hats?*

REREAD FOR FLUENCY

Beginning

- Review the high-frequency words **are**, **have**, **to**, **is**, and **play** using the **Read/Spell/Write** routine.

Intermediate/Advanced

- Use each word in a sentence that illustrates its use, such as: *We are happy. We like to play.* Gesture to the whole class and smile.

- Then provide sentence starters for children to complete. Where appropriate, act out children's responses. For example: *We are all friends.*

All Language Levels

- Guide children through a choral-reading of *Are Caps Hats?* Point to the exclamation mark at the end of the last sentence on page 8. Tell children that when a sentence ends in an exclamation mark, we read it as if we are very excited. Model reading the sentence and have children chorally repeat.

DEVELOP SPEAKING/LISTENING SKILLS

All Language Levels

- Have children reread *Are Caps Hats?* to a partner. Remind them to listen carefully and follow along in their book as their partner is reading. Work with children to read with accuracy and appropriate expression.

- Ask children to tell their partner about the pictures on each page. Then have the other partner describe the pictures. Circulate, listen in, and provide additional language as needed.

Beginning	Intermediate	Advanced
Confirm Understanding Point to the pictures for partners to identify. Ask: *What do you see?* Restate the correct answer in a complete sentence.	**Express Opinions** Ask partners to tell you which is their favorite picture in the book. Prompt them to explain why it is their favorite picture.	**Compare and Contrast** Have partners compare two different pictures and describe them. Prompt them to explain how they are alike and different.

ELL ENGLISH LANGUAGE LEARNERS

High-Frequency Words

Content Objective Spell high-frequency words correctly
Language Objective Write in complete sentences, using sentence frames
Materials • **Sound-Spelling WorkBoards** • **Sound-Spelling Cards** • **Photo Cards**

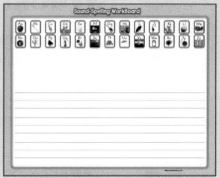

Sound-Spelling WorkBoard

Beginning/Intermediate

■ Write the high-frequency word **are** on the board. Have children copy the word on their **WorkBoards**. Then help children make up a sentence for the word. Provide the sentence starter *You are _____*.

Advanced

■ Children should first orally state their sentence. Correct as needed. Then they can draw a picture to complete the sentence. For children who are ready, help them spell words using their growing knowledge of English sound-spelling relationships. Model how to segment the word children are trying to spell and attach a spelling to each sound. Use the **Sound-Spelling Cards** to reinforce the spellings for each English sound.

Writing

All Language Levels

■ Say the word *hot* and ask children to write it. Pretend to place your hand near a hot fire as you say *hot*. Then use the word in context: *That fire is hot!* Have children write the word five times as they say *hot*. Demonstrate correct letter formation, as needed.

■ Then display a set of **Photo Cards**. Select at least five cards whose picture names begin with /h/ (hat, hand, helicopter, horse, hippo) and three whose picture names begin with /f/ (fish, fan, farm).

■ Say the name of each card, stretching or reiterating the initial sound to emphasize it. You may also need to model correct mouth formation when forming the sound. Use the articulation pictures and prompts on the back of the small Sound-Spelling Cards for support. Tell children to write the first letter of each picture name on their WorkBoards.

Phonemic Awareness/ Phonics

For English Language Learners who need more practice with this week's phonemic awareness and phonics skills, see the Approaching Level lessons. Focus on minimal contrasts, articulation, and those sounds that do not transfer from the child's first language to English. For a complete listing of transfer sounds, see pages T10–T31.

Weekly Assessment

Use your Quick Check observations and the assessment opportunities identified below to evaluate children's progress in key skill areas.

Skills	Quick Check Observations	Pencil and Paper Assessment
PHONEMIC AWARENESS/ PHONICS /h/h **h**	1309	Activity Book, pp. 4, 9–10, 12 Practice Book, pp. 121, 125–126
HIGH-FREQUENCY WORDS *are* **are**	1330	Activity Book, pp. 7–8 Practice Book, pp. 123–124
COMPREHENSION Identify Main Idea and Details	1320	Activity Book, pp. 5–6, 11 Practice Book, p. 122

Quick Check Rubric

Skills	1	2	3
PHONEMIC AWARENESS/ PHONICS	Does not connect the /h/ sound with the letter *Hh* and has difficulty blending the CVC words *hat, ham, Hap, hip, him, hop, had.*	Usually connects the /h/ sound with the letter *Hh* and blends the CVC words *hat, ham, Hap, hit, hip, him, hop, had* with only occasional support.	Consistently connects the /h/ sound with the letter *Hh* and blends the CVC words *hat, ham, Hap, hit, hip, him, hop, had.*
HIGH-FREQUENCY WORDS	Does not identify the high-frequency words.	Usually recognizes the high-frequency words with accuracy, but not speed.	Consistently recognizes the high-frequency words with speed and accuracy.
COMPREHENSION	Does not identify the main idea or supporting details using the pictures and text.	Usually identifies the main idea and supporting details using the pictures and text.	Consistently identifies the main idea and supporting details using the pictures and text.

DIBELS LINK

PROGRESS MONITORING

Use your DIBELS results to inform instruction.

IF...

Initial **S**ound **F**luency (**ISF**)	0–24
Phoneme **S**egmentation **F**luency (**PSF**)	0–17
Nonsense **W**ord **F**luency (**NWF**)	0–12

THEN...
Evaluate for Intervention

TPRI LINK

PROGRESS MONITORING

Use your TPRI scores to inform instruction.

IF...

Phonemic Awareness	Still Developing
Listening Name Identification	Still Developing
Letter to Sound Linking	Still Developing
Listening Comprehension	Still Developing

THEN...
Evaluate for Intervention

End-of-Week Assessment

Diagnose		Prescribe
Review the assessment answers with children. Have them correct their errors. Then provide additional instruction as needed.		
PHONEMIC AWARENESS/ PHONICS /h/h	**IF...** **Quick Check Rubric:** Children consistently score 1 or **Pencil and Paper Assessment:** Children get 0–2 items correct	**THEN...** Reteach Phonemic Awareness and Phonics Skills using the **Phonemic Awareness** and **Phonics Intervention Teacher's Editions**. *SPIRAL REVIEW* Use the Build Fluency lesson in upcoming weeks to provide children practice reading words with /h/h.
HIGH-FREQUENCY WORDS *are*	**Quick Check Rubric:** Children consistently score 1 or **Pencil and Paper Assessment:** Children get 0–2 items correct	Reteach High-Frequency Words using the **Phonics Intervention Teacher's Edition**. *SPIRAL REVIEW* Use the High-Frequency Words lesson in upcoming weeks to provide children practice reading the word *are*.
COMPREHENSION Skill: Identify Main Idea and Details	**Quick Check Rubric:** Children consistently score 1 or **Pencil and Paper Assessment:** Children get 0–2 items correct	Reteach Comprehension Skill using the **Comprehension Intervention Teacher's Edition**.

Response to Intervention

To place children in Tier 2 or Tier 3 Intervention use the *Diagnostic Assessment.*

- Phonemic Awareness
- Phonics
- Vocabulary
- Comprehension
- Fluency

Week 2 ★ At a Glance

Priority Skills and Concepts

 Comprehension
- **Genre:** Fiction, Expository, Folktale
- **Strategy:** Summarize
- **Skill:** Identify Main Idea and Details
- **Skill:** Identify Character

 High-Frequency Words
- *for*, *you*

Oral Vocabulary
- Build Robust Vocabulary: *admire*, *community*, *deliver*, *schedule*, *workers*

Fluency
- Echo-Read
- Word Automaticity

 Phonemic Awareness
- Phoneme Isolation
- Phoneme Blending
- Phoneme Segmentation

 Phonics
- *Dd, Rr*

Grammar
- Sentences

Writing
- Directions

Key   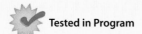 Tested in Program    Review Skill

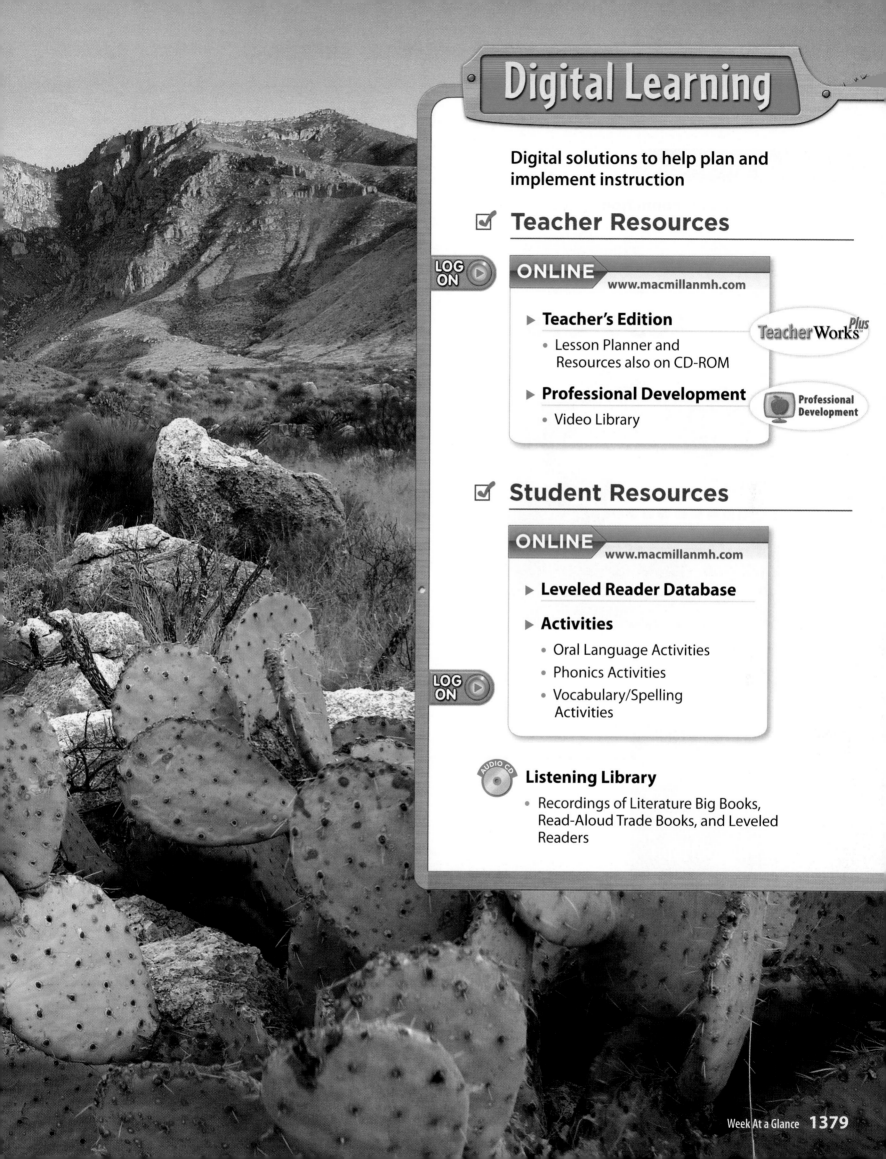

Digital Learning

Digital solutions to help plan and implement instruction

☑ Teacher Resources

LOG ON ▶

ONLINE
www.macmillanmh.com

▶ **Teacher's Edition**
- Lesson Planner and Resources also on CD-ROM

TeacherWorks Plus

▶ **Professional Development**
- Video Library

Professional Development

☑ Student Resources

ONLINE
www.macmillanmh.com

▶ **Leveled Reader Database**

▶ **Activities**
- Oral Language Activities
- Phonics Activities
- Vocabulary/Spelling Activities

LOG ON ▶

AUDIO CD **Listening Library**
- Recordings of Literature Big Books, Read-Aloud Trade Books, and Leveled Readers

Weekly Literature

Theme: People and Places

A mix of fiction and nonfiction

Big Book

Genre Fiction

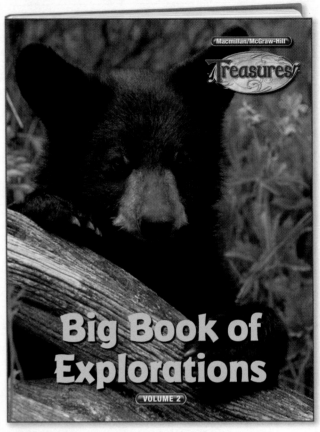

Big Book of Explorations

Genre Poetry

Support Literature

Interactive Read-Aloud Anthology

Genre Folktale

Oral Vocabulary Cards
- Listening Comprehension
- Build Robust Vocabulary

Decodable Reader

Resources for Differentiated Instruction

Leveled Readers

GR Levels Rebus-F

Genre	Fiction

- Same Theme
- Same Vocabulary/Phonics
- Same Comprehension Skills

Approaching Level

On Level

Beyond Level

ELL

Leveled Reader Database
Go to www.macmillanmh.com.

Practice

Activity Book

Practice Book

ELL Practice Book

Response to Intervention

Tier 2

- Phonemic Awareness
- Phonics
- Vocabulary
- Comprehension
- Fluency

Tier 3

Unit Assessment

Assess Unit Skills

- Phonemic Awareness
- Phonics
- High-Frequency Words
- Listening Comprehension

HOME-SCHOOL CONNECTION

- Family letters in English and Spanish
- Take-home stories and activities

Suggested Lesson Plan

Go to **www.macmillanmh.com** for Online Lesson Planner

TeacherWorks Plus
All-In-One Planner and Resource Center

Professional Development
Video Library

Big Book

WHOLE GROUP

ORAL LANGUAGE

	DAY 1	**DAY 2**

ORAL LANGUAGE

- **Oral Vocabulary**

- **Phonemic Awareness**

DAY 1

? Focus Question What are some places in your neighborhood? Who can you find there?
Build Background, 1390
Oral Vocabulary *admire, community, deliver, schedule, worker,* 1390

 Phonemic Awareness
Phoneme Isolation, 1393

DAY 2

? Focus Question How would you help your community ?
Oral Vocabulary *admire, community, deliver, schedule, worker,* 1398
Words That Compare, 1405

 Phonemic Awareness
Phoneme Blending, 1406

WORD STUDY

- **Phonics**

- **High-Frequency Words**

DAY 1

 Phonics
Introduce /d/d, 1394
Handwriting: Write *Dd*, 1395
Activity Book, 14
Practice Book, 127
High-Frequency Words
for, you, 1392

DAY 2

Phonics
Review /d/d, /m/m, /t/t, 1406
Blend with /d/d, 1407

Review High-Frequency Words, 1408

READING

- **Listening Comprehension**

- **Apply Phonics and High-Frequency Words**

- **Fluency**

DAY 1

Share the Big Book
Bus Stops
Strategy: Summarize, 1391
 Skill: Identify Main Idea and Details, 1391

Big Book

DAY 2

Reread the Big Book
Bus Stops
Strategy: Summarize, 1400
Skill: Identify Main Idea and Details, 1400
Retell, 1404
Decodable Reader:
Rod Can See It, 1408
Activity Book, 15–16
Practice Book, 128
Fluency Echo-Read, 1404

Big Book

LANGUAGE ARTS

- **Writing**

- **Grammar**

DAY 1

Shared Writing
Directions, 1397
Grammar
Sentences, 1396

DAY 2

Interactive Writing
Directions, 1409

ASSESSMENT

- **Informal/Formal**

DAY 1

Quick Check Phonemic Awareness, 1393

DAY 2

Quick Check Comprehension, 1404

 SMALL GROUP Lesson Plan > **Differentiated Instruction 1384–1385**

Priority Skills

Phonemic Awareness/Phonics /d/d, /r/r	High-Frequency Words *for, you*	Oral Vocabulary Words That Compare	Comprehension Strategy: Summarize Skill: Identify Main Idea and Details

Half-Day Kindergarten

Teach Core Skills
Focus on tested skill lessons, other lessons, and small group options as your time allows.

DAY 3

? Focus Question Where do people go for their work?

Oral Vocabulary *admire, community, deliver, schedule, worker,* 1410

Oral Vocabulary Cards: "Acrefoot, the Barefoot Mailman"

Phonemic Awareness
Phoneme Isolation, 1415

Phonics
Introduce /r/r, 1416

Handwriting: Write *Rr*, 1417

High-Frequency Words
for, you, 1414

Activity Book: "For You," 17–18

Practice Book, 129–130

Read for Fluency, 1414

Read the Big Book of Explorations
"The Park," 8

Literary Element: Word Choice/ Figurative Language, 1412

Big Book of Explorations

Independent Writing
Prewrite and Draft Directions, 1419

Grammar
Sentences, 1418

Quick Check	High-Frequency Words, 1414
	Phonemic Awareness, 1415

DAY 4

? Focus Question What are some ways you can help a neighbor?

Oral Vocabulary *admire, community, deliver, schedule, worker,* 1420

Words That Compare, 1423

Phonemic Awareness
Phoneme Blending, 1424

Phonics
Picture Sort, 1424

Blend with /r/r, 1425

Activity Book, 20

Practice Book, 132

Review High-Frequency Words, 1426

Interactive Read Aloud
Listening Comprehension, 1422

Read Aloud: "Ms. Mouse Needs a Friend"

Decodable Reader:
Rod Can See It, 1426

Read Aloud

Independent Writing
Revise and Edit Directions, 1427

Quick Check	Phonics, 1425

DAY 5
Review and Assess

? Focus Question What was the best story for you?

Oral Vocabulary *admire, community, deliver, schedule, worker,* 1428

Words That Compare, 1430

Phonemic Awareness
Phoneme Segmentation, 1431

Phonics
Read Words, 1432

Dictation, 1432

Activity Book, 22

High-Frequency Words
for, you, are, have, play, is, 1430

Read Across Texts
Strategy: Summarize, 1429

Skill: Identify Main Idea and Details, 1429

Activity Book, 21

Fluency Word Automaticity, 1430

Independent Writing
Publish and Present Directions, 1433

Weekly Assessment, 1460–1461

Differentiated Instruction

What do I do in small groups?

Teacher-Led Small Groups

Independent Activities

Focus on Skills

IF... children need additional instruction, practice, or extension based on your **Quick Check** observations for the following priority skills

 Phonemic Awareness
Phoneme Isolation, Blending, Segmentation

 Phonics
Dd, Rr

 High-Frequency Words
for , *you*

 Comprehension
Strategy: Summarize
Skill: Identify Main Ideas and Details

THEN... | Approaching | Preteach and
| ELL | Reteach Skills
| On Level | Practice
| Beyond | Enrich and Accelerate Learning

 LOG ON ▶ ## Suggested Small Group Lesson Plan

CD-ROM
TeacherWorks *Plus*
All-In-One Planner and Resource Center

	DAY 1	**DAY 2**
Approaching Level		
Tier 2 •**Preteach/Reteach** **Tier 2 Instruction**	• Oral Language, 1434 • High-Frequency Words, 1434 **ELL** High-Frequency Words Review, 1434 • Phonemic Awareness, 1435 • Phonics, 1435 **ELL** Sound-Spellings Review, 1435	• Oral Language, 1440 • High-Frequency Words, 1440 **ELL** • Phonemic Awareness, 1441 • Phonics, 1441
On Level •**Practice**	• High-Frequency Words, 1436 • Phonemic Awareness/Phonics, 1436 **ELL**	• Phonics, 1442
Beyond Level •**Extend/Accelerate** **Gifted and Talented**	• High-Frequency Words/Vocabulary, 1437 **ELL** Expand Oral Vocabulary, 1437 • Phonics, 1437	• Phonics, 1442
ELL •**Build English Language Proficiency** •**See ELL in other levels.**	• Oral Language Warm-Up, 1438 • Academic Language, 1438 • Vocabulary, 1439	• Access to Core Content, 1443

Small Group

Focus on Leveled Readers

Levels Rebus–F

Approaching

On Level

Beyond

ELL

Additional Leveled Readers

LOG ON **Leveled Reader Database**
www.macmillanmh.com

Search by

- Comprehension Skill
- Content Area
- Genre
- Text Feature
- Guided Reading Level
- Reading Recovery Level
- Lexile Score
- Benchmark Level

Subscription also available

Manipulatives

Sound-Spelling WorkBoards

Sound-Spelling Cards

Photo Cards

High-Frequency Word Cards

Visual Vocabulary Resources

DAY 3

- High-Frequency Words, 1444 **ELL**
- Phonemic Awareness, 1444
- Decodable Reader, 1445
- Phonics, 1445

- Decodable Reader, 1446 **ELL**

- Decodable Reader, 1446

- Access to Core Content, 1447
- Grammar, 1447

DAY 4

- Phonemic Awareness, 1448
- Phonics, 1448 **ELL**
- Leveled Reader Lesson 1, 1449

- Leveled Reader Lesson 1, 1450 **ELL**

- Leveled Reader Lesson 1, 1451
  Evaluate, 1451

- Leveled Reader, 1452–1453

DAY 5

- Phonemic Awareness, 1454
- Phonics, 1454 **ELL**
- Leveled Reader Lesson 2, 1455
- High-Frequency Words, 1455

- Leveled Reader Lesson 2, 1456

- Leveled Reader Lesson 2, 1457 **ELL**
- Expand Vocabulary, 1457

- Fluency, 1458
- High-Frequency Words, 1459
- Writing, 1459

Managing the Class

What do I do with the rest of my class?

- Activity Book
- Practice Book
- ELL Practice Book
- Leveled Reader Activities
- Literacy Workstations
- Online Activities
- Buggles and Beezy

Classroom Management Tools

Weekly Contract

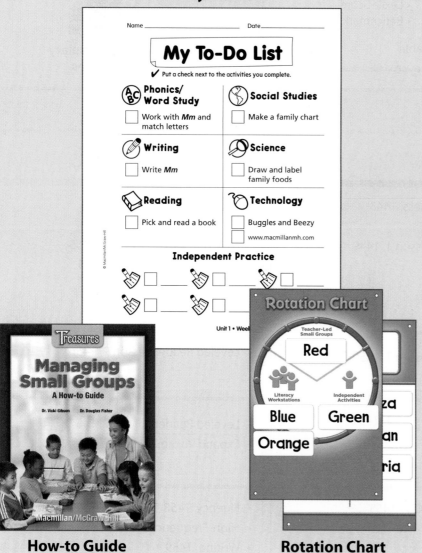

Name _____ Date _____

My To-Do List

✔ Put a check next to the activities you complete.

Phonics/Word Study
☐ Work with *Mm* and match letters

Social Studies
☐ Make a family chart

Writing
☐ Write *Mm*

Science
☐ Draw and label family foods

Reading
☐ Pick and read a book

Technology
☐ Buggles and Beezy
☐ www.macmillanmh.com

Independent Practice

Unit 1 • Week

How-to Guide

Rotation Chart

Rotation Chart
Teacher-Led Small Groups
Red
Literacy Workstations
Independent Activities
Blue   Green
Orange

Digital Learning

Phonics Activities

- Match Letters
- Match Letters to Sounds
- Blend Words

Meet the Author/Illustrator

Taro Gomi
- Taro was born in Tokyo, Japan, in 1945.
- He has published over 300 books!
- He also designs stationery and clothes, and makes animated videos for children.

Other books by Taro Gomi
- Gomi, Taro. *Spring Is Here*. New York: Macmillan/McGraw-Hill, 1993.
- Gomi, Taro. *My Friends*. New York: Macmillan/McGraw-Hill, 1997.

- Read Other Books by the Author or Illustrator

Practice

Activity Book

Practice Book

ELL Practice Book

Independent Activities

ONLINE INSTRUCTION www.macmillanmh.com

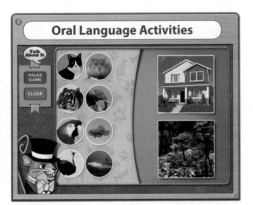

Oral Language Activities

- Focus on Unit Vocabulary and Concepts
- English Language Learner Support

Vocabulary/Spelling Activities

- Differentiated Lists and Activities

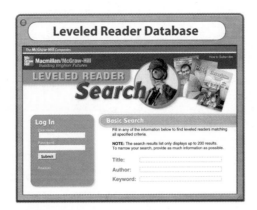

Leveled Reader Database

- Leveled Reader Database
- Search titles by level, skill, content area, and more

Available on CD

LISTENING LIBRARY
Recordings of selections
- Literature Big Books
- Read-Aloud Trade Books
- Leveled Readers
- ELL Readers

NEW ADVENTURES WITH BUGGLES AND BEEZY
Phonemic awareness and phonics activities

Leveled Reader Activities

People Who Help
by Susan Calder · illustrated by Ann Iosa

Approaching

This Is for You
by Lee Peters · illustrated by Noah Jones

On Level

The Good Idea
by Katherine Scraper

Beyond

For You
by Lee Peters · illustrated by Noah Jones

ELL

See inside cover of all Leveled Readers.

Literacy Workstations

Reading

Phonics/ Word Study

Writing

Science/ Social Studies

See lessons on pages 1388–1389

Managing the Class

What do I do with the rest of my class?

Reading

Objectives

- Read and talk about a book with a partner
- Read a book and retell the story

Phonics/Word Study

Objectives

- Sort pictures by their initial letters *d, h, r*
- Form words with the letters *d, h, r,* and *-im*

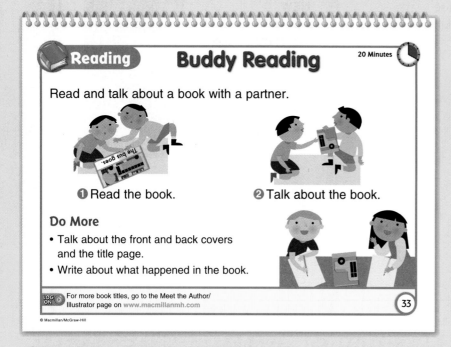

Reading — **Buddy Reading** — 20 Minutes

Read and talk about a book with a partner.

❶ Read the book.   ❷ Talk about the book.

Do More
- Talk about the front and back covers and the title page.
- Write about what happened in the book.

For more book titles, go to the Meet the Author/Illustrator page on www.macmillanmh.com

33

© Macmillan/McGraw-Hill

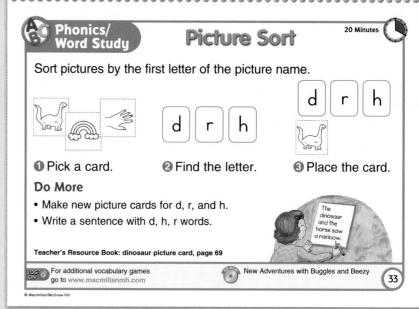

Phonics/Word Study — **Picture Sort** — 20 Minutes

Sort pictures by the first letter of the picture name.

❶ Pick a card.   ❷ Find the letter.   ❸ Place the card.

Do More
- Make new picture cards for d, r, and h.
- Write a sentence with d, h, r words.

Teacher's Resource Book: dinosaur picture card, page 69

For additional vocabulary games go to www.macmillanmh.com   New Adventures with Buggles and Beezy

33

© Macmillan/McGraw-Hill

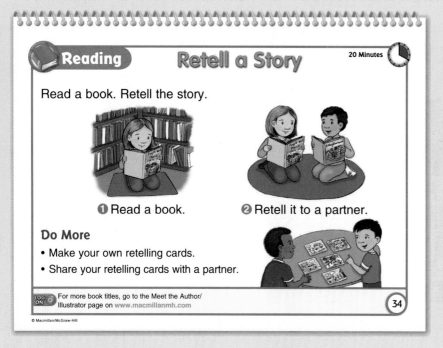

Reading — **Retell a Story** — 20 Minutes

Read a book. Retell the story.

❶ Read a book.   ❷ Retell it to a partner.

Do More
- Make your own retelling cards.
- Share your retelling cards with a partner.

For more book titles, go to the Meet the Author/Illustrator page on www.macmillanmh.com

34

© Macmillan/McGraw-Hill

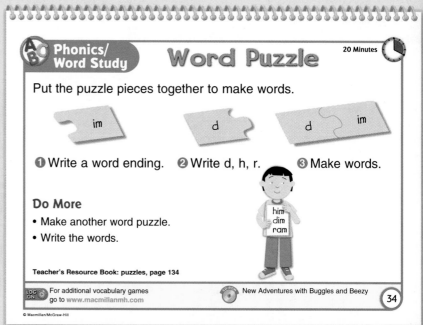

Phonics/Word Study — **Word Puzzle** — 20 Minutes

Put the puzzle pieces together to make words.

❶ Write a word ending.   ❷ Write d, h, r.   ❸ Make words.

Do More
- Make another word puzzle.
- Write the words.

Teacher's Resource Book: puzzles, page 134

For additional vocabulary games go to www.macmillanmh.com   New Adventures with Buggles and Beezy

34

© Macmillan/McGraw-Hill

Literacy Workstations

 Reading

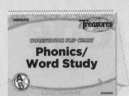 Phonics/ Word Study

 Writing

 Science/ Social Studies

Literacy Workstation Flip Charts

 **Writing**

Objectives

- Draw and label a neighborhood map
- Write a letter, using the words *for* and *you*

Content Literacy

Objectives

- Identify ways to recycle materials
- Plan and build a model neighborhood with a group

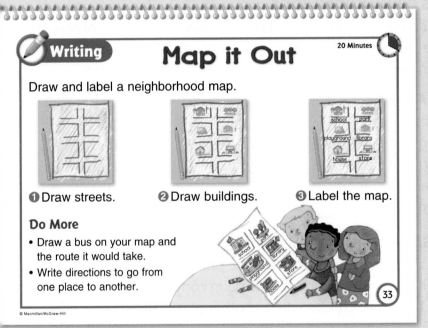

Writing — Map it Out — 20 Minutes

Draw and label a neighborhood map.

❶ Draw streets. ❷ Draw buildings. ❸ Label the map.

Do More
- Draw a bus on your map and the route it would take.
- Write directions to go from one place to another.

33

© Macmillan/McGraw-Hill

Science — Recycle It — 20 Minutes

Make something new from something old.

❶ Think about recycling. ❷ Choose an item. ❸ Make something new.

Do More
- Make a label to show what you have made.

LOG ON Internet Research and Inquiry Activity www.macmillanmh.com

34

© Macmillan/McGraw-Hill

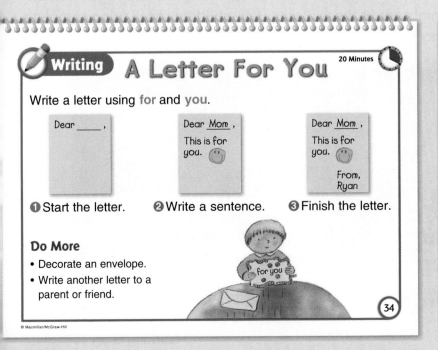

Writing — A Letter For You — 20 Minutes

Write a letter using **for** and **you**.

Dear _____ ,

Dear Mom , This is for you. 🙂

Dear Mom , This is for you. 🙂 From, Ryan

❶ Start the letter. ❷ Write a sentence. ❸ Finish the letter.

Do More
- Decorate an envelope.
- Write another letter to a parent or friend.

34

© Macmillan/McGraw-Hill

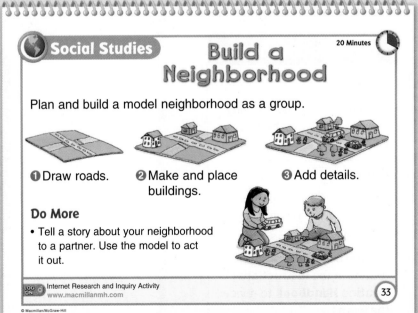

Social Studies — Build a Neighborhood — 20 Minutes

Plan and build a model neighborhood as a group.

❶ Draw roads. ❷ Make and place buildings. ❸ Add details.

Do More
- Tell a story about your neighborhood to a partner. Use the model to act it out.

LOG ON Internet Research and Inquiry Activity www.macmillanmh.com

33

Oral Language
- Build Background

✔ **Comprehension**
- Read *Bus Stops*
- Strategy: Summarize
- Skill: Identify Main Idea and Details

✔ **High-Frequency Words**
- Introduce *for, you*

✔ **Phonemic Awareness**
- Phoneme Isolation: /d/

✔ **Phonics**
- Introduce /d/*d*
- Handwriting: Write *Dd*

Grammar
- Sentences

Writing
- Shared Writing: Directions

SMALL GROUP

- Differentiated Instruction, pages 1434–1459

Oral Vocabulary

Week 2

admire	community
deliver	schedule
worker	

Review

borrow	equipment
frequently	neighborhood
organize	

Use the **Define/Example/Ask** routine in the **Instructional Routine Handbook** to review the words.

Oral Language

Talk About It

Build Background:
People and Places

INTRODUCE THE THEME

Tell children that this week they will be talking and reading books about places we go in our neighborhood.

Write the following questions on the board: *What are some places in your neighborhood? Who can you find there?* Read the sentence as you track the print. *When I come to the end of a line, I sweep back to the left and read the next line.* Prompt children to answer the questions.

ACCESS PRIOR KNOWLEDGE

A neighborhood is a **community**. *A community is a group of people who live or work together.* **Workers** *are people who do jobs in communities.*

Think Aloud Let's look at this picture. It is children playing baseball. I can tell that two children are on the same team because they both have the same uniform. (**Point to the children, baseball bat, and uniforms.**) I think they are playing in their community. Which sport would you like to play in your community?

DISCUSS THE PHOTOGRAPH

Look at and discuss with children the photograph of the baseball park. Talk about the things people do in communities, such as playing ball. Have children discuss other places they go, such as the post office, the supermarket, and the library. Discuss which workers they might see at these places. Have children speak using complete sentences.

Teaching Chart 40

Share the Big Book
Listening Comprehension

Big Book

PREVIEW AND PREDICT Display the cover. *I see a bus on a road. There are trees in the background* Point to the bus, road, and trees as you talk. *Have you ever ridden on a bus? Where did you go?*

Read the title and the name of the author/illustrator as you track the print. *What do you think this book will be about?*

GENRE:LITERARY TEXT/FICTION Tell children that this book is **fiction**. *The events in it did not really happen, but the book is about real things and places.*

STRATEGY Summarize

EXPLAIN/MODEL Have children listen for where the bus stops are at the beginning, middle, and end of the story.

Think Aloud I will stop occasionally and remind myself of what has happened in the story.

SKILL Identify Main Idea and Details

EXPLAIN Remind children that some books are about one topic or main idea. The facts and details in the book tell about the big idea.

Think Aloud The book is called *Bus Stops,* and we see a bus on the cover. I think the book will be about the many places a bus stops and the different people who get off it.

Read the Big Book

SET PURPOSE Tell children to think about the important details in the book as they listen. Use the **Define/Example/Ask** routine to teach the story words on the inside back cover.

Respond to Literature

MAKE CONNECTIONS Have children name their favorite part of the book. *What was the book about? Where in the **community** did the bus stop? Where in your community does the bus stop?*

Objectives
- Discuss the theme
- Understand and use oral vocabulary words *community* and *worker*
- Listen and respond to a story
- Summarize/identify main idea and details

Materials
- Teaching Chart 40
- Big Book: *Bus Stops*

ELL

Use the **Interactive Question-Response Guide** for *Bus Stops*, **ELL Resource Book** pages 162–169, to guide children through a reading of the book. As you read *Bus Stops*, make meaning clear by pointing to the pictures, demonstrating word meanings, paraphrasing text, and asking children questions.

Digital Learning

Story on **Listening Library Audio CD**

Objectives

- Read the high-frequency words *for, you*
- Review high-frequency words *have, is, are, play*
- Identify the words *for* and *you* in speech and text

Materials

- High-Frequency Word Cards: *for, you, have, is, are, play*
- Teaching Chart 41

ELL

Reinforce Vocabulary
Review the high-frequency words *for, you, have, is, are, play*. Display the **High-Frequency Word Cards** *for, you, have, is, are, play*. Hold different classroom objects and give them to children as you use the high-frequency words in sentences. For example: *I have a paint brush. This paint brush is for you, Sonia. I have this board game for Tommy and Raquel. They can play this game.*

High-Frequency Words

 for, you

| for | you |

INTRODUCE Display **High-Frequency Word Cards** for **for** and **you**. Use the **Read/Spell/Write** routine to teach the words.

- **Read** Point to and say the word *for*. *Please wait* for *me*.

- **Spell** *The word* for *is spelled* f-o-r. *What's the first sound in* for? *That's right. The first sound in* for *is /f/. That's why the first letter is* f. *After the* f, *I see the letters* or. *Let's read and spell* for *together.*

- **Write** *Now let's write the word* for *on our papers. Let's spell aloud the word as we write it:* f-o-r.

Repeat the routine for *you*.

REVIEW *have, is, are, play*
Display each card and have children read it.

| have | is |

READ THE RHYME AND CHIME Have children point to the words *for, you,* and *are* each time they hear them. Reread the Rhyme and Chime together for fluency. Then add *for* and *you* to the class Word Wall.

Run, Dinosaur, Run

Big Dinosaur,
Are you running in a race?
You have been running for days!
Hurry up! Pick up the pace!

High-Frequency Words: for, you
Phonics: /s/d, /r/r

Neighborhood Week 2 41

Teaching Chart 41

For Tier 2 instruction, see page 1434.

TIME TO MOVE!

Have children stand in a circle. Play music and have them pass a ball or other object from one to another and say *for you*.

Phonemic Awareness

Phoneme Isolation

Model

Display the Photo Card for *dolphin*.

Today we are going to learn a new sound. Listen for the sound at the beginning of *dolphin*: /d/, /d/, *dolphin*. *Dolphin* has /d/ at the beginning. Say the sound with me: /d/. What is the sound?

Repeat with the Photo Card for *deer*.

Let's raise a hand when we hear /d/ at the beginning of a word.

Read the "Run, Dinosaur, Run" Rhyme and Chime again. Have children raise a hand when they hear /d/.

Big Dinosaur,
Are you running in a race?
You have been running for days!
Hurry up! Pick up the pace!

Review /f/, /h/

Display the Photo Card for *hat*.

Repeat for *feet*.

This is a *hat*. The beginning sound in *hat* is /h/. **(Stretch the beginning sound.)** What is the sound?

Guided Practice/Practice

Display and name each Photo Card. Children identify the initial sound. Guide practice with the first card, using the same routine. Continue with the remaining Photo Cards.

Say each picture name with me. Tell me the sound you hear at the beginning of the word.

Quick Check

Can children identify initial /d/?

During **Small Group Instruction**

If No → **Approaching Level**   Provide additional practice, page 1435.

If Yes → **On Level**   Children are ready to blend words, page 1436.

Beyond Level   Children are ready to blend words, page 1437.

Objectives

- Identify initial /d/
- Review initial /f/ and /h/

Materials

- Photo Cards: *dog, doll, dolphin, deer, dime, hat, horse, hammer, helicopter, hippo, feet, feather, fan, five*

ELL

Pronunciation Display and have children name **Photo Cards** from this and prior lessons to reinforce phonemic awareness and word meanings. Point to a card and ask: *What do you see?* (a dolphin) *What is the sound at the beginning of the word* dolphin? (/d/). Repeat using Photo Cards with words that begin with the sounds /f/ and /h/.

Objectives

- Match the letter *d* to sound /d/
- Handwriting: write *Dd*

Materials

- Sound-Spelling Card: *Dolphin*
- Teaching Chart 41
- Handwriting
- Handwriting, Teacher's Edition
- Activity Book, p. 14
- Practice Book, p. 127

ELL

Variations in Languages
Speakers of Cantonese and Korean may have difficulty perceiving and pronouncing /d/. Use the Approaching Level Phonics lessons for additional pronunciation and decoding practice.

Sound Pronunciation

See **Sound Pronunciation CD** for a model of the /d/ sound. Play this for children needing additional models.

Phonics

✔ Introduce /d/d

Model

Display the *Dolphin* **Sound-Spelling Card**.

This is the *Dolphin* card. The sound is /d/. The /d/ sound is spelled with the letter *d*. Say it with me: /d/. This is the sound at the beginning of the word *dolphin*. Listen: /d/, *dolphin*. What is the name of this letter? What is the sound for this letter?

Read the "Run, Dinosaur, Run" Rhyme and Chime. Reread the title. Model placing a self-stick note below the *D* in *Dinosaur*.

Teaching Chart 41

Guided Practice/Practice

Read the rest of the rhyme. Stop after each line. Children place self-stick notes below words that begin with the letter *d*. Guide practice with the first line.

Let's put a sticky note below the word in the line that begins with the letter *d*. The word *Dinosaur* begins with capital letter *D*.

Corrective Feedback

If children need help with /d/, review the word *day. This is the /d/ sound at the beginning of* day: /d/ /ā/, day. *Let's blend* day *together:* /dāāā/, day. *Now it's your turn. Blend* day. *Repeat with* dot *and* dip.

Build Fluency: Sound-Spellings

 SPIRAL REVIEW Display the following **Word-Building Cards**: *a, c, d, f, h, i, m, n, o, p, s, t.* Have children chorally say each sound. Repeat and vary the pace.

Handwriting: Write *Dd*

MODEL Model holding up your writing hand. Say the handwriting cues as you write the capital and lowercase forms of *Dd* on the board. Then trace the letters on the board and in the air.

Straight down. Go back to the top. Around and in at the bottom.

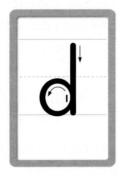

Circle back and around. Go to the top line. Straight down.

PRACTICE Ask children to hold up their writing hand.

- Say the cues together as children trace with their index finger the letters you wrote on the board.

- Have children write *D* and *d* in the air as they say /d/.

- Distribute handwriting practice pages. Observe children's pencil grip and paper position, and correct as necessary. Have children say /d/ each time they write *d*.

For Tier 2 instruction, see page 1435.

Daily Handwriting
Check that children form letters starting at the top and moving to the bottom. See **Handwriting Teacher's Edition** for ball-and-stick and slant models.

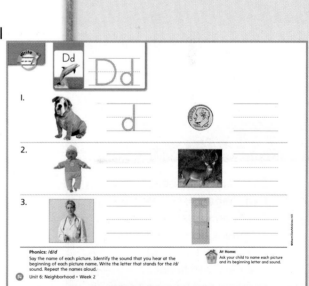

Activity Book, page 14
Practice Book, page 127

Objectives

Objectives

- Use complete sentences
- Identify prepositional phrases

Materials

- Photo Cards: *gate, astronaut, door, doctor, tree*
- Big Book: *Bus Stops*

Basic and Academic Language Display **Photo Cards** of workers, such as *astronaut, doctor,* and *nurse.* Pair English Language Learners with fluent speakers and have partners make up sentences that tell where the people on the photo cards work. For example: *The doctor works in a hospital.* Write children's sentences, read them chorally, and ask: *Where does the person in your sentence work?*

Grammar

Sentences

MODEL Use the **Big Book** *Bus Stops* to discuss sentences. Explain to children that a sentence tells a complete thought. Remind them that a sentence has to have a naming part and a telling part. *The naming part says who does something, and the telling part says what he or she does.*

- Display and read page 2. *An artist steps off.* Tell children that the naming part of the sentence is *An artist.* The telling part of the sentence is *steps off.*

- Read the sentence on page 8: *Four construction **workers** leap off.* Tell children that the naming part of the sentence is *Four construction workers;* the telling part of the sentence is *leap off.*

PRACTICE Show children **Photo Cards** for *gate, astronaut, door, doctor,* and *tree.*

- Have children identify each picture. Model saying sentences about each picture, such as:

> The **worker** opens the gate at the park.
>
> The doctor holds the chart for me.
>
> The tree in the yard is big.

- After each sentence, have children identify the naming part and the telling part. Then have children make up their own sentences.

- Point out that sometimes sentences have special words, such as *for, on, at,* and *in.* Sometimes these words are used before another word that name an object or person. For example: *on* the floor. The word *on* refers to the word *floor.* This group of words is called a prepositional phrase.

- Say simple sentences with prepositional phrases. *I will raise my hand when I hear the special words. The fish swam in the water.* (in the water) *The milk spilled on the floor.* (on the floor)

- *Now you will raise your hands when I say the special words. Please open the door for him.* (for him) *We will make puppets at school.* (at school)

Writing

Shared Writing: Directions

BRAINSTORM

Remind children that in the **Big Book** *Bus Stops,* they learned about people in the neighborhood and the jobs they do. *What are some jobs that you do in our classroom* **community**? *How do you do them?*

WRITE

- Display pages 30–31 of *Bus Stops.* Say: *The bus driver drives the bus. First, he picks people up. Then, he drops people off.*

- Create a list of classroom jobs. List children's suggestions.

- Select a job and then elicit two steps needed to do the job. Tell children that the words *first* and *next* are sequence words. Explain that sequence words can be used when writing directions. Write procedural text describing each step for the directions.

Classroom Helper
First, you fill the watering can.
Next, you water the plants.

- Read the sentences together as you track the print.

- *Today we wrote directions for doing a classroom job.* Have children identify the sequence words in the procedural text. *We wrote down what you need to do first and what you need to do next.*

- Save the sentences to refer to in other writing activities this week.

✎ Write About It

Ask children to draw a picture of a person who works in their school. Have them draw and label the picture in their Writer's Notebook.

Objective

- Write directions

Materials

- Big Book: *Bus Stops*

5-Day Writing

Procedural Text: Directions	
DAY 1	Shared: Directions
DAY 2	Interactive: Directions
DAY 3	Independent: Prewrite and Draft Directions
DAY 4	Independent: Revise and Edit Directions
DAY 5	Independent: Publish and Present

ELL

Prewriting Planning
Before children begin working on their Writer's Notebook, ask them to help you make a list of school workers, such as: *teacher, principal, janitor.* Discuss what each worker does.

Transitions That Teach

While lining up, have children tell about people in the **community**.

WHOLE GROUP

Oral Language
- Build Robust Vocabulary

✔ **Comprehension**
- Reread *Bus Stops*
- Strategy: Summarize
- Skill: Identify Main Idea and Details
- Fluency: Echo-Read

Vocabulary
- Words That Compare
- Story Words: *leap, dashes*

✔ **Phonemic Awareness**
- Phoneme Blending

✔ **Phonics**
- Review /d/d, /m/m, /t/t
- Blend with /d/d
- Decodable Reader: *Rod Can See It*

Writing
- Interactive Writing: Directions

SMALL GROUP

- Differentiated Instruction, pages 1434–1459

Oral Vocabulary

Week 2

admire   community
deliver   schedule   worker

Review

borrow   equipment
frequently   neighborhood
organize

Use the **Define/Example/Ask** routine in the **Instructional Routine Handbook** to review the words.

Oral Language

 Talk About It ## Build Robust Vocabulary

INTRODUCE WORDS
Tell children that today you are going to talk about the **Big Book** *Bus Stops*. Read pages 2–9 aloud. *Many people in a community are workers. A worker is a person who does a job. What kind of worker would you like to be? How would you help your community?* Have children speak in complete sentences.

Vocabulary Routine

Use the routine below to discuss the meaning of each word.

Define: A **community** is a place where people live, work, and play.
Example: We have a bank, a theater, and a grocery store in our little community.
Ask: What are some interesting places in your community? _____

Define: **Workers** are people who do jobs.
Example: The librarian and principal are school workers.
Ask: Who are some workers at a hospital?

CREATE A CHART
Create a three-column chart, or use **Teaching Chart G4**. Read the headings aloud as you track the print.

Think Aloud I see workers doing different jobs in my community. What are some of the jobs workers do in a community? Where are some of the places these people work?

Have children share information and ideas. Read the completed chart together as you track the print.

Places People Work

Job	What Workers Do	Where They Work
construction workers	build things	building site
baker	bakes bread	bakery
firefighter	puts out fires	in firehouse and all over town
nurse/doctor	cares for sick people	hospital
crossing guard	helps you cross the street	in front of the school

Listen for Rhythm

IDENTIFY RHYTHM

Tell children that rhythm is a regular or steady beat. *I'm going to clap to a rhyme about going to the market. Listen for the beat and then we will clap and say the rhyme together.* Recite "To Market, To Market" while clapping out the beat.

Let's say the rhyme together. Play the rhyme "To Market, to Market," using the **Listening Library Audio CD**. Then teach children the words. Recite and clap the rhyme together.

Ask children to identify the rhyming words. *(pig, jig; hog, jog)*

To Market, To Market

To market, to market to buy a fat pig;

Home again, home again, jiggity jig.

To market, to market to buy a fat hog;

Home again, home again, jiggity jog.

Objectives

- Discuss the theme
- Understand and use oral vocabulary words *community* and *worker*
- Complete a chart
- Identify rhythm

Materials

- Big Book: *Bus Stops*
- Graphic Organizer; Teaching Chart G4
- Listening Library Audio CD

Digital Learning

Rhyme on Listening Library Audio CD

ELL   ENGLISH LANGUAGE LEARNERS

Beginning	Intermediate	Advanced
Confirm Understanding Review oral vocabulary using the **Big Book** *Bus Stops*. Describe the places where the bus stops and the people who get off as you show the pictures. For example: *An artist gets off at the beach. Who gets off at the beach?* (an artist) *I see two sailboats. What do I see?* (two sailboats)	**Enhance Understanding** Display the same picture and ask: *How do you know this is a beach?* (There are two palms trees. There are two beach houses.) Ask children about other details. Guide them to answer in complete sentences. Continue with other pages.	**Make Connections** Have children imagine they are riding the bus. Ask them where they would get off and why. Help children elaborate on the reasons for getting off at a particular stop. For example: *What will you do at the beach?*

Objectives

- Summarize
- Identify main ideas and details
- Respond to a story
- Develop fluency

Materials

- Big Book: *Bus Stops*
- Activity Book, pp. 15–16
- Practice Book, p. 128

Big Book

Digital Learning

Story on **Listening Library Audio CD**

ELL

Gesture and Talk
Use gestures and talking to help make the text comprehensible.

pp. 2–3
artist: Gesture painting in the air with a paintbrush. Say: *I am an artist.* Have children repeat.

pp. 4–5
fisherman: Gesture casting a fishing line, then catching a fish. Say: *I am a fisherman.* Have children repeat.

Reread the Big Book
Listening Comprehension

CONCEPTS ABOUT PRINT Display the cover and read the title with children as you track the print. Have children tell what they remember about the story.

 STRATEGY Summarize

Explain to children that thinking about the beginning, middle, and end of a book can help them to understand it. Have children name some of the things that happened at different parts of the book.

 SKILL Identify Main Idea and Details

Tell children that some books have one main idea. A main idea is what the story is about. *Think about what is the main idea of this story.*

Think Aloud As I read the book, I will listen and think about what the story is about. I will look for details about where the bus goes in the **community** and the people who ride it.

Read the **Big Book** and use the prompts on the inside cover.

pages 2–3

 MAIN IDEA AND DETAILS
Think Aloud An artist gets off at the beach. I see that some towns have beaches and that artists are people in the neighborhood. I also see that there are sailboats on the beach.

The bus stops at the beach.
An artist steps off.

Can you find two sailboats?

pages 4–5

CONCEPT WORDS: SEQUENCE WORDS

- *What was the first stop?* (the beach) *What was the next stop?* (near the church)

The bus stops near an old church.
Two sightseers get off.

Can you find a fisherman?

Develop Comprehension

pages 6–7

⭐ SUMMARIZE

Think Aloud What important things have happened so far? The bus stopped at the beach, a church, and the edge of town. An artist, sightseers, and a salesperson got off.

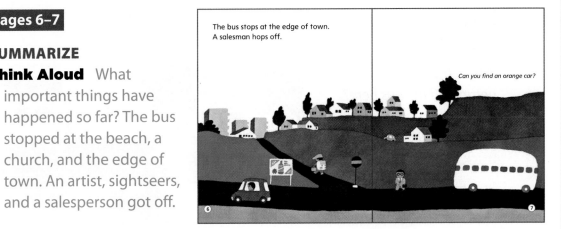

The bus stops at the edge of town.
A salesman hops off.

Can you find an orange car?

pages 8–9

⭐ MAIN IDEA AND DETAILS

- *What place in the neighborhood is shown here?* (building site) *What do you see there?* (Possible answers: a bulldozer, a crane, a fence)

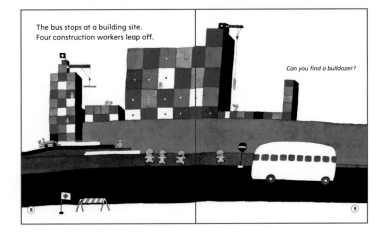

The bus stops at a building site.
Four construction workers leap off.

Can you find a bulldozer?

pages 10–11

PHONICS

- *What word starts with the /d/ sound?* (downtown) *What letter stands for the sound at the beginning of the word?* (d)

HIGH-FREQUENCY WORD

- *Can you point to the word you?*

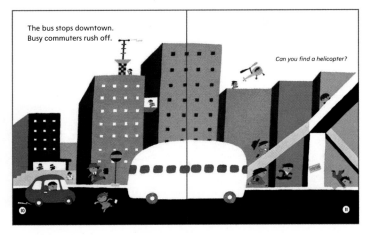

The bus stops downtown.
Busy commuters rush off.

Can you find a helicopter?

pages 12–13

⭐ MAIN IDEA AND DETAILS

- *Where is this?* (the fair) *Who do you see at the fair?* (parents and children)

The bus stops at a fair.
Some children and their parents run off.

Can you find a clown?

Comprehension

Summarize
- (pages 2–7) What important things have happened so far? The bus stopped at the beach, a church, and the edge of town. An artist, sightseers, and a salesperson got off.

Main Idea and Details
- (pages 8–9) A building site is another place in the neighborhood. Construction workers get off the bus there. What do you see there?

Story Words
(page 8) leap   (page 14) dashes

About the Author/Illustrator: Taro Gomi
Taro Gomi lives in Japan. He has written many children's books, including *Coco Can't Wait*, about a girl and her grandmother who travel across town many times in order to see each other.

**Big Book
Inside Back Cover**

ELL

pp. 6–7
edge of town: Demonstrate the *edge* by pointing out the edge of a table or chair. *This is the end of the table. It's the edge.* Point to the illustration. *This is the end of town. It's the edge of town.* Have children repeat.

pp. 8–9
construction workers: Act out hammering and building. *A construction worker is a person who makes a building.* Repeat gesturing and say *construction workers* with children.

pp. 10–11
downtown: Explain that *downtown* is the center of a city or town. There are many stores, workers, and offices *downtown.* Circle your hand around the group of buildings and say *downtown.* Repeat the gesture and ask children: *Where is this?*

pp. 12–13
fair: Point out the various rides in the illustration. *A fair is a fun place to go! What can you see at a fair?*

Main Idea and Details

Explain Remind children that when they answer a question, they must support their answer with text evidence.

Discuss Have children look at and listen to pages 18–19. Ask them what the bus does on every page so far. (the bus stops) Ask children what is the main idea. (the bus stops at many different places) Have them point to the evidence in the text or illustrations.

ELL

pp. 14–15
mechanic: Act out fixing a car engine. *A mechanic fixes cars. A mechanic is a person in the neighborhood.* Ask children to point to and name the mechanic.

pp. 16–17
baseball field: Gesture batting a ball. *A baseball field is where we play baseball.* Ask children to point to the baseball players.

pp. 18–19
hospital: Point out the nurse in the illustration. *A nurse works in a hospital to help sick people.* Do we have a nurse here at school?

pp. 20–21
shoppers: Act out shopping for items, putting them in a basket, and paying for them. Point to the various things being sold in the illustration. *What are some things the shoppers are buying?*

Develop Comprehension

pages 14–15

MAIN INFERENCES

■ *Why is the mechanic getting off the bus here?* (The mechanic is going to work to fix the broken truck.)

The bus stops near a restaurant. A mechanic dashes off.

Can you find a cow?

pages 16–17

⭐ SUMMARIZE

■ *What important things have happened in the book so far?* (The bus has stopped at many different places, including a beach, a building site, and a fair. People have gotten off at each place.)

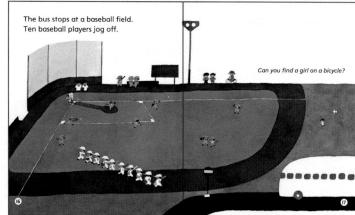

The bus stops at a baseball field. Ten baseball players jog off.

Can you find a girl on a bicycle?

pages 18–19

The bus stops at a hospital. A nurse comes out to meet it.

Can you find a jogger?

pages 20–21

SPIRAL REVIEW

✓ MAIN IDEA AND DETAILS

■ *Where has the bus stopped now?* (at the marketplace) *Who goes to the marketplace?* (shoppers) *What do you think they will do there?* (They will buy food and other things.)

The bus stops at the marketplace. Some shoppers get off.

Can you find a green van?

Develop Comprehension

pages 22–23

 SUMMARIZE

- *Who is getting off the bus here? Have people gotten off at all the other stops?*

The bus stops at a junkyard.
No one gets off.

What can you find here?

pages 24–25

GENERATE AND EVALUATE QUESTIONS

Think Aloud I'll ask myself why the actor runs off the bus. I see that the people are making a movie. The actor must be late and in a rush. That is why he is running.

The bus stops at a movie set.
An actor runs off.

Can you find a horse?

pages 26–27

CULTURAL PERSPECTIVES

Think Aloud The author/illustrator of this book is Japanese. I see that the signs on the drugstore are written in Japanese, which looks different from English. The sign on the cafe is written in English.

The bus stops in front of a drugstore.
Oops, a woman just missed the bus!

Can you find a man in a gray hat?

pages 28–29

IDENTIFY CHARACTER

Think Aloud The words on this page tell me that the person who is speaking is shown in the picture.

The bus stops outside our house.
We get off.

Can you find a dog?

ELL

pp. 22–23
junkyard: Explain that old things that we don't want anymore can be called *junk*. *My TV is old and broken. I am taking it to the junkyard.* Ask children to point to and name what they see in the junkyard.

pp. 24–25
actor: Act out some emotions, such as happy or sad. Explain that you are acting. Give examples of actors that children might know. *Actors can act in movies and on television.* Tell children to act out waking up in the morning. Say: *You are good actors!*

pp. 26–27
drugstore: Explain that a drugstore is a store that sells medicines. Give synonyms, such as *pharmacy*, or name drugstores in your city or town.

---

pages 30–31

MAIN IDEA AND DETAILS

Think Aloud The main idea of this book is that the bus stops at many different places. The details give information about where the bus stops and who gets off.

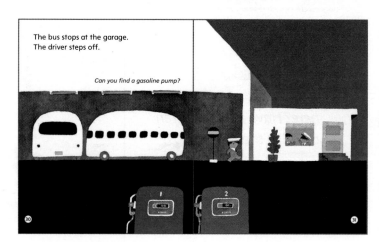

The bus stops at the garage.
The driver steps off.

Can you find a gasoline pump?

Name _____

Comprehension: Main Idea and Details Bus Stops
Look at the picture. Tell what you see speaking in complete sentences.
What is the picture mainly about? What is the main idea of *Bus Stops*?

At Home:
Ask your child to tell you what is happening in the picture.

Unit 6: Neighborhood • Week 2 15

Activity Book, pages 15–16
Practice Book, page 128

Respond to Literature

TALK ABOUT IT Have children talk about the words and illustrations that they liked.

- *Where does the bus stop at the end of the book?* (the garage) LOCATE

- *What did the bus do at all of the places that were shown in the book?* (The bus stopped.) COMBINE

- *Why is the bus important to this **community**?* (people in the community use the bus to get to places) CONNECT

Retell

GUIDED RETELLING
Remind children that as they listened to *Bus Stops*, they heard the words and looked at the illustrations. Now they will retell the story.

- *Where did the bus stop first? Where did it go next? Where did it go last?* (the beach, an old church, the garage)

- *Describe the characters that rode the bus. Where did each person get off the bus?*

- *What other things did you see in the **communities** the bus stopped in?*

Fluency: Echo-Read

MODEL Reread pages 6–7, emphasizing the action word *hops* and raising your voice at the end of the question on page 7. Then reread pages 8–11 and have children echo-read as you track the print.

Quick Check

Can children identify main idea and details to understand a story?

Retelling Rubric

4 Excellent

Retells the selection without prompting, in sequence, and using supporting details. Clearly describes the setting, main characters, and complete plot.

3 Good

Retells the selection with little guidance, in sequence, and using some details. Generally describes the setting, main characters, and plot.

2 Fair

Retells the selection with some guidance, mostly in sequence, and using limited details. Partially describes the setting, main characters, and plot.

1 Unsatisfactory

Retells the selection only when prompted, out of sequence, and using limited details. Does not describe the main characters or plot.

Vocabulary

Words That Compare

Chant the following jingle:

> *I see three balls;*
> *One is* small,
> *One is* smaller,
> *One is the* smallest!
> *I see three boxes;*
> *One is* big,
> *One is* bigger,
> *One is the* biggest!

- Repeat the first four lines and ask children to name the words that compare size. Repeat with other lines.

- Display the pocket chart with three paper squares of different sizes. Place squares in size order. As you point to each square, ask children to tell which is *big, bigger*, and *biggest*.

NAME WORDS THAT COMPARE Have children sort and arrange classroom objects, such as blocks, or pictures of objects in size order. Then have them point to the objects and say *big, bigger, biggest* or *small, smaller, smallest*.

Story Words: *leap, dashes*

Display page 8 of *Bus Stops* and point out the word *leap* and the picture of the construction **workers**. Explain that a *leap* is a jumping step. *The construction workers' legs show they are* leaping.

Display page 14 and point out the word *dashes* and the picture of the mechanic. *To dash is to move quickly. I dash around the corner to the bakery when I am hungry.* Talk about other words that mean to move quickly.

TIME TO MOVE!

Go on a Scavenger Hunt around the classroom. *Let's find something small. Now find something smaller. Let's find something big. Now find something bigger.* Have children say sentences such as: *The block is small. The crayon is smaller.*

Objectives

- Use words that compare
- Learn the story words *leap, dashes*

Materials

- Big Book: *Bus Stops*
- three paper squares, each a different size
- pocket chart
- pictures of objects that can be arranged by size

Digital Learning

 LOG ON For children who need additional language support and oral vocabulary development, use the activities found at **www.macmillanmh.com**.

ELL

Reinforce Meaning
Display classroom objects of different sizes such as crayons, books, or paper squares. Have children sort the objects into groups and model naming them accordingly: *small, smaller, smallest* or *big, bigger, biggest*.

Objectives

- Orally blend sounds to form words
- Match the letters *d, m, t,* to the sounds /d/, /m/, /t/
- Blend sounds in words with /a/*a,* /d/*d,* /i/*i,* /n/*n,* /o/*o,* /p/*p,* /t/*t,* /s/*s,* /m/*m,* /h/*h*

Materials

- Puppet
- Word-Building Cards
- pocket chart

Phonemic Awareness

✓ Phoneme Blending

Model

Use the **Puppet** to model how to blend the sounds in the word *dad*.

Repeat with the word *had*.

Happy is going to say the sounds in a word. Listen to Happy as he says each sound: /d/ /a/ /d/. Happy can blend these sounds to say the word: *dad*. Say the sounds with Happy: /d/ /a/ /d/, /daaad/, *dad*. Now say the word with Happy. (*dad*)

Guided Practice/Practice

Say the sounds. Have children blend the sounds to form words. Guide practice with the first word, using the same routine.

Happy is going to say the sounds in a word. Listen to Happy as he says each sound. Then blend the sounds to say the word.

/d/ /o/ /t/	/d/ /i/ /g/	/d/ /i/ /p/
/d/ /i/ /m/	/d/ /i/ /d/	/m/ /a/ /d/

Phonics

✓ Review

Model

Display **Word-Building Card** *d*.

Repeat the routine for the letters *m* and *t*.

This is the letter *d*. The letter *d* stands for /d/. You hear /d/ at the end of *mud*. What is the letter? What sound does this letter stand for?

Write the letter that stands for the sound.

Repeat the routine with *sat* and *rim*.

The ending sound in the word *pad* is /d/. The letter *d* stands for the /d/ sound. I'll write *d*.

Guided Practice/Practice

Say the word. Children write the letter that stands for the ending sound. Guide practice with the first word.

Listen as I say each word. Write the letter that stands for the ending sound.

had	him	sat	did
mad	mat	ham	sad

Build Fluency: Sound-Spellings

 Display the following **Word-Building Cards**: *a, c, d, f, h, i, m, n, o, p, s, t.* Have children chorally say each sound. Repeat and vary the pace.

 ## Blend with /d/*d*

Model

Place Word-Building Card *D* in the pocket chart.	This letter is capital *D*. It stands for the /d/ sound. Say /d/.	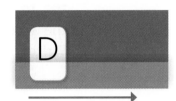
Place Word-Building Card *a* next to *D*. Move your hand from left to right.	This is the letter *a*. It stands for the /a/ sound. Listen as I blend the two sounds together: /daaa/. Now you say it. (/daaa/)	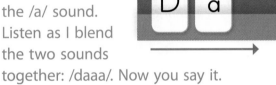
Place Word-Building Card *d* next to *Da*. Move your hand from left to right. Repeat the routine with *Dan*.	This is the letter *d*. It stands for /d/. Listen as I blend the three sounds together: /daaad/. Now you say it. (/daaad/, *Dad*)	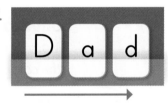

Guided Practice/Practice

Children blend sounds to form words. Guide practice with the first word, using the routine.

dad   sad   dot   dip

mad   had   dim   pad

Objectives

- Read decodable words with /d/*d*
- Read the high-frequency words *play, the, to, see, for, you*

Materials

- Decodable Reader: *Rod Can See It*
- High-Frequency Word Cards: *play, the, to, see, for, you*

Decodable Text

For additional decodable passages, see pages 21–22 of the **Teacher's Resource Book**.

Decodable Reader

Read *Rod Can See It*

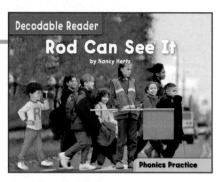

Rod Can See It

 REVIEW HIGH-FREQUENCY WORDS Display the **High-Frequency Word Cards** for **play**, **the**, **to**, **see**, **for**, and **you**. Review the words using the **Read/Spell/Write** routine.

MODEL CONCEPTS ABOUT PRINT
I hold the book so the words are right side up.
I read each page from top to bottom and from left to right.

PREDICT Ask children to describe the cover. *What are the children doing? Which person is Rod? What might Rod see?*

FIRST READ Turn to page 2. Have children point to each word, sounding out decodable words and saying the high-frequency words quickly. If children have difficulty, provide corrective feedback and continue to guide them page by page.

DEVELOP COMPREHENSION Ask the following: *What are Ron and Mom doing?* (Mom is teaching Ron to ride a bike.) *Where does Rod see the cat?* (on top of a raft)

 SECOND READ Have partners reread the book together. Circulate, listen in, and provide corrective feedback.

Rod can see Don hit it.
Don can hit the rim.

2

Rod can see Mom and Ron.
Mom ran to Ron.

3

Rod can see Tad mop.
Tad can dip the mop.

4

Rod can see Tim on a mat.
Can you nap on a mat?

5

Rod can see a cat.
The cat can sit on top.

6

Rod can see Rob.
Dot can pat him.

7

Rod can see a rip.
Mom can pin it for Dan.

8

Decodable Reader

Writing

Interactive Writing: Directions

REVIEW

Display the sentences that children created for the Shared Writing activity.

WRITE

- Tell children that today you will write directions for cleaning up the classroom.

- Collaborate with them to write procedural text with the following sentence frames, one word at a time.

> First, you pick up _____.
> Then, you put away _____.

- Have children suggest a word to complete the first sentence. Collaborate to write the word in the frame. Ask children to help you by writing all of the letters they know.

- Repeat the process with the second sentence.

- Read the completed sentences together as you track the print.

- Point out that the words *First* and *Then* are sequence words. They are followed by a comma.

- Work with children to write sentences using sequence words about their favorite classroom jobs.

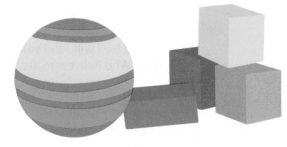

Write About It

Ask children to draw in their Writer's Notebooks. Suggest that they draw and label a picture of their class. Have them complete the caption *We are* _____.

Objectives

- Write directions
- Use letter knowledge to write letters in a word

Materials

- Shared Writing sentences from Day 1

5-Day Writing

	Procedural Text: Directions
DAY 1	Shared: Directions
DAY 2	Interactive: Directions
DAY 3	Independent: Prewrite and Draft Directions
DAY 4	Independent: Revise and Edit Directions
DAY 5	Independent: Publish and Present

ELL

Prewriting Planning
Remind children of classroom directions that they follow in sequence. For example: *First, you listen to me. Then, you repeat what I say.* Help children complete sentence frames with *First* and *Then*.

Transitions That Teach

While children are packing up, have them describe the roles that **workers** perform in their community.

Oral Language
- Build Robust Vocabulary
- Oral Vocabulary Cards: "Acrefoot, the Barefoot Mailman"

✓ **Comprehension**
- Read "The Park"

✓ **High-Frequency Words**
- Review *for*, *you*

✓ **Phonemic Awareness**
- Phoneme Isolation

✓ **Phonics**
- Introduce /r/r
- Handwriting: Write *Rr*

Grammar
- Sentences

Writing
- Independent Writing: Prewrite and Draft Directions

SMALL GROUP
- Differentiated Instruction, pages 1434–1459

Additional Vocabulary
To provide 15–20 minutes of additional vocabulary instruction, see Oral Vocabulary Cards 5-Day Plan. The pre- and posttests can be found in the **Teacher's Resource Book**, pages 224–225.

Oral Language

 Talk About It ## Build Robust Vocabulary

BUILD BACKGROUND

Introduce the story "Acrefoot, the Barefoot Mailman" using **Oral Vocabulary Card 1** and read the title aloud. *What kind of work do mail carriers do? How do mail carriers help our communities?* Ask children to tell what they think will happen in the story.

■ Read the story on the back of the cards. Pause at each oral vocabulary word and read the definition. Check children's understanding using the Use Illustrations, Generate Antonyms, and Pantomime prompts.

Oral Vocabulary Cards

Vocabulary Routine

Use the routine below to discuss the meaning of each word.

Define: To **admire** someone means "to like and respect someone." Say the word with me.
Example: I admire police officers and firefighters for their courage.
Ask: Whom do you admire in your community? Why?

Define: When you take something to someone, you **deliver** it. Say the word with me.
Example: I will send you to deliver a note to the music teacher.
Ask: Who delivers mail to your home?

Define: A **schedule** is a list of times things are supposed to be done. Say the word with me.
Example: I check the train schedule to find out what time the train is coming.
Ask: According to our classroom schedule, what time do we have lunch?

■ Use the routine on Card 1 to review the words **community** and **worker**.

 SPIRAL REVIEW

■ Review last week's words: *borrow, equipment, frequently, neighborhood,* and *organize*.

Listen for Alliteration

IDENTIFY ALLITERATION

Tell children that when two or more words begin with the same sound, it is called alliteration. Tongue twisters, such as "Peter Piper picked a peck of pickled peppers" use alliteration.

Tell children that they will recite a rhyme about someone running through the town. Have them listen for words that begin with the same sound. Play the rhyme and have children join in. Ask children to identify which words begin with the same sound.

Discuss the rhyme. Ask: *What is Wee Willie Winkie wearing?* (nightgown) *What question does he ask?* (Are the children in bed?) *What time is it in his town, or* **community**? (eight o'clock)

Wee Willie Winkie

Wee Willie Winkie
Runs through the town,
Upstairs and downstairs
In his nightgown.
Rapping at the window,
Crying through the lock,
"Are the children all in bed,
For now it's eight o'clock?"

Objectives

- Use oral vocabulary words *admire, community, deliver, schedule,* and *worker*
- Discuss the theme
- Recognize alliteration

Materials

- Oral Vocabulary Cards: "Acrefoot, the Barefoot Mailman"

Digital Learning

Rhyme on **Listening Library Audio CD**

Objectives

- Read and respond to a poem
- Identify word choice/ figurative language in poetry

Material

- Big Book of Explorations, Vol. 2: "The Park"

Vocabulary

dandelion a plant with bright yellow flowers and jagged leaves

dark having little or no light

still when something does not move

shine to make bright

Poetry

Genre

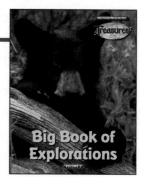

Big Book of Explorations

LITERARY TEXT: POETRY

Remind children that Acrefoot was a mailman from long ago. Talk about places in a community mail carriers today might see as they deliver the mail, such as stores, houses, and parks. Tell children that they will now read a **poem**. Some poems are fun and silly. *Some poems describe feelings or things in special ways. This poem will describe the way a park looks at night.*

LITERARY ELEMENT: WORD CHOICE/FIGURATIVE LANGUAGE

Explain/Model Tell children that writers of poetry choose words carefully. *A poet's words help make a picture in your mind.*

Think Aloud I am going to pay careful attention to the words in this poem. The words will help me picture the park the way the poet sees the park. I want to see the park the way the poet does.

READ "THE PARK"

- **Preview and Predict** Turn to "The Park" on page 8. Read the title and ask children what it tells them. Then read the poet's name. Point to the park lights in the picture. Have children predict how the writer of the poem might describe the park.

- **Vocabulary** Model using the vocabulary words *dark, shine, dandelion,* and *still*. For example, *After the sun sets, it gets* dark. Tell children that the dandelions are shown after they go to seed. Help children use the vocabulary words in sentences.

- **Set Purpose** Tell children that as they listen to the words of the poem, they should try to picture in their minds the park in the community that the poet is describing.

- Read the poem aloud as you track the print. Have children identify the words that describe the park lights and those that rhyme.

page 8

The Park

I'm glad that I
Live near a park

For in the winter
After dark

The park lights shine
As bright and still

As dandelions
On a hill.

—James Tippett

Retell and Respond

Talk About It Have children share responses to the poem.

- *Is the poet happy or sad that he lives near a park?* (happy) *Which word tells you?* (glad)

- *What does the poet compare the park lights to?* (dandelions)

Connect to Content

Social Studies Activity: National Parks

- Provide children with pictures of several national parks. Explain that a national park is a very large park with special features. Guide children to identify various geographic features, such as lakes, mountains, and plains.

- Have children draw and label a picture of one of the geographic features. Add their pictures to a class bulletin board.

Write About It

Have children draw a place that they like. Help them write words to describe their special place on their picture.

Objective

- Read the high-frequency words *for, you*

Materials

- High-Frequency Word Cards: *for, you, The, is, Are, the*
- pocket chart
- Photo Cards: *balloon, banana, bike, book, camera, doll, dime, envelope, guitar, hat, invitation, juice, kitten, pizza, ring, soup, yogurt, vegetables*
- 2 index cards with: period mark, question mark
- Activity Book, pp. 17–18
- Practice Book, pp. 129–130

Activity Book, pages 17–18
Practice Book, pages 129–130

High-Frequency Words

✔ *for, you*

| for | you |

REVIEW Display the **High-Frequency Word Card** for **for**. Review the word using the **Read/Spell/Write** routine.

Repeat the routine for the word **you**.

APPLY Build sentences in the pocket chart using High-Frequency Word Cards and **Photo Cards**. Read each sentence aloud, then have children chorally read it as you track the print with your finger. Use the sentence below and the following: *Are the vegetables for you? The juice is for you.*

The [☕] is for you .

READ FOR FLUENCY Chorally read the Take-Home Book with children. Then have children reread the book to review high-frequency words and build fluency.

Quick Check

Can children read the words *for* and *you*?

During **Small Group Instruction**

If No → **Approaching Level** Provide additional practice with high-frequency words, pages 1444.

If Yes → **On Level** Children are ready to read the Take-Home Book.

Beyond Level Children are ready to read the Take-Home Book.

TIME TO MOVE!

Put various items in a box. Have a child pick an item from the box. Ask the child to take the object to a classmate and say: *This is for you.* Continue until each child has selected and been given an object.

Phonemic Awareness

Phoneme Isolation

Model

Display the **Photo Card** for *rose*.

Today we are going to learn a new sound. Listen for the sound at the beginning of *rose*: /r/, /r/, *rose*. *Rose* has /r/ at the beginning. Say the sound with me: /r/. What is the sound? We'll raise our hand when we hear /r/ at the beginning of a word!

Say the Rhyme and Chime. Children raise a hand when they hear /r/.

Big Dinosaur,
Are you running in a race?
You have been running for days!
Hurry up! Pick up the pace!

Review /h/ and /d/

SPIRAL REVIEW

Display the **Photo Card** for *hand*.

This is a *hand*. The beginning sound in *hand* is /h/. Listen: /hhhand/. **(Stretch the beginning sound.)** What is the sound?

Repeat for *dog*.

Guided Practice/Practice

Display Photo Cards one at a time. Children identify initial sounds. Guide practice with the first card.

Say each picture name with me. Tell me the sound you hear at the beginning of the word.

Quick Check

Can children identify the initial sound /r/?

During **Small Group Instruction**

If No → **Approaching Level** Provide additional practice, page 1444.

If Yes → **On Level** Children are ready to blend words, page 1436.

Beyond Level Children are ready to blend words, page 1437.

Objectives

- Identify initial /r/
- Review initial /h/ and /d/

Materials

- **Photo Cards:** *deer, dog, dinosaur, doctor, hand, house, hippo, hook, rabbit, rake, ring, rock, rope, rose*

ELL

Pronunciation Display and have children name **Photo Cards** from this and prior lessons to reinforce phonemic awareness and word meanings. Point to a card and ask: *What do you see?* (a rose) *What is the sound at the beginning of the word* rose? (/r/) Repeat using Photo Cards with words that begin with the sounds /h/ and /d/.

- Match the letter *r* to the sound /r/
- Handwriting: write *Rr*

Materials

- Sound-Spelling Card: *Rose*
- Teaching Chart 41
- Handwriting
- Handwriting Teacher's Edition, pp. 62–64
- Activity Book, p. 19
- Practice Book, p. 131

ELL

Variations in Language
Speakers of Spanish, Hmong, Cantonese, Vietnamese, Korean, and Haitian Creole may have difficulty perceiving and pronouncing /r/. Use the Approaching Level Phonics lessons for additional pronunciation and decoding practice. Have children who need additional practice with the sound /r/ listen to the **Sound-Pronunciation CD**.

Corrective Feedback

Linguistic Differences
Many speakers of African American Vernacular English drop the /r/ sounds in words. For example, these children will say *sto'* for *store* or *do'* for *door*. Clearly pronounce these words, emphasizing the /r/ sound. Have children repeat several times, exaggerating the sound.

Phonics

✔ Introduce /r/r

Model

Display the *Rose* **Sound-Spelling Card**.

This is the *Rose* card. The sound is /r/. The /r/ sound is spelled with the letter *r*. Say it with me: /r/. This is the sound at the beginning of the word *rose*. Listen: /rrr/ . . . *ose, rose*.

What is the name of this letter? What is the sound for this letter?

Reread the "Run, Dinosaur, Run" Rhyme and Chime. Reread the title. Point out that the word *Run* in the title begins with the letter *R*. Model placing self-stick notes below the letter *R* in *Run*.

Teaching Chart 41

Guided Practice/Practice

Reread the Rhyme and Chime. Stop after each line. Children place self-stick notes below words that begin with the letter *r*. Guide practice with *running* in line 2.

Let's put a sticky note below the words in the line that begin with the letter *r*.

The word *running* begins with the letter *r*.

Build Fluency: Sound-Spellings

 Display the following **Word-Building Cards**: *a, c, d, f, h, i, m, n, o, p, r, s, t.* Have children chorally say each sound. Repeat and vary the pace.

Handwriting: Write *Rr*

MODEL Model holding up your writing hand. Say the handwriting cues as you write the capital and lowercase forms of *Rr* on the board. Then trace the letters on the board and in the air as you say /r/.

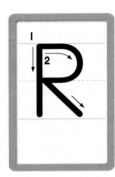 *Straight down. Go back to the top. Around and in at the dotted line. Slant down.*

 *Straight down. Curl forward.*

PRACTICE Ask children to hold up their writing hand.

- Say the cues together as children trace with their index fingers the letters you wrote on the board.

- Have children write *R* and *r* in the air as they say /r/.

- Distribute handwriting practice pages. Observe children's pencil grip and paper position, and correct as necessary. Have children say /r/ every time they write the letter *r*.

For Tier 2 instruction, see page 1444.

Daily Handwriting

Check that children form letters starting at the top and moving to the bottom. See **Handwriting Teacher's Edition** for ball-and-stick and slant models.

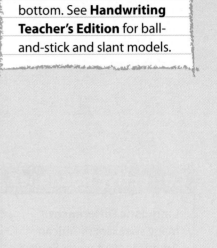

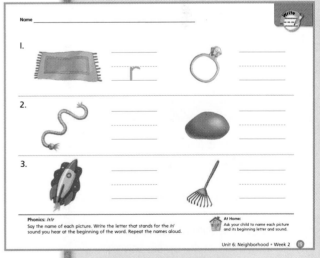

Activity Book, page 19
Practice Book, page 131

Objectives

- Recognize sentences
- Recognize prepositional phrases

Materials

- Photo Cards: *giraffe, bear, bird, cowboy, grapes, boat, boil, mix, jump, sing, write*
- pocket chart

Corrective Feedback

Linguistic Differences
Many speakers of African American Vernacular English have difficulties with subject-verb agreement when the verbs *do/does, have/has,* and *was/were* are used. Additional grammar instruction and practice will be needed.

ELL

Basic and Academic Vocabulary Display the **Photo Cards** from the lesson. Pair English Language Learners with fluent speakers and have partners make up sentences with the Photo Card names and these prepositions: *for, on, at, in.* Write partners' sentences, read them chorally, and say: *Tell me what preposition you used in your sentence. Show me where you used it. Let's circle the prepositional phrase.*

Grammar

Sentences

MODEL Explain to children that a sentence tells a complete thought. Remind them that a sentence needs to have a naming part and a telling part. *The naming part says* who *or* what *does something and the telling part says* what *he, she, or it does.*

- Tell children that you will say groups of words and they will say if the words make a complete sentence. If the sentence is incomplete, have children add to the sentence to make it complete. *The big cat; She is nice; are big; The apples.*

PRACTICE Display the **Photo Cards** for *giraffe, bear, bird, cowboy, jump,* and *mix* in the pocket chart. Use the first six sentence frames listed below and the Photo Cards to make complete sentences. Have children identify the *who* and *what* for each sentence.

The __giraffe__ is a tall animal.   The __bear__ looked at the tree.

Tim can __jump__ over the puddle.   The __bird__ flew in the sky.

Dan will __mix__ the batter.   The __cowboy__ rides on a horse.

- Use the remaining sentence frames to make complete sentences. Have children identify the *who* and *what* for each sentence.

Beth will __sing__ the national anthem in school.   The __boat__ is **scheduled** to leave at 9:00.

Dad will __boil__ water for tea.   The __grapes__ are on the table.

I will __write__ a list for mom.

- After children complete the above sentences, point out the prepositions: *for, on, at,* and *in.* Remind them that when there is a preposition and the object of the preposition, it is called a prepositional phrase. Identify the prepositional phrases with children. Guide with the first two sentences. (in school, at 9:00, for tea, on the table, for mom)

Writing

Independent Writing: Directions

Display the sentences from the Interactive Writing activity.

BRAINSTORM

WRITING TRAIT: ORGANIZATION Tell children that they will write directions for a classroom job. *Directions need to be in the right order.* Explain that they will generate ideas and formulate a plan to write about what to do first and what to do next.

Think Aloud I will write about feeding the classroom pet. What do I do first? First, I get the food. Then, I have to feed the pet.

Ask children to name ways they help in the classroom **community**. List their ideas on chart paper as a reference.

PREWRITE

Write the following sentence frames and read them aloud:

> First, you _____.
> Then, you _____.

- Complete the sentence frames by writing the words *get the food* and *feed the pet*. Read the sentences as you track the print.

- Have children select a job from the list to write about.

DRAFT

- Have children copy the sentence frames and complete each sentence by writing words that explain how to do a classroom job.

- Have children pause in the midst of writing and interpret what has been written.

- Collect and save children's work to use tomorrow.

Write About It

Ask children to draw and label a picture of themselves doing a classroom job.

Objectives

- **Write directions**
- **Use writing trait:** organization

Materials

- Interactive Writing from Day 2

5-Day Writing

Procedural Text: Directions

DAY 1	Shared: Directions
DAY 2	Interactive: Directions
DAY 3	Independent: Prewrite and Draft Directions
DAY 4	Independent: Revise and Edit Directions
DAY 5	Independent: Publish and Present

ELL

Use New Language Use the pictures in the **Big Book** *Bus Stops* to complete these sentence frames with children: *First, the bus stops at _____. Then the bus stops at _____.*

Transitions That Teach

While they are packing up, have children tell about people that they look up to or **admire**.

WHOLE GROUP

Oral Language
- Build Robust Vocabulary

✔ **Comprehension**
- Read Aloud: "Ms. Mouse Needs a Friend"

Vocabulary
- Words That Compare
- Story Words: *leap, dashes*

✔ **Phonemic Awareness**
- Phoneme Blending

✔ **Phonics**
- Picture Sort
- Blend with /r/r
- Decodable Reader: *Rod Can See It*

Writing
- Independent Writing: Revise and Edit Directions

SMALL GROUP

- Differentiated Instruction, pages 1434–1459

Oral Language

 Talk About It

Build Robust Vocabulary

HOW NEIGHBORS IN A COMMUNITY HELP EACH OTHER
Discuss problems that neighbors can help to solve together. Remind children that people in a **community** help one another. *With what problems would you ask neighbors to help you?* Have children speak using complete sentences.

CREATE A WORD WEB
Create a word web as shown, or use **Teaching Chart G1**.

Think Aloud Cleaning up a dirty park is a task you would need help to do. I will write that on the web. Who can name other ways that neighbors can help each other?

Have children' share their ideas. Read the completed web together.

How Neighbors Help
- clean up trash in park
- deliver groceries to elderly neighbors
- fix lunch for hungry people
- visit sick neighbors
- shovel snow
- help younger children
- plant trees

ELL   ENGLISH LANGUAGE LEARNERS

Beginning	Intermediate	Advanced
Confirm Understanding Display the photographs in the article "Helping Hands" to review how people help each other in a community. Say, for example: *Show me the photograph where children paint a mural.* Repeat with other photographs.	**Enhance Understanding** Use "Helping Hands" as a starting point to generate a list of ways people help each other and their communities. Have children dictate their ideas for you to write down.	**Share Experiences** Tell children to think of a community problem they or someone they know helped to solve. Ask, for example: *What problem did someone in our community have? How did neighbors help? What did you do to help?*

Listen for Rhythm

IDENTIFY RHYTHM

Remind children that rhythm is a regular or steady beat. Recite the rhyme with children. Have them clap out the rhythm.

MARKETING RHYME

Tell children that they will recite the rhyme "To Market, To Market" that they learned earlier in the week. Play the rhyme and have children join in.

Ask the following: *Could you buy a pig or hog in your **community**? What type of **worker** might take care of it?*

Discuss and compare different types of communities, such as a farming community and a city community. A worker in a farming community might **deliver** animal feed to the farmers. A worker in the city might deliver pizza.

To Market, To Market

To market, to market to buy a fat pig;

Home again, home again, jiggity jig.

To market, to market to buy a fat hog;

Home again, home again, jiggity jog.

Objectives

- Discuss the theme
- Discuss neighborhood problem-solvers
- Contribute ideas for a web
- Understand and use oral vocabulary words *admire, community, deliver, schedule,* and *worker*
- Identify a regular beat

Materials

- Big Book of Explorations, Vol. 1, "Helping Hands"
- Graphic Organizer; Teaching Chart G1

Oral Vocabulary

Have children use each word in a sentence about this week's stories.

admire	community
deliver	schedule
worker	

Review Work with children to review last week's words. *What type of* equipment *do you need to play baseball? If you read* frequently, *why might it be better to* borrow *books from the library instead of buying them? How is your* classroom organized? *Name a* worker *in your* neighborhood.

borrow	equipment
frequently	neighborhood
organize	

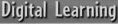

Rhyme on **Listening Library Audio CD**

Objective

- Listen and respond to a folktale

Materials

- Read-Aloud Anthology: "Ms. Mouse Needs a Friend," pp. 88–92
- Story Patterns; Teacher's Resource Book, pp. 171–198

ELL

Reinforce Comprehension
Make and display cutouts of a rabbit, mink, fox, and bear. Say: *In this story four animals try to help Ms. Mouse. Try to remember what happened to each one.* As you read the story aloud, point to the cutouts of the animals and say their names, one by one, as they appear.

Readers Theater

BUILDING LISTENING AND SPEAKING SKILLS
Distribute copies of "The Three Little Pigs," Read-Aloud Anthology pages 169–184. Have children practice performing the play throughout the unit. Assign parts and have children present the play or perform it as a dramatic reading at the end of the unit.

Interactive
Read Aloud

Listening Comprehension

Read Aloud

GENRE: LITERARY TEXT/FOLKTALE
Explain that this story is a **folktale** about an animal **community**. In the story a mouse asks one animal after another for help. Stories such as this make good bedtime stories. The tale can be made longer by adding more animals and ends when everyone has fallen asleep.

CULTURAL PERSPECTIVES
Tell children that "Ms. Mouse Needs a Friend" is a folktale told by the Chucha people of northern Siberia. Siberia is a region of Russia with long, cold winters.

READ "MS. MOUSE NEEDS A FRIEND"

- **MODEL ASKING QUESTIONS AND SUMMARIZING** Use the Think Alouds provided at point of use in the folktale.

- **MODEL FLUENT READING** Read aloud the folktale with fluent expression. Stop occasionally so that children can predict what will happen next.

- **EXPAND VOCABULARY** See page 88 of the **Read-Aloud Anthology** to teach new words using the **Define/Example/Ask** routine.

Respond to Literature

TALK ABOUT IT Ask children to discuss the big idea of this folktale.

- *How did Ms. Mouse get stuck to the pond?*

- *Why did Ms. Mouse have to keep asking different friends for help?*

- *How could Ms. Mouse have acted differently and not lost her tail?*

Write About It
Have children draw a picture of Ms. Mouse and some of the friends she asked for help. Ask them to write a sentence that Ms. Mouse might say to her friends.

Vocabulary

Words That Compare

REVIEW WORDS THAT COMPARE

Listen as I read. Raise your hand when you hear words that compare.

> *We got a puppy last year. We named him* Small Pup. *That is because he was the* smallest *puppy at the animal shelter.*

> *What are the words that compare?*

> *The puppy ate lots of food. He grew* big, *then* bigger! *We changed his name to* Biggest Pup.

> *What are the words that compare?*

Display pictures of the same item in different sizes. Have children sort the pictured items into categories of "big, bigger, biggest" or "small, smaller, smallest".

Story Words: *leap, dashes*

Display page 8 of *Bus Stops*. Point to the leaping construction **workers**. *Animals* leap, *too*. Read page 26 of *Animal Babies ABC: Yak calves live with their mothers in a herd. They run,* leap, *and climb*.

Display page 14 of *Bus Stops* and page 27 of *Animal Babies ABC*.

The mechanic dashes *across the street. The zebra* dashes *through the grass.*

Tell children to create sentences with the words *leap* and *dashes*. Have them describe how they could *leap* or *dash*.

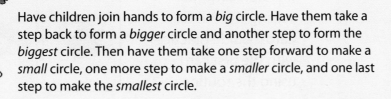

TIME TO MOVE!

Have children join hands to form a *big* circle. Have them take a step back to form a *bigger* circle and another step to form the *biggest* circle. Then have them take one step forward to make a *small* circle, one more step to make a *smaller* circle, and one last step to make the *smallest* circle.

Objectives

- **Use words that compare**
- **Identify and sort pictures of objects into categories**
- **Review story words** *leap, dashes*

Materials

- **pictures of the same item in different sizes**
- **Big Books:** *Bus Stops; Animal Babies ABC*

ELL

Reinforce Vocabulary
Write *big, bigger, biggest* on the outside of three different-size paper bags. Have children collect classroom items to put in the bags. Next write *small, smaller, smallest* on other bags. Have children put other items in those bags. Take items out of each bag, and help children describe them in complete sentences, for example: *The eraser is small. The chalk is smaller. The pencil is the biggest item.*

Objectives

- Blend sounds to form words with /r/
- Sort words by initial sound/letter /d/d, /h/h, /r/r
- Blend letter-sounds in words with /r/r

Materials

- Puppet
- Word-Building Cards
- pocket chart
- Photo Cards: *rake, doctor, deer, dog, horse, helicopter, hat, rock, ring, rose, ruby, rabbit, door, dinosaur, dolphin, hand, hair*
- Activity Book, p. 20
- Practice Book, p. 132

ELL

Pronunciation Display and have children name **Photo Cards** from this and prior lessons to reinforce sound-letter relationships and word meanings. Point to a card and ask: *What do you see?* (a ring) *What is the sound at the beginning of the word ring?* (/r/). *What is the letter?* (r) Repeat with other cards.

Phonemic Awareness

✔ Phoneme Blending

Model

Use the **Puppet** to model how to blend the word *red*.

Repeat with the word *rat*.

Happy is going to say the sounds in a word. Listen to Happy: /r/ /e/ /d/. Happy can blend these sounds together: /rrreeed/. Now you say the sounds with Happy: /r/ /e/ /d/. Now blend the sounds to say the word with Happy: *red*.

Guided Practice/Practice

Children blend sounds to form words.

Guide practice with the first word using the same routine.

Happy is going to say sounds in a word. Listen to Happy as he says each sound. Then blend the sounds to say the word.

/r/ /o/ /k/	/r/ /u/ /n/	/r/ /i/ /p/
/r/ /i/ /b/	/r/ /a/ /t/	/r/ /ā/ /k/

Phonics

✔ Picture Sort

r   h   d

Model

Place **Word-Building Card** *r* in the pocket chart.

This is the letter *r*. The sound for this letter is /r/. The letter *r* stands for the /r/ sound.

Follow the routine for *h* and *d*.

This is the letter *h*. The letter *h* stands for the /h/ sound.

Hold up the **Photo Card** for *rake*.

Here is the picture of a *rake*. *Rake* begins with /r/. I will put *rake* under *r*.

Repeat with *horse*.

Guided Practice/Practice

Children continue sorting the Photo Cards. Guide practice with the first card, using the routine.

Build Fluency: Sound-Spellings

  Display the following **Word-Building Cards**: *a, c, d, f, h, i, m, n, o, p, r, s, t.* Have children chorally say each sound. Repeat and vary the pace.

✦ Blend with /r/r

Model

Place Word-Building Card *r* in the pocket chart.

This letter is *r*. The sound for this letter is /r/. Say /r/.

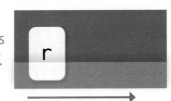

Place Word-Building Card *a* next to *r*. Move your hand from left to right below the letters.

This is the letter *a*. The sound for this letter is /a/. Listen as I blend the two sounds together: /rrraaaa/. Now you say it. (/rrraaa/)

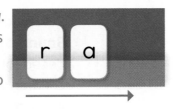

Place Word-Building Card *n* next to *ra*. Move your hand from left to right below the letters.

Repeat with the word *rip*.

This is the letter *n*. The sound for this letter is /n/. Listen as I blend the three sounds together: /rrraaannn/. Now you say it. (/rrraaannn/, ran)

Guided Practice/Practice

Children blend sounds to form words. Guide practice with the first word.

ram	rat	rod	rid
Ron	rim	rot	rap

Corrective Feedback

Blending: Sound Error Model the sound that children missed, then have them repeat the sound. For example, for the word *rat*, say: *My turn.* Tap under the letter *t* in the word *rat* and say: *Sound? What's the sound?* Then return to the beginning of the word. Say: *Let's start over.* Blend the word with children again.

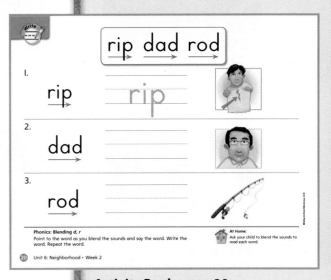

Activity Book, page 20
Practice Book, page 132

Objectives

- Read decodable words with /r/r
- Review high-frequency words for, you, is, play, see, the, to
- Reread for fluency

Materials

- Decodable Reader: *Rod Can See It*
- High-Frequency Word Cards: *for, you, is, play, see, the, to*
- Sound-Spelling Cards: *Dolphin, Rose*

Decodable Text

For additional decodable passages, see pages 21–22 in the **Teacher's Resource Book**.

Decodable Reader

Read *Rod Can See It*

Rod Can See It

REVIEW Review this week's high-frequency words and phonics skills using the word lists on the inside back cover of *Rod Can See It*.

Review the high-frequency words **for**, **you**, **is**, **play**, **see**, **the**, and **to** using the **Read/Spell/Write** routine. Then have children chorally read the high-frequency word list.

Review the phonics skills /d/d and /r/r using the *Dolphin* and *Rose* **Sound-Spelling Cards**. Then have children chorally read the decodable word list. Model blending as needed and take note of children who struggle while reading these words. Provide additional instruction and practice during Small Group time.

MODEL CONCEPTS ABOUT PRINT

Guide children to follow along. *I open the book by turning the cover. The first page I see is the title page. Then I turn each page as I read it, starting with the first page and ending with the last page. Now I want you to read the book.*

SECOND READ Have children reread the book with a partner. Have partners turn to each other to ask and answer questions about the text. Circulate and listen in, providing corrective feedback as needed. Then have children reread the book independently.

Rod can see Don hit it. Don can hit the rim.

Rod can see Mom and Ron. Mom ran to Ron.

Rod can see Tad mop. Tad can dip the mop.

Rod can see Tim on a mat. Can you nap on a mat?

Rod can see a cat. The cat can sit on top.

Rod can see Rob. Dot can pat him.

Rod can see a rip. Mom can pin it for Dan.

Decodable Reader

Writing

Independent Writing: Directions

REVISE AND EDIT

Distribute children's directions from yesterday. Have them reread them and check for the following:

- Did I write my name at the top of the paper?

- Did I write a set of directions?

- Are my directions in the right order?

- Did I use *first* and *then* or *first* and *next* to make the order clear?

 Circulate and help children as they review and revise their sentences. Have children share their sentences with a partner.

Cairon

First you pick up.

Then you put away.

 Write About It

Ask children to draw a picture of a job someone in their family does. Have them label their drawing.

Proofreading

Tell children they may need to revise and edit their writing after reading it to classmates. By asking for suggestions on how to make sure their writing supports what they want to express, they can make the appropriate revisions.

Objectives

- Revise and edit sentences
- Use letter knowledge to write words and sentences

Materials

- children's writing from Day 3
- Writer's Checklist; Teacher's Resource Book, p. 205

5-Day Writing

Procedural Text: Directions

DAY 1	Shared: Directions
DAY 2	Interactive: Directions
DAY 3	Independent: Prewrite and Draft Directions
DAY 4	Independent: Revise and Edit Directions
DAY 5	Independent: Publish and Present

ELL

Use New Language Explain the importance of writing directions in the correct order or sequence. Demonstrate doing a classroom task in the wrong order, such as putting away unwashed paintbrushes. Emphasize how the words *first* and *then* help the reader understand the sequence.

Transitions That Teach

While children line up for recess, have them talk about people who **deliver** things in their community.

Oral Language
- Build Robust Vocabulary

✓ **Comprehension**
- Strategy: Summarize
- Skill: Identify Main Idea and Details
- Read Across Texts

✓ **Vocabulary**
- High-Frequency Words
- Build Fluency
- Words That Compare

✓ **Phonemic Awareness**
- Phoneme Segmentation

✓ **Phonics**
- Read Words
- Dictation

Writing
- Independent Writing: Publish and Present

- Differentiated Instruction, pages 1434–1459

Review and Assess
Oral Language
Build Robust Vocabulary

REVIEW WORDS

Review this week's oral vocabulary words with children. Explain that all of the words will be used to discuss activities in the community.

Use the following questions to check children's understanding:

- What type of **worker delivers** the mail?

- Why would you **admire** someone who volunteers at a hospital?

- How would you describe a **community** garden?

- Why is it important for a bus to make all the stops on its **schedule**?

REVIEW RHYMES

Recite the rhyme "Wee Willie Winkie" and ask children to join you. Remind children that when a group of words begins with the same sound, it is called alliteration. Ask children to identify the words with the same beginning sound after you recite the rhyme.

Explain to children that the line "Crying through the lock" means calling out or shouting—not crying with tears. Explain that "Rapping at the window" means tapping loudly for someone to hear you.

Have children stand up and recite the poem again. Children will act out running in place for the line "Runs through the town." They will stand on tiptoes for "Upstairs" and bend at the knees for "downstairs." Children will point to their clothing for "nightgown." They will gesture "rapping" at the window and then say the rest of the rhyme.

Recite "To Market, To Market" with the children. Explain that the word "jiggity" is a nonsense word that helps keep the rhythm of the rhyme. To demonstrate, have children recite the poem without the word "jiggity." Then say it again with "jiggity." Discuss the difference.

Review and Assess
Comprehension

 STRATEGY Summarize

REFLECT ON THE STRATEGY Remind children that recalling the most important parts of the beginning, middle, and end of the story will help them understand and summarize the story.

 SKILL Identify Main Idea and Details

Lead children in reviewing *Bus Stops* and "Ms. Mouse Needs a Friend" to help them recall how they identified main events in each selection.

■ *Where in the **community** did the bus in* Bus Stops *go? Which **workers** rode the bus? Who else rode the bus?*

■ *What was the big idea of the book?*

■ *Why did the rabbit, mink, and fox decide not to help Ms. Mouse?*

■ *What lesson does Ms. Mouse learn?*

Reading Across Texts

Create a chart like the one shown to compare the realistic fiction story *Bus Stops* and the folktale "Ms. Mouse Needs a Friend."

Bus Stops	Ms. Mouse Needs a Friend
fiction	folktale
illustrations	no illustrations; we have to use our imaginations
could really happen	could not really happen
has a happy ending	unhappy ending with a lesson

Objectives

- Recognize alliteration
- Review the strategy and skill
- Compare and contrast genres

Materials

- Big Book: *Bus Stops*
- Read-Aloud Anthology: "Ms. Mouse Needs a Friend," pp. 88–92
- Activity Book, p. 21

Activity Book, page 21

Objectives

- Review high-frequency words *for, you, are, have, play, is*
- Review words that compare
- Build fluency

Materials

- High-Frequency Word Cards; Teacher's Resource Book, pp. 103–110
- High-Frequency Word Cards: *for, you, are, have, play, is*
- three paper squares of different sizes
- pocket chart

Fluency

Connected Text Have children reread this week's **Decodable Reader** with a partner. Circulate, listen in, and note those children who need additional instruction and practice reading this week's decodable and sight words.

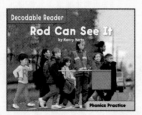

Review and Assess
Vocabulary

 ## High-Frequency Words

Distribute one of the following **High-Frequency Word Cards** to children: **for**, **you**, **are**, **have**, **play**, and **is**.

When you hear the word that is on your card, stand and hold up your Word Card.

- *We* are *leaping* for *joy.*
- *I* have *something that belongs to* you.
- *The gifts* are for *them.*
- You play *with the ball.*
- *What* is *your name?*

Build Fluency: Word Automaticity

Rapid Naming Display the High-Frequency Word Cards. Point quickly to each card, at random, and have children read the word as fast as they can.

for	you	are
have	play	is

Words That Compare

Display the pocket chart with paper squares of three consecutively smaller squares. Say the words *small, smaller, smallest.* Sort the squares so that the smallest is first. Then have children point to and say words to compare the sizes using *big, bigger, biggest.*

TIME TO MOVE!

Show children how to crouch down to look small. Show them how to stretch up tall. Point to individuals, say: *You are tall. You are taller. You are tallest.* Have children follow your descriptions.

Review and Assess
Phonemic Awareness

 ## Phoneme Segmentation

Guided Practice

Use the **Sound Box**.

Repeat with *rod*.

Let's break the word *rock* into its sounds: /r/ /o/ /k/. Say the sounds in *rock* again and let's put a marker in a box for each sound: /r/ /o/ /k/.

There are three sounds in *rock*. Say the sounds again with me: /r/ /o/ /k/.

Practice

Distribute Sound Boxes and markers.

Children place a marker in the box as they segment the sounds in a word.

Break each word into its sounds. Put a marker in a box as you say each sound.

rat, /r/ /a/ /t/   *red, /r/ /e/ /d/*
rim, /r/ /i/ /m/   *rip, /r/ /i/ /p/*
ram, /r/ /a/ /m/   *fat, /f/ /a/ t/*

Objective

- Segment sounds in words

Materials

- Sound Box
- WorkBoard Sound Boxes; Teacher's Resource Book, p. 136
- markers

Objectives

- Build words with /d/d, /r/r
- Read and write simple one-syllable words

Materials

- Word-Building Cards
- 6 index cards with: *The, hat, is, for, Ron,* period mark
- 6 index cards with: *The, ham, is, for, Dad,* period mark
- Sound Box
- WorkBoard Sound Boxes; Teacher's Resource Book, p. 136
- Activity Book, p. 22

Activity Book, page 22

Review and Assess
Phonics

Build Fluency: Sound-Spellings

Rapid Naming Display the following **Word-Building Cards**: *a, c, d, f, h, i, m, n, o, p, r, s, t.* Have children chorally say each sound as quickly as they can.

 ## Read Words

Apply

Distribute the first set of index cards. Have children stand in sequence.	Let's read the sentence together. The hat is for Ron.
Repeat, using the other set of cards.	Let's read the sentence together. The ham is for Dad.

Dictation

Dictate sounds for children to spell.	Listen as I say a sound. Repeat the sound, then write the letter that stands for the sound. /a/ /t/ /r/ /f/ /d/ /k/ /o/ /h/ /n/ /i/
Then dictate words for children to spell. Model for children how to use the Sound Boxes to segment the sounds in the words. Have them repeat.	Now let's write some words. I will say a word. I want you to repeat the word, then think about how many sounds are in the word. Use your Sound Boxes to count the sounds. Then write one letter for each sound you hear.
Write the letters and words on the board for children to self-correct.	

dad	hop	mad	rim
dot	Ron	rap	hat
ram	rat	fan	mop

Review and Assess
Writing

Independent Writing: Directions

PUBLISH

Explain to children that you will gather their directions to make a bulletin board display of jobs in the classroom **community**.

- Brainstorm ideas for a title, such as "Classroom Helpers." Write the title on a banner. Have children illustrate the banner.
- Place children's directions on the bulletin board.

PRESENT

Have children take turns reading their directions to the class.

LISTENING, SPEAKING, AND VIEWING

PARTNERS

- Remind children to speak clearly and to be good listeners when a classmate is speaking. Guide children to identify the topic of each classmate's writing and discuss related details.
- Display children's work. Children may wish to add copies of their work to their Writing Portfolios.

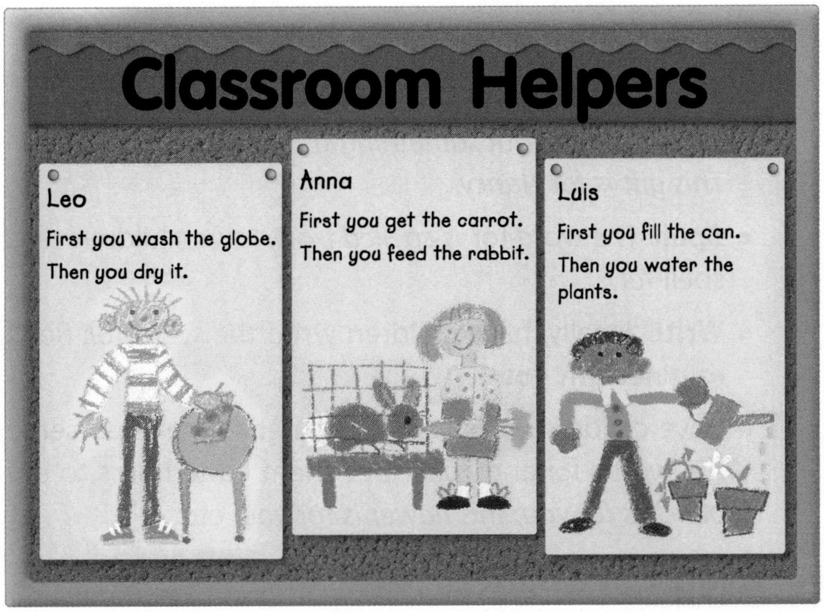
Classroom Helpers
Leo
First you wash the globe.
Then you dry it.
Anna
First you get the carrot.
Then you feed the rabbit.
Luis
First you fill the can.
Then you water the plants.

Write About It

Ask children to draw how they might help in the playground. Have them label their drawing.

Objective

- Publish and present directions

Materials

- children's writing from Day 4
- paper for banner

5-Day Writing

Procedural Text: Directions	
DAY 1	Shared: Directions
DAY 2	Interactive: Directions
DAY 3	Independent: Prewrite and Draft Directions
DAY 4	Independence: Revise and Edit Directions
DAY 5	Independent: Publish and Present

Transitions That Teach

While in line, have children recall the class **schedule** for the day or week.

ON YOUR OWN

My Community

Have children draw a picture of people and places in their community. Ask children to share their pictures with the class and tell about their community.

ELL

Partners When pairing children to make up sentences, pair English Language Learners with children who are more proficient. Write their sentences, read them together, and point out the high-frequency words.

Approaching Level

Oral Language

Objective	Preteach oral vocabulary
Materials	• none

PRETEACH THEME WORDS: *community, worker*

- Tell children the meanings for **community** and **worker**. *A* community *is a group of people who live or work together. Our school is part of a community.* Workers *are people who do jobs. Firefighters and police are workers in our community.*

- Discuss the words with children. Ask: *What places are in your community? What kinds of workers have you seen in your community?*

- Have children use the following sentence frames to generate oral sentences using the words: *A community is a place that has _____. A worker in my community is a _____.*

High-Frequency Words

Objective	Preteach high-frequency words
Materials	• **High-Frequency Word Cards:** *for, you*

PRETEACH WORDS: *for, you*

- Display the **High-Frequency Word Card** for **for**.

- **Read** Point to and say the word *for. This is the word* for. *It can be used to talk about something that is meant to belong to someone. This gift is for Nancy.*

- **Spell** *The word* for *is spelled* f-o-r. Have children read and spell *for*.

- **Write** Finally, have children write the word *for*. Repeat the routine with **you**.

- Have children work with a partner to make up sentences using the words *for* and *you*. Have them hand items to each other: *This pencil is for you; this flower is for you,* etc.

HIGH-FREQUENCY WORDS REVIEW

Display the High-Frequency Word Cards for words previously taught, one card at a time, and have children chorally read and spell the word. Mix and repeat. Note words children need to review.

Tier 2

Approaching Level

Phonemic Awareness

Objective   Identify initial sound /d/
Materials   • **Photo Cards:** *deer, dog, doll, door, doctor, dolphin*

✔ PHONEME ISOLATION

Model

- Display the **Photo Card** for *deer. This is a deer. Listen for the beginning sound in* deer: */d/, /d/, /d/,* deer. *Deer begins with /d/.* Repeat for *dog.*

Guided Practice/Practice

- Display the Photo Cards. Have children take turns selecting a picture, naming it, and saying the initial sound of the picture name: *This is a _____. _____ begins with /d/.*

Phonics

Objective   Recognize words that begin with /d/d
Materials   • **Sound-Spelling Card:** *Dolphin*   • **Word-Building Cards**
               • **Photo Cards:** *deer, dog, doll, door, doctor, dolphin*

✔ RECOGNIZE /d/d

Model

- Display Photo Cards for *dog* and *doctor* and the *Dolphin* **Sound-Spelling Card**. Say: *This is the letter* d. D *stands for the /d/ sound at the beginning of* dog. *I will place the letter* d *on the picture of the* dog *because* dog *begins with /d/.* Repeat with *doctor.*

- Say /d/. Trace the *d* on your **Word-Building Card** as you say /d/.

Guided Practice/Practice

- Display the Photo Cards. *This is the picture of a deer. What sound do you hear at the beginning of* deer? *What letter stands for /d/? Let's place the letter* d *on the deer because* deer *begins with /d/.* Repeat with the remaining Photo Cards.

- Guide children to trace the letter *d* on their Word-Building Cards.

- For additional practice, point out children and objects with names that begin with /d/ (Donna, Dan, desk, doll). Hold the *d* card next to each while children say the name chorally.

SOUND-SPELLINGS REVIEW

Display Word-Building Cards *m, a, s, p, t, i, n, c, o, f, h,* and *d,* one at a time. Have children chorally say the sound. Repeat and vary the pace.

Tier 2

Corrective Feedback

Mnemonic Display the *Dolphin* Sound-Spelling Card. *This is a* dolphin. *The first sound is /d/. The /d/ sound is spelled with the letter* d. *Say /d/ with me: /d/, /d/, /d/. This is the sound at the beginning of* dolphin. *What is the letter? What is the sound? What word begins with /d/?* Dolphin *is the word we can use to remember the sound for* d, /d/.

ELL

Extra Practice Provide additional practice in recognizing and naming letters for children whose native languages do not use the symbols of the Latin alphabet.

On Level

High-Frequency Words

Objective Review high-frequency words *for, you, is, are,* and *play*

Materials • **High-Frequency Word Cards:** *for, you, is, are, play*

REVIEW

- Display the **High-Frequency Word Card** for **you**. Say the word and have children repeat it.

- **Read** Point to and say the word *you. This is the word* you. *It names the person I'm talking to. You are my friend.*

- **Spell** *The word* you *is spelled* y-o-u. Have children read and spell *you*.

- **Write** Finally, have children write the word *you*.

- Repeat with **for**, **is**, **are**, and **play**. Then have partners make up sentences using the words *for, you, is, are,* and *play*. Have them talk about things they like to play with together.

Phonemic Awareness/Phonics

Objective Blend sounds to form words; Review recognizing initial /a/a, /d/d, /h/h,/ /i/i, and /r/r

Materials • **Puppet** • **Word-Building Cards** • pocket chart

PHONEME BLENDING

Model

- Hold up the **Puppet**. *Happy is going to say the sounds in a word*: /d/ /u/ /k/. *Happy can blend these sounds together:* /duuuk/, duck. *Say the sounds with Happy:* /d/ /u/ /k/, /duuuk/, duck. *Now say the word with Happy:* duck. Repeat with *rock*.

Practice

- Have the Puppet say /g/ /ō/ /t/. Ask children to repeat. *Now blend the sounds and say the word with Happy:* /gōōōt/, goat. Repeat with the following: *pig, rat, ant, cat, dog, yak,* and *sheep*.

REVIEW /d/d, /a/a, /h/h, /i/i, /r/r

- Display **Word-Building Card** d. *This is the letter is* d. D *stands for the /d/ sound we hear at the beginning of* dog. *What is the sound? I'll hold up the* d *card because* dog *begins with /d/.* Repeat with *a, h,* and *i.* Repeat routine with *r* on Day 3.

- Distribute small Word-Building Cards to children. Say: *rabbit, ant, hippo, doll, insect, apple, rake, ham, ink,* and *dime.* Children hold up their Word-Building Cards and say the initial sound of the word you name. Guide practice with the first two words.

Puppet

Beyond Level

High-Frequency Words/Vocabulary

Objective Review high-frequency words
Materials • none

ACCELERATE

- Write *help* and *good* on the board.
- **Read** Point to and say the word *help. This is the word* help. *It means "to do what is needed." My son helps me wash the car.*
- **Spell** *The word* help *is spelled* h-e-l-p. Have children read and spell *help*.
- **Write** Finally, have children write the word *help*.
- Repeat the routine with *good*.
- Have children work with a partner to make up oral sentences using the words *help* and *good*.

EXPAND ORAL VOCABULARY

Gifted Talented

- **Suffixes** Explain that a *suffix* is a word part added to the end of a word to form a new word.
- Say: *The suffix* -er *at the end of* worker *means "person who." A* worker *is a person who works. Another word with the suffix* -er *is* writer. *A writer is a person who writes.*

- Have children take turns using the new word *writer* in a sentence. Then tell children that they will work with a partner to name and define other words with the suffix -*er*.

Phonics

Objective Read words with *d* and *r*
Materials • **Sound-Spelling Cards:** *Dolphin, Rose* • **Word-Building Cards**
• pocket chart

ENRICH

- Say the following sounds and have children blend them: /d/ /o/ /g/, /r/ /i/ /p/, /d/ /r/ /i/ /p/.
- Display the *Dolphin* **Sound-Spelling Card**. Remind children that the /d/ sound is spelled with the letter *d*. Dolphin *begins with /d/. What other words begin with /d/?* Repeat with *Rose*.
- Have children apply their skills to more complex words with *d* or *r*. Write these words on the board: *rack, deck, rash, dent, rush, dill, dash, rent, dish, rips, rest, rich.* Model blending with the first word.
- Display **Word-Building Cards** *a, b, i, e, m, n, d, h, g, p, r, s, t.* Have partners make as many words as they can.

ELL

Partners When pairing children to make up sentences, pair English Language Learners with children who are more proficient. Write their sentences, read them together, and point to the high-frequency words.

ELL ENGLISH LANGUAGE LEARNERS

Oral Language Warm-Up

Content Objective Learn theme vocabulary
Language Objective Repeat and act out a rhyme to demonstrate understanding
Materials • **Listening Library Audio CD** • **Big Book:** *Bus Stops*

BUILD BACKGROUND KNOWLEDGE

All Language Levels

> **To Market, To Market**
> To market, to market to buy a fat pig;
> Home again, home again, jiggity jig.
> To market, to market to buy a fat hog;
> Home again, home again, jiggity jog.

- Continue developing vocabulary around the unit theme "Neighborhood" using "To Market, To Market." Display a picture of a marketplace, such as the one on pages 20–21 of *Bus Stops*. Teach the word *market* as you point to the picture. Point out that *marketplace* and *market* are the same.

- Play "To Market, To Market" on the **Listening Library Audio CD**. Act out each line; for example, walk in place at the beginning of each line and make a wide circle with your arms for "fat pig."

- Then teach children words related to markets. Emphasize key words such as *buy* and *pig*.

- Ask children to tell what they know about markets. Build on their responses, for example: *We can buy many things at a market.*

Academic Language

Language Objective Use academic language in classroom conversations

All Language Levels

- This week's academic words are **boldfaced** throughout the lesson. Define the word in context and provide a clear example from the selection. Then ask children to generate an example or a word with a similar meaning.

Cognates

Help children identify similarities and differences in pronunciation and spelling between English and Spanish cognates:

Cognates

admire	*admirar*
community	*comunidad*
compare	*comparar*
idea	*idea*
details	*detalles*

Academic Language Used in Whole Group Instruction

Oral Vocabulary Words	Vocabulary and Grammar Concepts	Strategy and Skill Words
admire community deliver schedule worker	words that compare sentences	big idea details summarize sentence

ELL ENGLISH LANGUAGE LEARNERS

Vocabulary

Language Objective Demonstrate understanding and use of key words by discussing places in the neighborhood

Materials • **Visual Vocabulary Resources**

Visual Vocabulary Resources

PRETEACH KEY VOCABULARY

All Language Levels

Use the **Visual Vocabulary Resources** to preteach the weekly oral vocabulary words *admire, community, deliver, schedule,* and *worker.* Focus on one or two words per day. Use the following routine that appears in detail on the cards.

- Define the word in English and provide the example given.
- Define the word in Spanish, if appropriate, and indicate if the word is a cognate.
- Display the picture and explain how it illustrates or demonstrates the word.
- Then engage children in structured partner-talk about the image, using the key word.
- Ask children to chorally say the word three times.
- Point out any known sound-spellings or focus on a key aspect of phonemic awareness related to the word.

PRETEACH FUNCTION WORDS AND PHRASES

All Language Levels

Use the Visual Vocabulary Resources to preteach the function phrases *come out of* and *step off.* Focus on one phrase per day. Use the detailed routine on the cards.

- Define the word in English and, if appropriate, in Spanish. Point out if the word is a cognate.
- Refer to the picture and engage children in talk about the word. For example, children will partner-talk using sentence frames, or they will listen to sentences and replace a word or phrase with the new function phrase.
- Ask children to chorally repeat the word three times.

TEACH BASIC WORDS

Beginning/Intermediate

Use the Visual Vocabulary Resources to teach the basic words *garage, bulldozer, drugstore, junkyard, downtown,* and *commuters.* Teach these words about "town and city sights and places" using the routine provided on the card.

Approaching Level

Oral Language

Objective   Reinforce oral vocabulary
Materials   • none

THEME WORDS: *community, worker*

- Say: *We've talked about places in the **community**. A community is where people live and work together. A community also has **workers**. These are people who do jobs.* Remind children to use complete sentences when speaking.

- *What places are in the same community as our school?*

- *Who is a worker in our school? What does he or she do?*

- *A community includes workers who help people. Who are some of those people? How do they help people?*

High-Frequency Words

Objective   Reteach high-frequency words
Materials   • **High-Frequency Word Cards:** *for, you*
                      • **Sound-Spelling WorkBoards**

RETEACH WORDS: *for, you*

Tier 2

- Distribute a **WorkBoard** to each child. Then display the **High-Frequency Word Card** for **for**.

- Use the **Read/Spell/Write** routine to reteach the word. Point to and say the word. *This is the word* for. *It is a word we use to talk about something that you are giving to someone: This pencil is for you. For is spelled* f-o-r. Have children read and spell *for*. Repeat the routine with *you*. Then have them write the words on their WorkBoards.

 - Have children work with a partner to make up sentences using the words *for* and *you*. Ask them to talk about what they will give to each other.

CUMULATIVE REVIEW

Display the High-Frequency Word Cards for words previously taught, one card at a time. Have children chorally read and spell the word. Mix and repeat. Note words children need to review.

Drawings for You

Have children draw a picture of something they would like to give a community worker. Have them title their pictures *For you!*

ELL

Partners When pairing children to make up sentences, pair English Language Learners with children who are more proficient. Write their sentences, read them together, and point out the high-frequency words.

Approaching Level

Phonemic Awareness

Objective Blend sounds
Materials • **Puppet**

Puppet

PHONEME BLENDING

Tier 2

Model

- Hold up the **Puppet**. *Happy is going to say the sounds in a word: /d/ /o/ /g/. Happy can blend these sounds together: /dooog/. Now you can say the sounds: /d/ /o/ /g/. Say the word with Happy:* dog. Repeat the routine with *dot*.

Guided Practice/Practice

- Have the Puppet say /d/ /o/ /l/. Ask children to repeat. *Now you blend the sounds and say the word with Happy: /dooolll/,* doll. Repeat with the following:

/d/ /i/ /p/	/d/ /a/ /n/	/d/ /o/ /t/	/h/ /i/ /t/	/h/ /i/ /p/
/d/ /i/ /m/	/d/ /i/ /g/	/d/ /a/ /d/	/n/ /o/ /t/	/f/ /a/ /n/

Corrective Feedback

Blending Error If children have difficulty blending the word *dog*, say: *My turn: /d/ /o/ /g/. I say each sound and then blend: /dooog/. What is the word? Let's start over.* Repeat with the word *dip* for children to blend the sounds.

Phonics

Objective Reinforce sound-letter correspondence for /d/*d*
Materials • **Sound-Spelling Card:** *Dolphin* • **Word-Building Cards**
　　　　　　• **Sound-Spelling WorkBoards** • **Decodable Reader:** *Rod Can See It*

RECOGNIZE /d/*d*

Model

- Display the *Dolphin* **Sound-Spelling Card**. *The letter* d *stands for the /d/ sound as in* dog. *What is this letter? What sound does it stand for?* Repeat with *doll*.

- Trace *d* on a small **Word-Building Card**. *I will say a sentence. We will trace* d *on the cards when we hear /d/.* Say: *Don's dog likes ducks.*

Guided Practice/Practice

- Distribute a **WorkBoard** to each child. Say: *dog, doll, door, hippo, bat, dice, mop, doctor*. Children write *d* on their WorkBoard when they hear a word with /d/. Guide them with the first two words.

- **Read the Decodable Reader** Read *Rod Can See It* with children. Have them echo-read each page. Chorally reread the story.

CUMULATIVE REVIEW

Display Word-Building Cards *m, a, s, p, t, i, n, c, o, f, h,* and *d,* one at a time. Point to the letters in a random order. Have children chorally say the sound. Repeat and vary the pace.

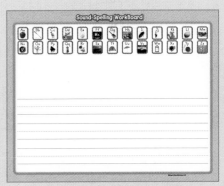

Sound-Spelling WorkBoard

Decodable Reader

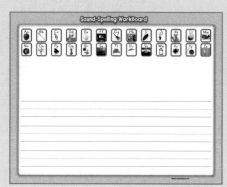

Sound-Spelling WorkBoard

Decodable Reader

On Level

Phonics

Objective Review blending initial /a/*a*, /d/*d*, /h/*h*,/ /i/*i*, and /r/*r*

Materials
- **Word-Building Cards**   • pocket chart
- **Sound-Spelling WorkBoards**   • **Decodable Reader:** *Rod Can See It*

REVIEW *Dd*

- Display **Word-Building Card** *d*. The name of this letter is d. D *stands for the /d/ sound we hear at the beginning of* dolphin. *What is the sound? I'll hold up the* d *card because* dolphin *begins with /d/.* Repeat with *a, h, i,* and *r*.

- **Blend Words** Place Word-Building Cards *h, a,* and *d* in the pocket chart. Point to each letter for children to identify. Move your hand from left to right below the letters as you blend the word. *Now listen as I blend the three sounds together: /haaad/,* had. *What's the word? Repeat with* hid *and* rid.

- Have children write *h, a, d; h ,i, d;* and *r, i, d* several times on their **WorkBoards** as they say /h/ /a/ /d/, /h/ /i/ /d/, /r/ /i/ /d/.

- **Read the Decodable Reader** Read *Rod Can See It* with children. Have them reread each page. Then chorally reread the story.

Beyond Level

Phonics

Objective Review and read words with *d* and *r*

Materials • **Word-Building Cards** • pocket chart

ACCELERATE

- Display Word-Building Cards *s, n, a, p* in a pocket chart. Point to the letters as you say each sound. *The word* snap *has four sounds: /s/ /n/ /a/ /p/. Let's say the sounds together: /s/ /n/ /a/ /p/. Listen as I blend the sounds: /sssnnnaaap/.* Cover the *s* to show *nap. Sometimes we can find a smaller word within a word.* Blend /nnnaaap/, *nap.* Uncover the *s* and blend /sssnnnaaap/, *snap.* Change the *sn* to *tr.* Then blend the new sounds to make *trap.*

- Help children read words with initial blends. Write the following words on the board: *brush, step, still, spin, snip, trash, swim, snack, snap, broom, trip, flip, flop, clip, clap.* Model blending as needed.

Corrective Feedback

If children have difficulty blending words with /d/, demonstrate the /d/ sound while modeling the correct mouth position. *This is the /d/ sound at the beginning of* dog. *Let's blend* dog *together: /dooog/,* dog. Repeat with *deer* and *Dan.*

ELL ENGLISH LANGUAGE LEARNERS

Access to Core Content

Content Objective Develop listening comprehension
Language Objective Discuss text using key words and sentence frames
Materials • **ELL Resource Book**, pp. 162–169

PRETEACH BIG BOOK

All Language Levels

Use the Interactive Question-Response Guide on **ELL Resource Book** pages 162–169 to introduce children to *Bus Stops*. Preteach half of the selection on Day 1 and half on Day 2.

- Use the prompts provided in the guide to develop meaning and vocabulary. Use the partner-talk and whole-class responses to engage children and increase student talk. Remind children to listen attentively and face the child speaking.

- When completed, revisit the selection and prompt children to talk about the photographs. Provide sentence starters as needed and build on children's responses to develop language.

ELL Resource Book

Big Book

Beginning	Intermediate	Advanced
Use Visuals During the Interactive Reading, select several pictures. Describe them and have children summarize what you said.	**Summarize** During the Interactive Reading, select a few lines of text. After you read them and explain them, have children summarize the text.	**Expand** During the Interactive Reading, select a larger portion of text. After you read it and explain it, have children summarize the text.

Approaching Level

High-Frequency Words

Objective Recognize high-frequency words *for, you, are, play, is*

Materials
- **High-Frequency Word Cards:** *for, you, are, play, is*
- **Word-Building Cards**

REVIEW WORDS: *for, you, are, play, is*

- Display the **High-Frequency Word Card** for **for**. Say the word and have children repeat it. Point to each letter and have children name it.

- Distribute **Word-Building Cards** *f, o,* and *r*. Model putting the letters together to form *for*. Then have children form *for*.

- Repeat the above routines with the words **you**, **are**, **play**, and **is**.

- Ask a question with the word *for*: *Is this pen for me?* Have children use *for* to answer the question. Continue with the other words.

CUMULATIVE REVIEW

Display the High-Frequency Word Cards for words previously taught, one card at a time. Have children chorally read and spell the word. Mix and repeat. Note words children need to review.

Phonemic Awareness

Objective Identify initial sound /r/r

Materials
- **Photo Cards:** *rose, rabbit, rake, ring, rock, rope*
- **Sound-Spelling Card:** *Rose*

PHONEME ISOLATION

Tier 2

Model
- Display the **Photo Card** for *rock*. *This is a rock. Listen for the beginning sound in* rock: */rrroook/.* Rock *begins with /r/.* Repeat for *rose* and *rabbit*.

- Distribute the small *Rose* **Sound-Spelling Card**. Point out the articulation picture. *See how my lips are slightly open when I say /r/. When I say /r/, I put my teeth together and push my lips out.*

Guided Practice/Practice
- Display the Photo Cards. Have children take turns selecting a picture, naming it, and saying the initial sound of the picture name: *This is a _____. _____ begins with /r/.*

- Have children note the position of their lips as they say /r/. *Are your lips together or apart when you say /r/?*

Approaching Level

Phonics

Objective Recognize words that begin with /r/r
Materials
- **Sound-Spelling Card:** *Rose* • **Word-Building Cards**
- **Photo Cards:** *rose, rabbit, rake, ring, rock, rope*

TEACH /r/r

Tier 2

Model

■ Display **Photo Cards** for *rose* and *rabbit,* and the *Rose* **Sound-Spelling Card**. Say: *The name of this letter is* r. R *stands for the /r/ sound that you hear at the beginning of* rose. *I will place the letter* r *on the picture of the* rose *because* rose *begins with /r/.* Repeat with *rake*.

■ Say /r/. Trace the *r* on your **Word-Building Card** as you say /r/.

Guided Practice/Practice

■ Display the remaining Photo Cards. Say: *This is the picture of a* ring. *What sound do you hear at the beginning of* ring? *What letter stands for /r/? Let's place the letter* r *on the ring because* ring *begins with /r/.* Repeat with remaining Photo Cards.

■ Guide children to trace the letter *r* on their small Word-Building Cards.

■ For additional practice, point out children and objects in the classroom with names that begin with initial /r/ (room, ribbon, rubber band, ring, rug, ruler, rack, raincoat, reading corner). Hold the *r* card next to each while children say the name chorally.

Decodable Reader

Objective Teach Decodable Reader *Rod Can See It*
Materials • **Decodable Reader:** *Rod Can See It*

PRETEACH *Rod Can See It*

■ Display the cover of the book and read the title. Open to the title page and point out the title. *Let's read the title together.* Have children sound out each word as you run your finger under it. *What do you think Rod can see?*

■ Page through the book. Ask children what they see in each picture. Ask them to find the words *for* and *you*.

■ Read the book chorally with children. Have them point to each word as they read it. Provide corrective feedback.

■ Ask children to use *for* to talk about the pictures. *The mop is for Tad.*

■ After reading, ask children to recall things they read about.

Corrective Feedback

Association Error If children have difficulty identifying initial /r/, say: *My turn: /rok/, rock. I hear the /r/ sound at the beginning of rock: /rrroook/. What is the sound? What is the letter? Let's start over.* Repeat the word *rock* for children to identify the position of /r/.

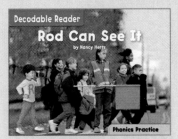

Decodable Reader

ON YOUR OWN

Draw What You Can See

Have children draw what you would see if you came to their neighborhood. Have them draw a picture and write a caption. Provide this sentence frame: *You can see _____.*

You can see a firehouse.

On Level

Decodable Reader

Objective   Reread *Rod Can See It* to develop fluency
Materials   • **Decodable Reader:** *Rod Can See It*

REREAD FOR FLUENCY

- Ask children to look at the illustrations in *Rod Can See It*. Have them use their own words to retell what the book was about.

- Have children reread a page or two of *Rod Can See It*. Work with them to read with accuracy and expression. Model reading a page. Point out how to make the reading sound natural: *I pause at certain places. For example, on page 2, I read the sentence like this:* Rod can see Don hit it. *I pause at the period before reading the next sentence.*

- Provide time to listen as children read their page(s). Comment on their accuracy and expression and provide corrective feedback by modeling proper fluency.

Decodable Reader

Beyond Level

Decodable Reader

Objective   Reread *Rod Can See It* to reinforce fluency and phonics
Materials   • **Decodable Reader:** *Rod Can See It*

REREAD FOR FLUENCY

- Have partners reread *Rod Can See It*.

- Listen as children read. Comment on their accuracy and expression. Model fluency to provide corrective feedback.

- Have partners take turns asking and answering questions from each other.

INNOVATE

- Brainstorm names that start with *R* and *D*. List them in two columns. Have children choose a name and create a story with a new setting. For example, children can create the cover for *Dan Can See It,* with Dan observing an elephant at the zoo.

ELL ENGLISH LANGUAGE LEARNERS

Access to Core Content

Content Objective Develop listening comprehension
Language Objective Discuss text using key words and sentence frames
Materials • **ELL Resource Book**, pp. 170–171

PRETEACH BIG BOOK OF EXPLORATIONS

All Language Levels

Use the Interactive Question-Response Guide on **ELL Resource Book** pages 170–171 to preview the **Big Book of Explorations** selection "The Park." Preteach half of the selection on Day 3 and half on Day 4.

Grammar

Content Objective Identify complete sentences
Language Objective Speak in complete sentences, using sentence frames
Materials • **Listening Library Audio CD** • **Photo Cards**

SENTENCES

All Language Levels

- Review sentences. Tell children that a sentence tells a complete thought. It has a naming part and a telling part. The naming part tells who the sentence is about. The telling part tells what happens.

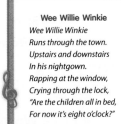

> **Wee Willie Winkie**
> *Wee Willie Winkie*
> *Runs through the town.*
> *Upstairs and downstairs*
> *In his nightgown.*
> *Rapping at the window,*
> *Crying through the lock,*
> *"Are the children all in bed,*
> *For now it's eight o'clock?"*

- Play "Wee Willie Winkie " from the **Listening Library Audio CD**. Tell children to listen for a sentence at the beginning of the rhyme.

- Point out the sentence "Wee Willie Winkie runs through the town." Ask: *What is the telling part? What does Wee Willie Winkie do?* (runs through the town) Provide a naming part: *The teacher; A tree; My mom.* Have children provide a telling part.

PEER DISCUSSION STARTERS

All Language Levels

- Distribute **Photo Cards** of people, such as *nurse, umpire, cowboy,* and *doctor*. Name each card and provide meanings as needed.

- Pair children and have them complete sentence frames such as: *The nurse _____.* Ask them to expand on their sentences by providing as many details as they can. For example: *The nurse works at the hospital.* Circulate, listen in, and take note of each child's language use and proficiency.

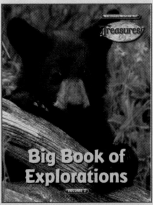

Big Book of Explorations

Puppet

Corrective Feedback

Sound Error If children miss making the sound-letter correspondence, say: *My turn: rod, /rrroood/. I hear /r/ at the beginning of rod, /rrroood/. I'll hold up my* r *card because /rrroood/ begins with /r/. What is the sound? What letter stands for that sound? Let's start again.*

Corrective Feedback

Linguistic Differences Some speakers of African American Vernacular English drop the /r/ sound in words. For example, these children will say *sto'* for *store* and *do'* for *door*. Clearly pronounce these words, emphasizing the /r/ sound. Have children repeat several times, exaggerating the sound.

ELL

Minimal Contrasts Provide additional practice in pronouncing and blending vowel sounds that do not transfer directly to the native language of children by practicing pronouncing minimal-contrast word pairs such as *hat/hit* and *sit/sat*.

Approaching Level

Phonemic Awareness

Objective Blend sounds to form words
Materials • **Puppet**

PHONEME BLENDING

Tier 2

Model

■ Hold up the **Puppet**. *Listen as Happy says the sounds in a word: /r/ /o/ /d/. Now Happy will blend the sounds: /rrroood/, /rod/,* rod. *Happy put /r/ /o/ and /d/ together to say the word* rod. *Now listen again. I'll do another word.* Repeat blending with the words *rip* and *rock*.

Guided Practice/Practice

■ Have three children stand side by side. Ask the first child to say the /r/ sound. Have the next child say the /a/ sound. Have the third child say the /m/ sound. Have them say the sounds in order and blend them: /rrraaammm/, *ram*. Continue with *rag, rim, rig, ran, rod,* and *rub*.

Phonics

Objective Blend with /r/r
Materials • **Word-Building Cards** • pocket chart

REVIEW SKILLS

Tier 2

Model

■ Place **Word-Building Cards** *r, a,* and *n* in the pocket chart. *The name of this letter is* r. *The letter* r *stands for the /r/ sound. Say /r/. The name of this letter is* a. *The letter* a *stands for the /a/ sound. Say /a/. The name of this letter is* n. *The letter* n *stands for the /n/ sound. Say /n/.*

■ Walk by the word and say the sound each letter stands for: */r/ /a/ /n/. Now I will blend the three sounds together: /rrraaannn/,* ran.

Guided Practice/Practice

■ Keep the Word-Building Cards in the pocket chart. Have children take turns walking by the cards, saying the letter sounds, and blending the word: /r/ /a/ /n/, /rrraaannn/, *ran*. Repeat with *rat, mat, mad, sad, dad, had, hat, hit, fit,* and *sit*. Guide practice as necessary.

Approaching Level

Leveled Reader Lesson 1

Objective Read *People Who Help* to apply skills and strategies
Materials • **Leveled Reader:** *People Who Help*

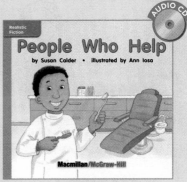

Leveled Reader

BEFORE READING

- **Preview and Predict** Read the title and the name of the author. *Who do you see on the cover? What is he doing?* Turn to the title page and point out that it also has the title and the author's name. *Who do you think the book is about?*

- **Model Concepts About Print** Demonstrate book handling. Guide children as they follow along. *I hold the book so that the cover is on the front and the words are not upside down. I open the book by turning the cover. Then I turn each page as I read it, starting with the first page and ending with the last page.*

- **Review High-Frequency Words** Write **for** and **you** and read the words aloud. Guide children as they name the letters in each word. Have children find each word in the book and point to the word as they read it.

- **Page Through the Book** Name unfamiliar terms and identify the rebus pictures.

- **Set a Purpose for Reading** *Let's find out who helps and what they do.*

DURING READING

- Remind children to use the rebuses and illustrations to gain information and to look for the high-frequency words *for* and *you.*

- Show children how to self-correct if a word doesn't sound right or doesn't make sense in the sentence. *On page 8, I see a word that starts with* d *below the rebus. This man looks like a doctor, so I think it says, "I am the doctor." But when I look more closely at the picture, I see a toothbrush and a dentist's chair. The "d" word must be* dentist, *not* doctor. *"I am the dentist." That makes sense.*

- Monitor children's reading and provide help as needed.

AFTER READING

- Ask children to point out words that they had trouble reading and to share strategies they used to help them.

- Ask children to retell the story and to share personal responses. *Did the story remind you of people in your own community? Who else is in your community?*

Digital Learning

 Use the **Leveled Reader Audio CD** for fluency building *after* children read the book with your support during Small Group time.

ON YOUR OWN

Summarize

Have children make a main idea picture web for *People Who Help.* Have them write the word *help* in the center circle and draw lines coming out of the circle. Ask children to draw pictures of ways people help around the web.

Leveled Reader

ELL

Retell Use the Interactive Question-Response Guide Technique to help English Language Learners understand *This Is for You.* As you read, make meaning clear by pointing to pictures, demonstrating word meaning, paraphrasing text, and asking children questions.

ON YOUR OWN

Make a Gift

Make available a selection of craft materials. Provide time to make a simple gift, such as a decorated pencil can or a place mat for a family member. Provide slips of paper for gift cards and have children write a message to a recipient.

The mat is for you.

On Level

Leveled Reader Library

Leveled Reader Lesson 1

Objective   Read *This Is for You* to apply skills and strategies

Materials   • **Leveled Reader:** *This Is for You*

BEFORE READING

- **Preview and Predict** Read the title and the name of the author. *Who do you see on the cover? What is the little girl on the cover doing?* Open and page through the book. Name unfamiliar items.

- **Model Concepts About Print** Demonstrate book handling. *I hold the book so that the cover is on the front and the words are not upside down. I open the book by turning the cover. Then I turn each page as I read it.*

- **Review High-Frequency Words** Write **for** and **you** on chart paper. Have children find each word in the book and point to the word as they read it.

- **Set a Purpose for Reading** *Let's find out what the girl gives to people.*

DURING READING

- Have children turn to page 2 and begin by whisper-reading the first two pages.

- Remind children to look for the new high-frequency words and to use the illustrations.

- Monitor children's reading and provide help. Stop during the reading and ask open-ended questions to facilitate discussion, such as: *What does the mother give the girl at the end? Why does she do this?* Build on children's responses to develop deeper understanding of the text.

AFTER READING

- Ask children to point out words they had trouble reading and to share strategies they used. Reinforce good behaviors. For example: *Rita, I noticed that you put your finger under each word as you sounded it out. After you read it, you looked carefully at the picture.*

- **Retell** Ask children to retell the story. Help them make a personal connection. *Who are the people that receive gifts from you? What would you like to give a friend?*

Beyond Level

Leveled Reader Lesson 1

Objective Read *The Good Idea* to apply skills and strategies
Materials • **Leveled Reader:** *The Good Idea*

Leveled Reader

BEFORE READING

- **Preview and Predict** Read the title and the name of the author. *Where are the girl and her father? What are they doing?* Turn to the title page and point out that it also has the title and the name of the author. Page through the book with children and pause to name unfamiliar items. Ask children what this story will be about.

- **Introduce Story Words** Point to the word *trash* on page 2. Read the sentence. Have children give another word for *trash*. (*garbage*) Repeat with *dip* on page 10.

- **Set a Purpose for Reading** *Let's find out what the good idea is.*

DURING READING

- Remind children that when they come to an unfamiliar word, they can look for familiar chunks in the word, break the word into syllables and sound out each part, or think about what the word might mean. If the word does not sound right or make sense in the sentence, children can self-correct.

- Monitor children's reading and provide help as needed.

AFTER READING

- Ask children to point out words they had trouble reading and to share the strategies they used.

- Ask children to retell the story and to share personal responses. *Can you tell us about a time when you had a good idea?*

- **Evaluate** *Do you think Help Clean the Park Day was successful? What would you have done differently if you planned the project?*

- Have children work in pairs to name projects that require a group effort, such as planting a neighborhood garden. Have them think about the tasks involved and the equipment needed.

- **Model** Tell children to choose a project and write a flier asking for help. Encourage them to mention the project's goal. Write an example on the board: *Make Wilson Park pretty! Come and help plant flowers on Saturday at 9 a.m. Please bring rakes and shovels.*

ON YOUR OWN

Write Questions

Have children draw themselves asking a friend if they can play. Have them write a sentence to go with their picture.

Can you play drums?

Leveled Reader

Vocabulary

Preteach Vocabulary Use the routine in the **Visual Vocabulary Resources** pages 333–334 to preteach the ELL Vocabulary listed in the inside front cover of the Leveled Reader.

ELL ENGLISH LANGUAGE LEARNERS

Leveled Reader

Content Objective Read to apply skills and strategies
Language Objective Retell information using complete sentences
Materials • **Leveled Reader:** *For You*

BEFORE READING

All Language Levels

- **Preview** Read the title *For You*. Ask: *What's the title? Say it again.* Repeat with the author's name. Point to the cover illustration and say: *I see a girl giving something to a woman.* Point to the girl and the woman as you name them. *What does the girl say? Maybe she says, "This is for you."* Now turn to a partner and tell about this picture.

- **Page Through the Book** Use simple language to tell about the illustration on each page. Immediately follow up with questions such as: *Do you see the picture she gave to the man? Point to it.*

- **Review Skills** Use the inside front cover to review the phonics skill and high-frequency words.

- **Set a Purpose** Say: *Let's read to find out what the girl gives different people.*

DURING READING

All Language Levels

- Have children whisper-read each page, or use the differentiated suggestions below. Circulate, listen in, and provide feedback.

- **Retell** Stop after every two pages and ask children to state what they have learned so far. Reinforce language by restating children's comments when they have difficulty using story-specific words. Provide differentiated sentence frames to support children's responses and engage children in partner-talk where appropriate.

Beginning	Intermediate	Advanced
Echo-Read Have children echo-read after you.	**Choral-Read** Have children choral-read with you.	**Choral-Read** Have children choral-read.
Check Comprehension Point to pictures and ask questions such as: *Do you see the rose? Point to the rose.*	**Check Comprehension** Ask questions/prompts such as: *Describe what you see in this picture. What does the girl give the woman?*	**Check Comprehension** Ask: *What did you learn about the girl? Who do you think sent her the card?*

ELL ENGLISH LANGUAGE LEARNERS

AFTER READING

All Language Levels

Book Talk Children will work with peers of varying language abilities to discuss their books for this week. Display the four **Leveled Readers** read this week: *The Good Idea* (Beyond Level), *This Is for You* (On Level), *People Who Help* (Approaching Level), and *For You* (English Language Learners).

Ask the questions and provide the prompts below. Call on children who read each book to answer the questions or respond to the prompt. If appropriate, ask children to find the pages in the book that illustrate their answers.

- Name the people in the book.
- What do the people do?
- How do they help?
- Which person did you think was the nicest?
- Who is your favorite person from the book? Tell about him or her.

Develop Listening and Speaking Skills Tell children to remember the following:

- Share information in cooperative learning interactions. Remind children to work with their partners to retell the story and complete any activities. Ask: *What happened next in the story?*

- Employ self-corrective techniques and monitor their own and other children's language production. Children should ask themselves: *What parts of this passage were confusing to me? Can my classmates help me clarify a word or sentence that I don't understand?*

- Use high-frequency English words to describe people, places, and objects.

- Narrate, describe, and explain with specificity and detail. Ask: *Where did the story take place? Can you describe the setting? What else did you notice?*

- Express opinions, ideas, and feelings on a variety of social and academic topics. Ask: *What do you think about the characters in the story?*

Approaching Level

Phonemic Awareness

Objective Segment sounds in words

Materials
- **Sound Box** • markers
- **WorkBoard Sound Boxes; Teacher's Resource Book**, p. 136

PHONEME SEGMENTATION

Tier 2

Model
- Use the **Sound Box**. *I am going to say the sounds in* rat. *Listen:* /r/ /a/ /t/, rat. *I will place a marker in a box as I say each sound in* rat. *There are three sounds in* rat: /r/ /a/ /t/. *Say the sounds with me:* /r/ /a/ /t/. Repeat with *red*.

Guided Practice/Practice
- Distribute Sound Boxes and markers. *I will say a word. Say each sound in the word as you place a marker in a box. Then tell me the sounds.* Say these words and have children say each sound as they place a marker in a box: *rip, /r/ /i/ /p/; rid, /r/ /i/ /d/; rim, /r/ /i/ /m/; rock, /r/ /o/ /k/; ram, /r/ /a/ /m/; rod, /r/ /o/ /d/.*

Phonics

Objective Identify initial sounds /d/d, /h/h, /r/r, /t/t, /f/f and build fluency

Materials
- **Photo Cards:** *dolphin, dog, doll, deer, door, hand, hat, helicopter, horse, hammer, rose, rabbit, rake, ring, rock, table, teeth, tiger, turtle, top, fan, feather, feet, farm, fire* • **Word-Building Cards** • pocket chart
- **Sound-Spelling WorkBoards**

Sound-Spelling WorkBoard

BUILD FLUENCY: SOUND/LETTER CORRESPONDENCE

Tier 2

Model
- Place **Word-Building Cards** *d, h, r, t, f* in the top row of the pocket chart. Shuffle the **Photo Cards** and place them facedown in a stack. Pick the first card, name the picture, and identify its initial sound. Place the Photo Card under the letter that stands for the beginning sound.

Guided Practice/Practice
- Have each child choose a Photo Card, say the name of the picture, identify its initial sound, and place it in the pocket chart under the correct letter. Guide practice with the first Photo Card.

Build Fluency
- Display Word-Building Cards *a, c, d, f, h, i, m, n, o, p, r, s, t.* Have children name each letter as quickly as they can. Then ask them to write the letters on their **WorkBoards** several times as they say the sounds.

ELL

Extra Practice Provide additional practice in recognizing and naming letters for children whose native languages do not use the symbols of the Latin alphabet.

Approaching Level

Leveled Reader Lesson 2

Objective   Reread *People Who Help* to reinforce fluency and to identify main idea and details

Materials   • **Leveled Reader:** *People Who Help*

FOCUS ON FLUENCY

- Tell children that you will read one page of the book and they should read that page right after you. They should follow along in their books and try to read at the same speed and with the same expression that you use.

SKILL   IDENTIFY MAIN IDEA AND DETAILS

- *What is this book about? How do different people help?*

REREAD PREVIOUSLY READ BOOKS

- Distribute copies of the past six **Leveled Readers**. Tell children that rereading the books helps them develop their skills.

- Ask children to make connections to how the ideas in the different books are alike and different.

- Circulate and listen in as children read. Stop them periodically and ask them how they are figuring out words or checking their understanding. Tell children to read other previously read Leveled Readers during independent reading time.

High-Frequency Words

Objective   Review high-frequency words *for, you, are, play,* and *is*

Materials   • **High-Frequency Word Cards:** *for, you, are, play, is*

BUILD WORD AUTOMATICITY: *for, you, are, play, is*

- Distribute copies of the **High-Frequency Word Card** for **for**. Say the word and have children repeat it. Have children name the letters in the word. Repeat with the words **you**, **are**, **play**, and **is**.

- **Build Fluency** Use the High-Frequency Word Cards to review previously taught words. Repeat, guiding children to read the words more rapidly.

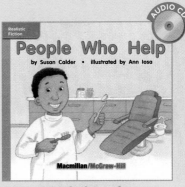

Leveled Reader

Meet Grade-Level Expectations

As an alternative to this day's lesson, guide children through a reading of the On Level Leveled Reader. See page 1450. Since both books contain the same vocabulary, phonics, and comprehension skills, the scaffolding you provided will help most children gain access to this more challenging text.

ON YOUR OWN

People Who Help

Children can draw pictures of people who help in their communities. Have children display and discuss their pictures.

Leveled Reader

Write About a Gift

Give children blank paper. Have them write: *This is for you.* Have them draw something that people give to each other as a gift.

This is for you.

On Level

Leveled Reader Lesson 2

Objective Reread to apply skills and strategies to retell a story

Materials • **Leveled Reader:** *This Is for You*

BEFORE READING

■ Ask children to look through *This Is for You* and recall what the book is about. Reinforce vocabulary by repeating children's sentences using more sophisticated language. For example: *Yes, the girl gives many gifts. She is very generous, isn't she?*

DURING READING

■ Have children join you in a choral-reading of the story. Model reading with expression. *When I read page 2, I emphasized the word* rose *a little stronger. I used the same strong emphasis when I read* picture *on page 3. I wanted to emphasize the different gifts that the girl is giving.* Ask children to use the same kind of expression when they read.

■ Assign each child a page. Have children practice by whisper-reading. *Follow along as other children read, and be ready to come in when it is your turn. Remember, use lots of expression.*

AFTER READING

■ Have children retell an important event in the story.

■ *The book is all about a girl who gives gifts to people. What are some of the gifts, and who are the people who receive them?*

Beyond Level

Leveled Reader Lesson 2

Objective Reread to apply skills and strategies to retell a story
Materials • **Leveled Reader:** *The Good Idea*

BEFORE READING

■ Ask children to look back at *The Good Idea*. Ask them to describe the big idea of the story. (There are many ways to clean the park.) *What are some ways to clean the park?*

DURING READING

■ Assign each child a page of the book to read aloud. Have children practice by whisper-reading. *Follow along as each child reads, and be ready to come in when it is your turn. Remember, use lots of expression.*

AFTER READING

■ Explain that summarizing is telling the most important ideas in the story. Model the strategy: *The story tells about a problem at the park. There was trash in the fountain. Pam solved the problem. She found a net to use to take out the trash.* Guide children in creating their own summaries of the story.

Expand Vocabulary

Objective Identify opposites
Materials • **Leveled Reader:** *The Good Idea*

ENRICH: WORDS FOR OPPOSITES

■ Reread the title of the book. Point out the word *good. The word* good *has a word that means the opposite. That word is* bad.

■ Make a two-column chart. Write *good* in one column and *bad* in the other. Ask children to use *good* and *bad* in sentences.

■ Have children look through the book to find other words that have opposites: *sad* (happy), *yes* (no), *in* (out). Add them to the chart.

■ Have children think of other opposite pairs. Write them on the chart and have children use them in sentences.

Leveled Reader

ON YOUR OWN

Clean the Park

Have pairs work together to draw a picture that shows how they can help clean the park. Have them write what they say.

ELL

Partners When children draw pictures and write about how they can help clean the park, pair English Language Learners with children who are more proficient. Ask pairs: *What can you do together to help clean the park?*

ELL ENGLISH LANGUAGE LEARNERS

Fluency

Content Objectives Reread the Decodable Reader to develop fluency; develop speaking skills

Language Objective Tell a partner what a selection is about

Materials • **Decodable Reader:** *Rod Can See It*

REREAD FOR FLUENCY

Beginning

- Review the high-frequency words **for**, **you**, **have**, **is**, **are**, and **play** using the **Read/Spell/Write** routine.

Intermediate/Advanced

- Use each word in a sentence, such as: *Here is a flower for you*. Gesture smelling a flower and giving it to a child.

- Then provide sentence starters for children to complete. Where appropriate, act out children's responses.

All Language Levels

- Guide children through a choral-reading of *Rod Can See It*. Point to the question mark on page 5 of *Rod Can See It*. Tell children that when a sentence ends in question mark, our voice goes up at the end. Model reading the question and have children chorally repeat.

DEVELOP SPEAKING/LISTENING SKILLS

All Language Levels

- Have children reread *Rod Can See It* to a partner. Remind them to listen carefully and follow along in their book as their partner is reading. Work with children to read with accuracy and appropriate expression.

- Ask children to tell their partner about the pictures on each page. Then have the other partner describe the pictures. Circulate, listen in, and provide additional language as needed.

Beginning	Intermediate	Advanced
Confirm Understanding Point to the pictures for partners to identify. Ask: *What do you see?* Restate the correct answer in a complete sentence.	**Share Preferences** Ask partners to tell you which is their favorite picture in the book. Prompt them to explain why it is their favorite picture.	**Compare and Contrast** Have partners compare two different pictures and describe them. Prompt them to explain how they are alike and different.

ENGLISH LANGUAGE LEARNERS

High-Frequency Words

Content Objective Spell high-frequency words correctly

Language Objective Write in complete sentences, using sentence frames

Materials • **Sound-Spelling WorkBoards** • **Sound-Spelling Cards** • **Photo Cards**

Beginning/Intermediate

- Write the high-frequency words **for** and **you** on the board. Have children copy the words on their **WorkBoards**. Then help them say, and then write, a sentence with the words. Provide the sentence starter *This _____ is for you*.

Advanced

- Children should first orally state their sentence. Correct as needed. Then they can draw a picture to complete the sentence. For children who are ready, help them spell words using their growing knowledge of English sound-spelling relationships. Model how to segment the word children are trying to spell and attach a spelling to each sound. Use the **Sound-Spelling Cards** to reinforce the spellings for each English sound.

Writing

All Language Levels

- Say the word *dip* and ask children to write it. Pretend to dip a paintbrush in some paint as you say *dip*. Then use the word in context: *I dip my brush in the paint*. Have them write the word five times as they say *dip*. Demonstrate correct letter formation, as needed. Repeat with *ran*.

- Then display a set of **Photo Cards**. Select at least five cards whose picture names begin with /d/ (*deer, doctor, dog, doll, dolphin*) and five whose picture names begin with /r/ (*rose, rock, rope, ring, rabbit*).

- Say the name of each card, stretching the initial sound to emphasize it. You may also need to model the correct mouth formation when forming the sound. Use the articulation pictures and prompts on the back of the small Sound-Spelling Cards for support. Tell children to write the first letter of each picture name on their WorkBoards.

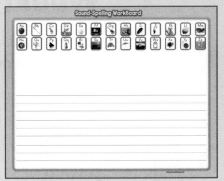
Sound-Spelling WorkBoard

Phonemic Awareness/ Phonics

For English Language Learners who need more practice with this week's phonemic awareness and phonics skills, see the Approaching Level lessons. Focus on minimal contrasts, articulation, and those sounds that do not transfer from the child's first language to English. For a complete listing of transfer sounds, see pages T10–T31.

Weekly Assessment

Use your Quick Check observations and the assessment opportunities identified below to evaluate children's progress in key skill areas.

Skills	Quick Check Observations	Pencil and Paper Assessment
PHONEMIC AWARENESS/ PHONICS /d/d, /r/r **d** **r**	1393, 1415	Activity Book, pp. 14, 19, 20, 22 Practice Book, pp. 127, 131–132
HIGH-FREQUENCY WORDS *for, you* **you** **for**	1414	Activity Book, pp. 17–18 Practice Book, pp. 129–130
COMPREHENSION Identify Main Idea and Details	1404	Activity Book, pp. 15–16, 21 Practice Book, p. 128

Quick Check Rubric

Skills	1	2	3
PHONEMIC AWARENESS/ PHONICS	Does not connect the sounds /d/, /r/ with the letters *Dd, Rr* and has difficulty blending the CVC words *Dad, mad, sad, had, fad, pad, dim, Dom, dot, dip, rim, ram, rat, Ron.*	Usually connects the sounds /d/, /r/ with the letters *Dd, Rr* and blends the CVC words *Dad, mad, sad, had, fad, pad, dim, Dom, dot, dip, rim, ram, rat, Ron* with only occasional support.	Consistently connects the sounds /d/, /r/ with the letters *Dd, Rr* and blends the CVC words *Dad, mad, sad, had, fad, pad, dim, Dom, dot, dip, rim, ram, rat, Ron.*
HIGH-FREQUENCY WORDS	Does not identify the high-frequency words.	Usually recognizes the high-frequency words with accuracy, but not speed.	Consistently recognizes the high-frequency words with speed and accuracy.
COMPREHENSION	Does not identify the main idea or details using the pictures and text.	Usually identifies the main idea or details using the pictures and text.	Consistently identifies the main idea or details using the pictures and text.

DIBELS LINK

PROGRESS MONITORING

Use your DIBELS results to inform instruction.

IF...

Initial **S**ound **F**luency (**ISF**)	0–24
Phoneme **S**egmentation **F**luency (**PSF**)	0–17
Nonsense **W**ord **F**luency (**NWF**)	0–12

THEN...
Evaluate for Intervention

TPRI LINK

PROGRESS MONITORING

Use your TPRI scores to inform instruction.

IF...

Phonemic Awareness	Still Developing
Letter Name Identification	Still Developing
Letter to Sound Linking	Still Developing
Listening Comprehension	Still Developing

THEN...
Evaluate for Intervention

End-of-Week Assessment

Diagnose		Prescribe
Review the assessment answers with children. Have them correct their errors. Then provide additional instruction as needed.		
PHONEMIC AWARENESS/ PHONICS /d/d, /r/r	**IF...** **Quick Check Rubric:** Children consistently score 1 or **Pencil and Paper Assessment:** Children get 0–2 items correct	**THEN...** Reteach Phonemic Awareness and Phonics Skills using the **Phonemic Awareness** and **Phonics Intervention Teacher's Editions.** SPIRAL REVIEW Use the Build Fluency lesson in upcoming weeks to provide children practice reading words with /d/d and /r/r.
HIGH-FREQUENCY WORDS *for, you*	**Quick Check Rubric:** Children consistently score 1 or **Pencil and Paper Assessment:** Children get 0–2 items correct	Reteach High-Frequency Words using the **Phonics Intervention Teacher's Edition.** SPIRAL REVIEW Use the High-Frequency Words lesson in upcoming weeks to provide children practice reading the words *for* and *you*.
COMPREHENSION Skill: Identify Main Idea and Details	**Quick Check Rubric:** Children consistently score 1 or **Pencil and Paper Assessment:** Children get 0–2 items correct	Reteach Comprehension Skill using the **Comprehension Intervention Teacher's Edition.**

Response to Intervention

To place children in Tier 2 or Tier 3 Intervention use the *Diagnostic Assessment*.

- Phonemic Awareness
- Phonics
- Vocabulary
- Comprehension
- Fluency

Week 3 ★ At a Glance

Priority Skills and Concepts

 ### Comprehension
- **Genre:** Fiction, Expository, Folktale
- **Strategy:** Summarize
- **Skill:** Retell
 - **Skill:** Identify the Main Idea and Details

 ### High-Frequency Words
- *are* , *for* , *you*

Oral Vocabulary
- Build Robust Vocabulary: *alert* , *celebration* , *job* , *precise* , *repair*

Fluency
- Echo-Read
- Word Automaticity

 ### Phonemic Awareness
- Phoneme Categorization
- Phoneme Blending
- Phoneme Segmentation

 ### Phonics
- *Dd, Hh, Rr*

Grammar
- Sentences

Writing
- Sentences

Key 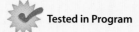 Tested in Program  Review Skill

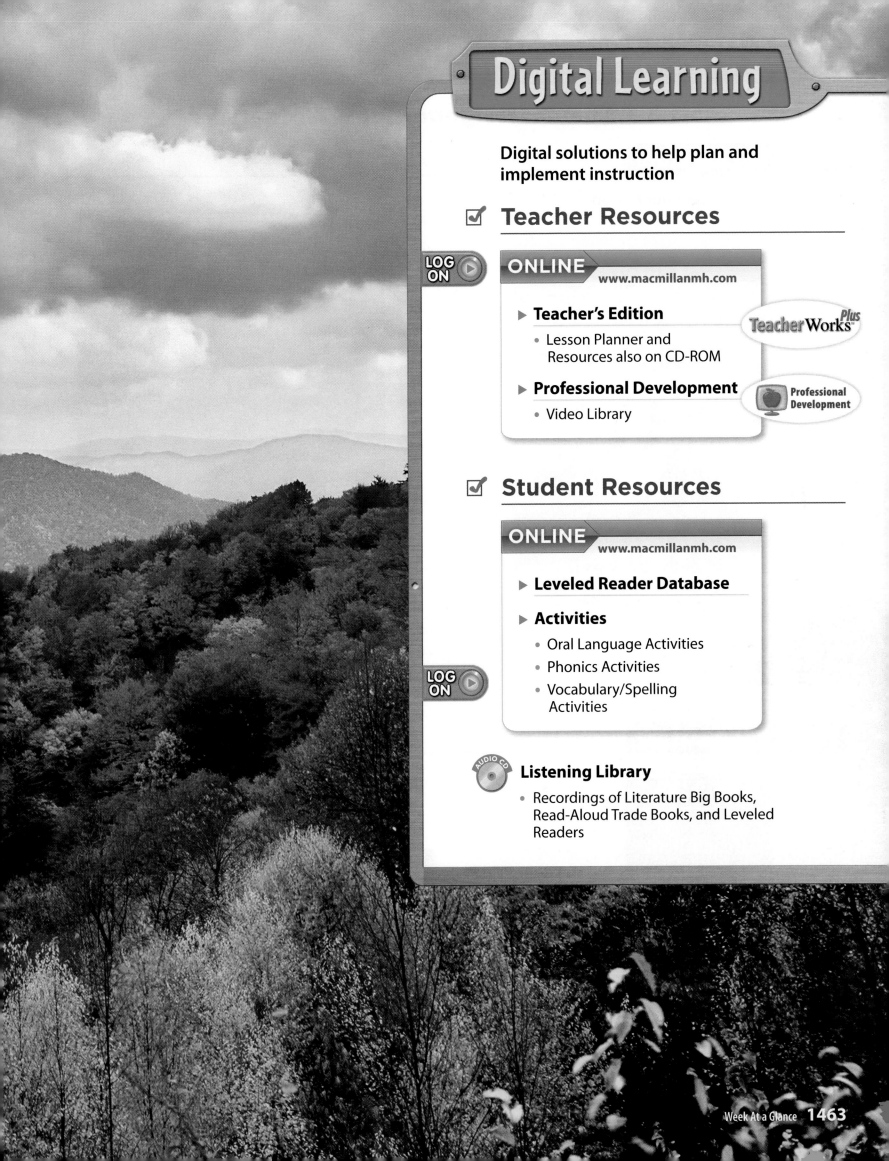

Digital Learning

Digital solutions to help plan and implement instruction

☑ Teacher Resources

LOG ON ▶

ONLINE www.macmillanmh.com

▶ **Teacher's Edition**
- Lesson Planner and Resources also on CD-ROM

TeacherWorks Plus

▶ **Professional Development**
- Video Library

Professional Development

☑ Student Resources

ONLINE www.macmillanmh.com

▶ **Leveled Reader Database**

▶ **Activities**
- Oral Language Activities
- Phonics Activities
- Vocabulary/Spelling Activities

LOG ON ▶

AUDIO CD

Listening Library
- Recordings of Literature Big Books, Read-Aloud Trade Books, and Leveled Readers

Theme: Neighborhood Workers

Student Literature

A mix of fiction and nonfiction

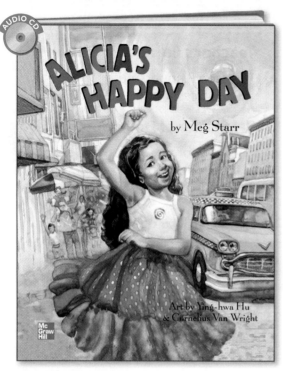

Trade Book

Genre Fiction

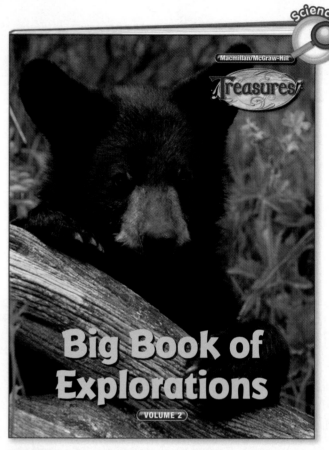

Big Book of Explorations

Genre Expository

Support Literature

**Interactive
Read-Aloud Anthology**

Genre Folktale

Oral Vocabulary Cards
- Listening Comprehension
- Build Robust Vocabulary

Decodable Reader

Resources for Differentiated Instruction

Leveled Readers

GR Levels Rebus–F

Genre	Fiction

- Same Theme
- Same Vocabulary/Phonics
- Same Comprehension Skills

We Work for You
by Mindy Krupa • illustrated by Nicole Rutten

Approaching Level

B

Panda House
by Marie Stone • illustrated by John Wallner

On Level

F

Bunny Town Helpers
by Fran Anne • illustrated by Carol Nicklaus

Beyond Level

A

A House For You
by Marie Stone • illustrated by John Wallner

ELL

LOG ON ▶ **Leveled Reader Database**
Go to www.macmillanmh.com.

Practice

AUDIO CD

Activity Book

Practice Book

English Language Learner Practice Book

ELL Practice Book

Response to Intervention

Tier 2

- Phonemic Awareness
- Phonics
- Vocabulary
- Comprehension
- Fluency

Tier 3

Unit Assessment

Unit and Benchmark Assessment

Assess Unit Skills
- Phonemic Awareness
- Phonics
- High-Frequency Words
- Listening Comprehension

🏠 HOME-SCHOOL CONNECTION

Home-School Connection

- Family letters in English and Spanish
- Take-home stories and activities

Go to **www.macmillanmh.com** for Online Lesson Planner

 **TeacherWorks** *Plus*
All-In-One Planner and Resource Center

Professional Development
Video Library

Trade Book

WHOLE GROUP

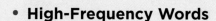

ORAL LANGUAGE

- Oral Vocabulary

- Phonemic Awareness

WORD STUDY

- Phonics

- High-Frequency Words

READING

- Listening Comprehension

- Apply Phonics and High-Frequency Words

- Fluency

LANGUAGE ARTS

- Writing

- Grammar

ASSESSMENT

- Informal/Formal

DAY 1

❓Focus Question Who do you see in your neighborhood?

Build Background, 1474

Oral Vocabulary *alert, celebration, job, precise, repair*, 1474

Phonemic Awareness
Phoneme Categorization, 1477

Phonics
Review /d/d, /h/h, /r/r, 1478
Handwriting: Review *Dd, Hh, Rr*, 1479)
Activity Book, 24
Practice Book, 137

High-Frequency Words
are, *for*, *you*, 1476

Share the Trade Book
Alicia's Happy Day
Strategy: Summarize, 1475
Skill: Retell, 1475

Trade Book

Shared Writing
Lists, 1481
Grammar
Sentences, 1480

 Quick Check Phonemic Awareness, 1477

DAY 2

❓Focus Question What are some things neighborhood workers do for you?

Oral Vocabulary *alert, celebration, job, precise, repair*, 1482

Sequence Words, 1489

Phonemic Awareness
Phoneme Blending, 1490

Phonics
Review /d/d, /h/h, /r/r, /f/f, 1490
Blend with -*ad*, 1491

Review High-Frequency Words, 1492

Reread the Trade Book
Alicia's Happy Day
Strategy: Summarize, 1484
Skill: Retell, 1488
Decodable Reader:
Dad Can Pin It On, 1492
Activity Book, 25–26
Practice Book, 134
Fluency Echo-Read, 1488

Trade Book

Interactive Writing
Sentences, 1493

Quick Check Comprehension, 1488

 SMALL GROUP Lesson Plan ▷ **Differentiated Instruction 1468–1469**

Priority Skills

Phonemic Awareness/Phonics /d/d, /h/h, /r/r	High-Frequency Words *are, for, you*	Oral Vocabulary Sequence Words	Comprehension Strategy: Summarize Skill: Retell

Half-Day Kindergarten

Teach Core Skills
Focus on tested skill lessons, other lessons, and small group options as your time allows.

DAY 3

❓ Focus Question What would be the best job for you someday?

Oral Vocabulary *alert, celebration, job, precise, repair,* 1494
Oral Vocabulary Cards: "The Elves and the Shoemakers"
Phonemic Awareness
Phoneme Segmentation, 1499

Phonics
Review, 1500
Blend with *-at, -an*, 1501

High-Frequency Words
are, *for*, *you*, 1498
Activity Book: "Are You?" 27–28
Practice Book, 135–136
Read for Fluency, 1498

Read the Big Book of Explorations
"Is This the Job for You?" 9–12
Text Feature: Labels, 1496

Big Book of Explorations

Independent Writing
Prewrite and Draft Sentences, 1503
Grammar
Sentences, 1502

Quick Check High-Frequency Words, 1498

DAY 4

❓ Focus Question What do you think a Road Builder or a River Drinker does?

Oral Vocabulary *alert, celebration, job, precise, repair,* 1504
Words That Compare, 1507

Phonemic Awareness
Phoneme Blending, 1508

Phonics
Review, 1508
Blend with *-ap, -am*, 1509
Activity Book, 29–30
Practice Book, 137–138
Review High-Frequency Words, 1510

Interactive Read Aloud
Listening Comprehension, 1506
Read Aloud: "Why the Moon Is in the Sky"
Decodable Reader:
Dad Can Pin It On, 1510

Read Aloud

Fluency Reread for Fluency, 1510

Independent Writing
Revise and Edit Sentences, 1511

Quick Check Phonics, 1509

DAY 5
Review and Assess

❓ Focus Question What are some jobs we read about? Which ones did you find most interesting?

Oral Vocabulary *alert, celebration, job, precise, repair,* 1512
Sequence Words, 1514

Phonemic Awareness
Phoneme Segmentation, 1515

Phonics
Read Words, 1516
Dictation, 1516
Activity Book, 32

High-Frequency Words
are, *for*, *you*, *is*, *play*, *have*, 1514

Read Across Texts
Strategy: Summarize, 1513
Skill: Retell, 1513
Activity Book, 31

Fluency Word Automaticity, 1514

Independent Writing
Publish and Present Sentences, 1517

Weekly Assessment, 1544–1545

Differentiated Instruction

What do I do in small groups?

Teacher-Led Small Groups

Independent Activities

Focus on Skills

IF... children need additional instruction, practice, or extension based on your **Quick Check** 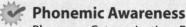 observations for the following priority skills

✓ **Phonemic Awareness**
Phoneme Categorization, Blending, Segmentation

✓ **Phonics**
Dd, Hh, Rr

✓ **High-Frequency Words**
are, *for*, *you*

✓ **Comprehension**
Strategy: Summarize
Skill: Retell

THEN...

Approaching	Preteach and
ELL	Reteach Skills
On Level	Practice
Beyond	Enrich and Accelerate Learning

 Suggested Small Group Lesson Plan

Approaching Level	DAY 1	DAY 2
Tier 2 • **Preteach/Reteach** **Tier 2 Instruction**	• Oral Language, 1518 • High-Frequency Words, 1518 **ELL** High-Frequency Words Review, 1518 • Phonemic Awareness, 1519 • Phonics, 1519 **ELL** Sound-Spellings Review, 1519	• Oral Language, 1524 • High-Frequency Words, 1524 **ELL** • Phonemic Awareness, 1525 • Phonics, 1525
On Level • **Practice**	• High-Frequency Words, 1520 • Phonemic Awareness/Phonics, 1520 **ELL**	• Phonics, 1526
Beyond Level • **Extend/Accelerate** **Gifted and Talented**	• High-Frequency Words/Vocabulary, 1521 **ELL** Expand Oral Vocabulary, 1521 • Phonics, 1521	• Phonics, 1526
ELL • **Build English Language Proficiency** • See **ELL** in other levels.	• Oral Language Warm-Up, 1522 • Academic Language, 1522 • Vocabulary, 1523	• Access to Core Content, 1527

Small Group

Focus on Leveled Readers

Levels Rebus–F

Approaching

On Level

Beyond

ELL

Additional Leveled Readers

LOG ON **Leveled Reader Database**
www.macmillanmh.com

Search by
- Comprehension Skill
- Content Area
- Genre
- Text Feature
- Guided Reading Level
- Reading Recovery Level
- Lexile Score
- Benchmark Level

Subscription also available

Manipulatives

Sound-Spelling WorkBoards

Sound-Spelling Cards

Photo Cards

High-Frequency Word Cards

Visual Vocabulary Resources

DAY 3

- High-Frequency Words, 1528 **ELL**
- Phonemic Awareness, 1528
- Decodable Reader, 1529
- Phonics, 1529

- Decodable Reader, 1530

- Decodable Reader, 1530

- Access to Core Content, 1531
- Grammar, 1531

DAY 4

- Phonemic Awareness, 1532
- Phonics, 1532 **ELL**
- Leveled Reader Lesson 1, 1533

- Leveled Reader Lesson 1, 1534 **ELL**

- Leveled Reader Lesson 1, 1535
  Analyze, 1535

- Leveled Reader, 1536–1537

DAY 5

- Phonemic Awareness, 1538
- Phonics, 1538 **ELL**
- Leveled Reader Lesson 2, 1539
- High-Frequency Words, 1539

- Leveled Reader Lesson 2, 1540

- Leveled Reader Lesson 2, 1541 **ELL**
- Expand Vocabulary, 1541

- Fluency, 1542
- High-Frequency Words, 1543
- Writing, 1543

Managing the Class

What do I do with the rest of my class?

- Activity Book
- Practice Book
- ELL Practice Book
- Leveled Reader Activities
- Literacy Workstations
- Online Activities
- Buggles and Beezy

Classroom Management Tools

Weekly Contract

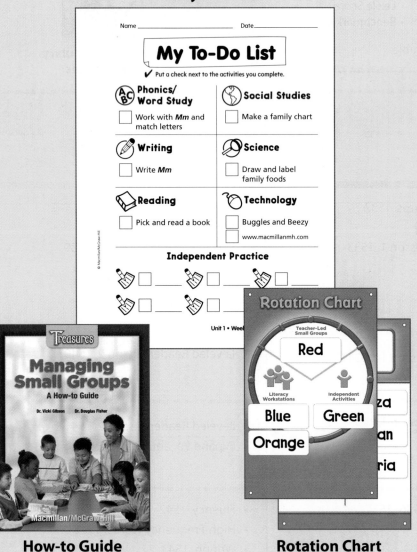

My To-Do List

✔ Put a check next to the activities you complete.

(ABC) Phonics/Word Study
☐ Work with *Mm* and match letters

Social Studies
☐ Make a family chart

Writing
☐ Write *Mm*

Science
☐ Draw and label family foods

Reading
☐ Pick and read a book

Technology
☐ Buggles and Beezy
☐ www.macmillanmh.com

Independent Practice

Unit 1 • Week

How-to Guide

Treasures
Managing Small Groups
A How-to Guide
Dr. Vicki Gibson Dr. Douglas Fisher
Macmillan/McGraw-Hill

Rotation Chart

Rotation Chart
Teacher-Led Small Groups
Red
Literacy Workstations   Independent Activities
Blue   **Green**
Orange

Digital Learning

Phonics Activities

- Match Letters
- Match Letters to Sounds
- Blend Words

Meet the Author/Illustrator

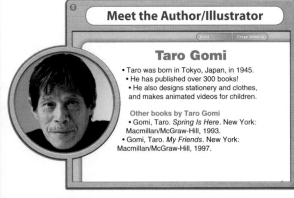

Taro Gomi
- Taro was born in Tokyo, Japan, in 1945.
- He has published over 300 books!
- He also designs stationery and clothes, and makes animated videos for children.

Other books by Taro Gomi
- Gomi, Taro. *Spring Is Here*. New York: Macmillan/McGraw-Hill, 1993.
- Gomi, Taro. *My Friends*. New York: Macmillan/McGraw-Hill, 1997.

- Read Other Books by the Author or Illustrator

Practice

Activity Book

Practice Book

ELL Practice Book

Independent Activities

ONLINE INSTRUCTION www.macmillanmh.com

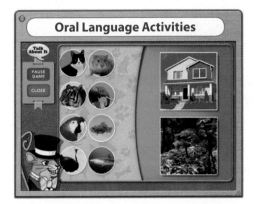

Oral Language Activities

- Focus on Unit Vocabulary and Concepts
- English Language Learner Support

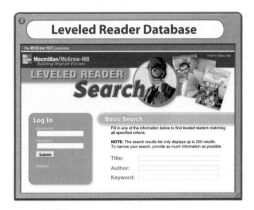

Leveled Reader Database

- Leveled Reader Database
- Search titles by level, skill, content area, and more

Vocabulary/Spelling Activities

- Differentiated Lists and Activities

Available on CD

LISTENING LIBRARY
Recordings of selections
- Literature Big Books
- Read-Aloud Trade Books
- Leveled Readers
- ELL Readers

NEW ADVENTURES WITH BUGGLES AND BEEZY
Phonemic awareness and phonics activities

Leveled Reader Activities

Approaching   **On Level**   **Beyond**   **ELL**

See inside cover of all Leveled Readers.

Literacy Workstations

See lessons on pages 1472–1473.

Managing the Class

What do I do with the rest of my class?

Reading

Objectives

- Select a book to read independently
- Read a book; add a page to a book to tell what might happen next

Phonics/Word Study

Objectives

- Identify rhyming words; find different ways to sort words
- Complete word webs for *d*, *h*, and *r*

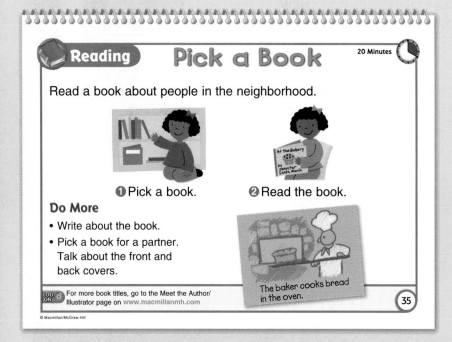

Reading — **Pick a Book** — 20 Minutes

Read a book about people in the neighborhood.

❶ Pick a book. ❷ Read the book.

Do More
- Write about the book.
- Pick a book for a partner. Talk about the front and back covers.

The baker cooks bread in the oven.

For more book titles, go to the Meet the Author/Illustrator page on www.macmillanmh.com

35

© Macmillan/McGraw-Hill

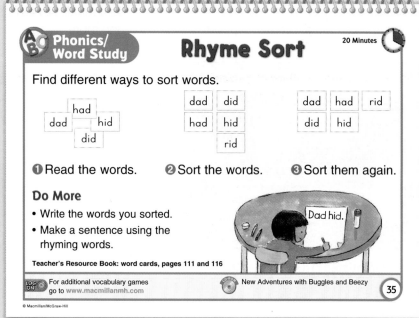

Phonics/Word Study — **Rhyme Sort** — 20 Minutes

Find different ways to sort words.

❶ Read the words. ❷ Sort the words. ❸ Sort them again.

Do More
- Write the words you sorted.
- Make a sentence using the rhyming words.

Dad hid.

Teacher's Resource Book: word cards, pages 111 and 116

For additional vocabulary games go to www.macmillanmh.com

New Adventures with Buggles and Beezy

35

© Macmillan/McGraw-Hill

Reading — **Read It, Add to It** — 20 Minutes

Read a book and add a new page to it.

❶ Read a book. ❷ What could happen next? ❸ Write a new page.

Do More
- Share your new page with a partner.
- Make a new cover for the book.

For more book titles, go to the Meet the Author/Illustrator page on www.macmillanmh.com

36

© Macmillan/McGraw-Hill

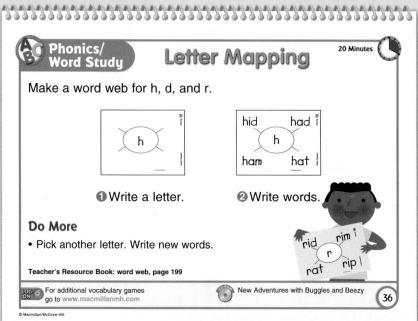

Phonics/Word Study — **Letter Mapping** — 20 Minutes

Make a word web for h, d, and r.

❶ Write a letter. ❷ Write words.

Do More
- Pick another letter. Write new words.

Teacher's Resource Book: word web, page 199

For additional vocabulary games go to www.macmillanmh.com

New Adventures with Buggles and Beezy

36

© Macmillan/McGraw-Hill

Literacy Workstations

 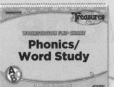  

Literacy Workstation Flip Charts

Writing

Objectives

- Write a greeting card; leave appropriate space between words when writing
- Make a list of words that can be read in the classroom

Content Literacy

Objectives

- Draw pictures that show how a neighborhood changes in different seasons
- Make a puzzle of a neighborhood worker

Writing — **Write Greeting Cards** — 20 Minutes

Write a card to Alicia on her special day.

Dear Alicia,

Dear Alicia, Have a happy day! Carlos

Dear Alicia, Have a happy day! Carlos

❶ Start your card. ❷ Finish your card. ❸ Draw pictures for Alicia.

Do More
- Make an envelope for your card.
- Make more cards.

Alicia

35

© Macmillan/McGraw-Hill

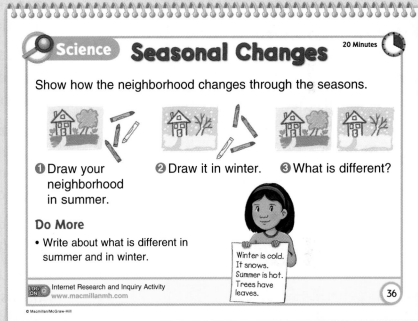

Science — **Seasonal Changes** — 20 Minutes

Show how the neighborhood changes through the seasons.

❶ Draw your neighborhood in summer. ❷ Draw it in winter. ❸ What is different?

Do More
- Write about what is different in summer and in winter.

Winter is cold. It snows. Summer is hot. Trees have leaves.

LOG ON — Internet Research and Inquiry Activity
www.macmillanmh.com

36

© Macmillan/McGraw-Hill

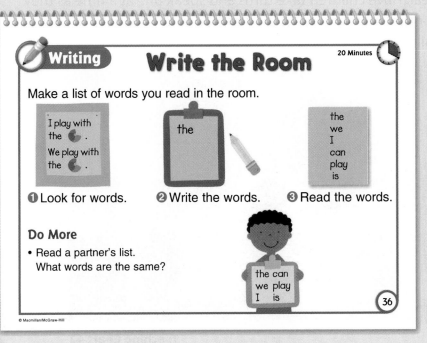

Writing — **Write the Room** — 20 Minutes

Make a list of words you read in the room.

I play with the ●. We play with the ●.

the

the we I can play is

❶ Look for words. ❷ Write the words. ❸ Read the words.

Do More
- Read a partner's list. What words are the same?

the can we play I is

36

© Macmillan/McGraw-Hill

Social Studies — **Neighborhood Worker Puzzles** — 20 Minutes

Make a puzzle of a worker.

❶ Draw a worker. ❷ Cut it into 4 pieces. ❸ Put it together.

Do More
- Share your puzzle with a partner.
- Write about a neighborhood worker.

LOG ON — Internet Research and Inquiry Activity
www.macmillanmh.com

35

© Macmillan/McGraw-Hill

Oral Language
• Build Background

✔ **Comprehension**
• Read *Alicia's Happy Day*
• Strategy: Summarize
• Skill: Retell

✔ **High-Frequency Words**
• Review *are, you, for*

✔ **Phonemic Awareness**
• Phoneme Categorization

✔ **Phonics**
• Review /d/d, /h/h, /r/r
• Handwriting: Review *Dd, Hh, Rr*

Grammar
• Sentences

Writing
• Shared Writing: Lists

SMALL GROUP

• Differentiated Instruction, pages 1518–1543

Oral Vocabulary

Week 3

| alert | celebration | job |
| precise | repair | |

Review

| admire | community | deliver |
| schedule | workers | |

Use the **Define/Example/Ask** routine in the **Instructional Routine Handbook** to review the words.

Oral Language

 Talk About It

Build Background:
Neighborhood Workers

INTRODUCE THE THEME

Tell children that this week they will be talking and reading about **jobs** people do, such as driving a bus or preparing food.

Write the following question on the board: *Who do you see in your neighborhood?* Guide children to chant the question and to identify syllables in words. Say the word *see* and clap the beat. *How many beats did you hear?* Then have children segment *neigh-bor-hood* and clap. *How many beats did you hear?* Prompt children to answer the question on the board.

ACCESS PRIOR KNOWLEDGE

Have children tell about workers they see in their neighborhood. Explain that workers do jobs.

Think Aloud Let's look at this picture. I see a girl and a man. She is smiling. He is using a tool to look in her ear. (**Point to the girl, man, tool, and ear as you describe the picture.**) I think the man is a doctor.

What do doctors do to help people? How do workers in the neighborhood make the neighborhood a better place to live?

DISCUSS THE PHOTOGRAPH

Discuss what the doctor in the photograph is doing to help the child. Tell children that the doctor is using an otoscope to look into the child's ear. Have children take turns and speak one at a time as they discuss other jobs workers in the neighborhood do that help children.

Teaching Chart 42

Share the Trade Book

Listening Comprehension

PREVIEW Display the cover. *I see a girl in front of buildings and traffic. Maybe she is in a city. Let's read about a girl and her community.* Guide children to read the title. Have them use the title and illustration to help them predict what might happen.

Trade Book

GENRE Explain that the genre of this story is **realistic fiction**. The story did not really happen, but the girl does things a real child could do.

STRATEGY Summarize

EXPLAIN/MODEL Tell children that it is important to think about the main events from the beginning, middle, and end of stories.

Think Aloud When I read a few pages of the story, I will recall the important things that happened so far.

SKILL Retell

EXPLAIN/MODEL Tell children that a good way to understand a story is to remind themselves of what is happening in it as they listen and read. Point out that this will help them retell the story. Display pages 2–3.

Think Aloud I see a girl and her mother leaving a building in the city. There are other people on the street. The girl looks happy.

Read the Trade Book

SET PURPOSE Discuss with children the purpose for listening to this story. Elicit that they will become involved in imagined events and will enjoy language. Use the **Define/Example/Ask** routine to teach the story words on the inside back cover.

Respond to Literature

MAKE CONNECTIONS Have children name their favorite part of the book. *Why did Alicia feel happy? What kind of **celebration** takes place in the book? Tell about a time when you celebrated something.*

Objectives

- Discuss the purpose for listening to a story
- Identify the number of syllables in words
- Identify people who work in a neighborhood
- Use oral vocabulary words *job* and *celebration*
- Summarize/retell a story

Materials

- Teaching Chart 42
- Read-Aloud Trade Book: *Alicia's Happy Day*

ELL

Use the Interactive Question-Response Guide for *Alicia's Happy Day*, **ELL Resource Book** pages 172–177, to guide children through a reading of the book. As you read *Alicia's Happy Day*, make meaning clear by pointing to pictures, demonstrating word meanings, paraphrasing text, and asking children questions.

Digital Learning

Story on **Listening Library Audio CD**

Objectives

- Read the high-frequency words *are, for, you*
- Review the high-frequency words *play, is*
- Identify the words *are, for,* and *you* in speech and text

Materials

- High-Frequency Word Cards: *are, for, you, play, is*
- Teaching Chart 43

ELL

Reinforce Vocabulary
Display the High-Frequency Word Cards *are, for, you, play, is*. Hold different classroom objects and address individual children as you say, for example: *Beto, this pencil is for you.* Then address pairs and say, for example: *Lupe and Tita, these crayons are for you. Kentaro and Rosa, you can play with the ball.* Repeat pointing to other children and holding other objects.

High-Frequency Words

 are, for, you

are	for

you

REVIEW
Display the **High-Frequency Word Cards** for **are**, **for**, and **you**. Use the **Read/Spell/Write** routine to teach the words.

- **Read** Point to and say the word *are*. *We* are *in school.*

- **Spell** *The word* are *is spelled* a-r-e. *Let's read and spell* are *together.*

- **Write** *Now let's write the word* are *on our papers. Let's spell aloud the word as we write it:* are, a-r-e.

Repeat the routine for *for* and *you*.

SPIRAL REVIEW **REVIEW** *is, play* Display each card and have children read the word.

is	play

READ THE RHYME AND CHIME
Ask children to point to the words *are, for,* and *you* each time they see them. Repeat the rhyme together for fluency.

Hop, Dance, and Run

Are you ready for some fun?
Are you ready for this game?
Hop, dance, and run!
Then shout out your name.

Unit 6
Rhyme and Chime

High-Frequency Words: are, for, you
Phonics: /uh/, /d/, /r/

Neighborhood Week 3 43

Teaching Chart 43

For Tier 2 instruction, see page 1518.

TIME TO MOVE!

Have children stand in a circle. Pass a "phone" to the first child and say: *It's for you.* The child says a few words and passes the phone to the next child: *It's for you.*

Phonemic Awareness

Phoneme Categorization

Model

Say the "Hop, Dance, and Run" Rhyme and Chime again.

Hop, Dance, and Run

Are you ready for some fun? Are you ready for this game? Hop, dance, and run! Then shout out your name.

Model how to categorize initial sounds.

Repeat with *for, fun,* and *hop.*

I will say some words from the Rhyme and Chime: *run, ready, name. Run* and *ready* begin with the /r/ sound. *Name* does not begin with the /r/ sound. It does not belong.

Display and name the **Photo Cards** for *door, hay, dog.*

Listen to the names of these three pictures: *door, dog, hay. Door* and *dog* begin with the /d/ sound. *Hay* does not. It does not belong.

Guided Practice/Practice

Show sets of three Photo Cards and name them.

I will say some picture names. Two of the names begin with the same sound. Tell me which name doesn't belong.

Children identify initial sounds. Guide practice with the first card, using the same routine.

Objective

- Recognize groups of words that begin with the same spoken onset for /d/, /h/, /r/

Materials

- Photo Cards: *door, dog, hay; hand, hat, rock; horse, doctor, hammer; rabbit, hair, rake; helicopter, rope, ring; deer, rose, dinosaur; hook, house, ruby; dolphin, hippo, dime*

ELL

Pronunciation Display and have children name Photo Cards from this and prior lessons to reinforce phonemic awareness and word meanings. Point to a card and ask: *What do you see?* (a door) *What is the sound at the beginning of the word* door? (/d/) Repeat using Photo Cards with words that begin with the /h/ and /r/ sounds.

Quick Check

Can children categorize words by initial /d/, /h/, /r/ sounds?

During **Small Group Instruction**

If No → **Approaching Level** Provide additional practice, page 1519.

If Yes → **On Level** Children blend words with /d/ and /h/, page 1520.

Beyond Level Children read words with *d, h,* and *r,* page 1521.

Objectives

- Match the letters *d, h,* and *r* to the sounds /d/, /h/, and /r/
- Recognize the difference between a letter and a word
- Handwriting: Review *Dd, Hh, Rr*

Materials

- Word-Building Cards
- Teaching Chart 43
- Handwriting
- Handwriting Teacher's Edition
- Activity Book, p. 24
- Practice Book, p. 137

Phonics

✔ Review

Model

Display **Word-Building Card** *d*.

Repeat for the letters *h* and *r*.

This letter is *d*. The letter *d* stands for /d/. What is the name of this letter? What sound does this letter stand for?

Read the "Hop, Dance, and Run" Rhyme and Chime. Reread the title. Point out that *Dance* begins with *D*. Model placing a self-stick note below the *D* in *Dance*. Guide children to understand the difference between a letter and a word.

Teaching Chart 43

Guided Practice/Practice

Reread the Rhyme and Chime. Children place self-stick notes below words that begin with *d*. Guide practice with *dance* in line 3. Repeat with *h* and *r*.

Let's place a sticky note below the word in line 3 that begins with the letter *d*. *Dance* begins with *d*. Do any words in the line begin with the letter *h*? Let's place a sticky note under the word *Hop*.

Corrective Feedback

Model saying the /d/ sound in the word *dance*. Model the correct mouth position as you emphasize the sound. *This is the /d/ sound at the beginning of* dance: /d/ /a/ /n/ /s/, dance. Repeat with *duck*.

Build Fluency: Sound-Spellings

 Display the following **Word-Building Cards**: *a, c, d, f, h, i, m, n, o, p, r, s, t*. Have children chorally say each sound. Repeat and vary the pace.

Handwriting: Review *Dd, Hh, Rr*

MODEL Model holding up your writing hand. Say the handwriting cues from **Handwriting Teacher's Edition** pages 62–64 as you write the capital and lowercase forms of *Dd, Hh,* and *Rr* on the board. Then trace the letters on the board and in the air.

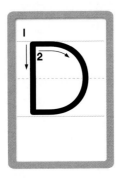 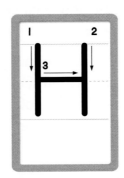 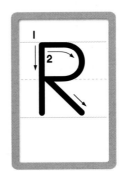

PRACTICE Ask children to hold up their writing hand.

- Say the cues together as children trace with their index finger the letters you wrote on the board.

- Have children write *D* and *d* in the air as they say /d/ multiple times. Then ask children to write *R* and *r* in the air as they say /rrr/. Finally, have children write *H* and *h* in the air as they say /h/ multiple times.

- Distribute handwriting practice pages. Observe children's pencil grip and paper position, and correct as necessary. Have children say /d/ each time they write *d,* /h/ each time they write *h,* and /rrr/ each time they write *r.*

For Tier 2 instruction, see page 1519.

See Handwriting Teacher's Edition for ball-and-stick and slant models.

Daily Handwriting
Check that children form letters starting at the top and moving to the bottom. See Handwriting Teacher's Edition for ball-and-stick and slant models.

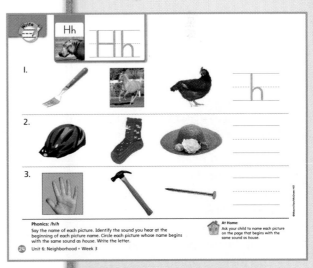

Activity Book, page 24
Practice Book, page 137

Objective

- Use complete simple sentences

Materials

- **Read-Aloud Trade Book:** *Alicia's Happy Day*
- **Photo Cards:** *ball, book, box, camera, chair, dime, envelope, feather, fork, game, globe, graph, hook, jar, jump rope, map, newspaper, paint, pen, penny, plate, quarter, soap, spoon, string, table, thermometer, watermelon, window, yarn*

ELL

Basic and Academic Language Display Photo Cards of objects from this and prior lessons. Pair English Language Learners with fluent speakers. Have partners complete the sentence frame by using the Photo Card objects as subjects of their sentences. Then ask them to complete their sentences by telling where they think the objects are.

Grammar

Sentences

MODEL Ask children what a sentence is. Confirm that a sentence tells a complete thought. Elicit that a sentence has two parts: a naming part that tells *who* and a telling part that tells *what*.

- Turn to pages 2–5 of the **Trade Book** *Alicia's Happy Day* and read the sentences: *May you have a day that's twirly-swirly. May you hear salsa and start to dance.* Explain that these are sentences because they tell who and what people do on a happy day. The *who* is the reader. The *what* is a twirly-swirly day, hearing salsa, and dancing.

- Ask two children to stand. Make up a sentence about them. For example: *Marco and Kendall like to build with blocks.* Tell children that the naming part of the sentence is *Marco and Kendall;* the telling part of the sentence is *like to build with blocks.*

PRACTICE

Display and name the **Photo Card** for *book.* Show children the sentence frame and read it together.

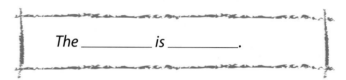

The _____ is _____.

Explain that you will make a sentence using the sentence frame and the Photo Card. *I can fill out the first part of the sentence frame using the picture:* The book is. *What can I tell about a book? I can tell about what it looks like. The book is brown. I can also tell about where it is. The book is in the bookcase. That is the sentence I want to use. The book is in the bookcase. What is the naming part of the sentence?* (book) *What is the telling part of the sentence?* (is in the bookcase)

- Distribute the Photo Cards to children and have them name the cards. Ask children to use the sentence frame to make a sentence about the item pictured on their card.

- After each sentence, ask children to identify the naming part and the telling part of the sentence.

Writing
Shared Writing: Lists

BRAINSTORM
Remind children that in the **Trade Book** *Alicia's Happy Day,* Alicia saw many special things as she walked through her neighborhood and **celebrated** her birthday. *What were some of the things she saw?*

WRITE
Create two lists as shown, or use **Teaching Chart G3**. Read each title together as you track the print.

■ Tell children they will list some things that happened in the story. Model by reading pages 4–5. *A man in a store waves to Alicia, so I will write* man in the store *under* What She Sees, *and* waves *under* What They Do.

■ Continue by reading pages 6–7, 8–9, and 18–19. Have children suggest what you should write in each list. Share the pen with children who can write words on the chart, such as *stop* or *a.*

■ Read the completed lists together. Point out that lists can help you retell what happened in the story.

■ Save the list to refer to in other writing activities this week.

What She Sees	What They Do
man in the store	waves
flags	fly
taxicabs	stop
orange lady	gives a peel

Write About It
Ask children to draw and label a picture of someone Alicia met in the book.

Objective
• Dictate information for a list

Materials
• Read-Aloud Trade Book: *Alicia's Happy Day*
• Graphic Organizer; Teaching Chart G3

5-Day Writing

	Sentences
DAY 1	Shared: Lists
DAY 2	Interactive: Sentences
DAY 3	Independent: Prewrite and Draft Sentences
DAY 4	Independent: Revise and Edit Sentences
DAY 5	Independent: Publish and Present

ELL

Prewriting Planning
Have children page through *Alicia's Happy Day.* Ask what is happening in the pictures. Have children respond by dictating a sentence to describe each picture. Be sure to identify each character before children work on their notebook entries.

Transitions That Teach

While lining up, have children tell about a **celebration** that they have attended.

WHOLE GROUP

Oral Language
- Build Robust Vocabulary

✔ **Comprehension**
- Reread *Alicia's Happy Day*
- Strategy: Summarize
- Skill: Retell
- Fluency: Echo-Read

Vocabulary
- Sequence Words
- Story Words: *twirly-swirly, ribbon*

✔ **Phonemic Awareness**
- Phoneme Blending

✔ **Phonics**
- Review /d/d, /h/h, /r/r, /f/f
- Blend with -ad
- Decodable Reader: *Dad Can Pin It On*

Writing
- Interactive Writing: Sentences

SMALL GROUP

- Differentiated Instruction, pages 1518–1543

Oral Vocabulary

Week 3

alert	celebration	job
precise	repair	

Review

admire	community
deliver	schedule	workers

Use the **Define/Example/Ask** routine in the **Instructional Routine Handbook** to review the words.

Oral Language

 Talk About It

Build Robust Vocabulary

INTRODUCE WORDS

Tell children that today they will talk about the book *Alicia's Happy Day*. *A celebration is a joyful gathering for a special occasion. Birthdays are a time for celebration. How does Alicia celebrate her birthday? How do you celebrate special occasions?*

Alicia sees many people doing their jobs as she celebrates her special day around the neighborhood. Who does Alicia see? What kind of work do they do? Did you see people doing their jobs as you went to school today? Who were they? What were they doing? Read pages 2–9 aloud.

Vocabulary Routine

Use the routine below to discuss the meaning of each word.

Define: A **job** is the work you do. Say the word with me.
Example: A cab driver's job is to drive people from place to place.
Ask: What neighborhood job would you like to do?

Define: A **celebration** is a joyful gathering for a special occasion. Say the word with me.
Example: We bought balloons for my sister's graduation celebration.
Ask: What events or holidays are good reasons for celebrations?

CREATE A STORY MAP

Create a story map like the one shown. Read the title aloud, tracking the print. *We will show some of the workers Alicia sees doing their jobs. Who is the first worker Alicia sees?*

Guide children to use complete sentences when speaking. Write the names of the workers Alicia sees and add a drawing for each one. Read the completed chart together as you track the print.

Alicia's Neighborhood Workers

music store man	cab driver	orange lady	icey man	baker

Listen for Alliteration

IDENTIFY ALLITERATION

Tell children that sometimes words that tell an idea all begin with the same sound. For example, point out that most of the words in this sentence begin with the /b/ sound: *The baby boy bounces the ball.*

RHYME ABOUT WORK

Let's recite a rhyme about working in the neighborhood. Play the rhyme "One Man Went to Mow," using the **Listening Library Audio CD**. Explain to children that a *meadow* is a field of grass. Say the sentence *Many men mowed a meadow.* Ask children if most of the words begin with the same sound. Ask: *What beginning sound do you hear?*

Discuss the rhyme. *What is the rhyme about? What is the man's job? How might the dog help him?*

Say the words *man, mow, meadow.* Ask: *What sound do you hear in these words?* Guide children to replace the word *mow* with another action word that begins with /m/, such as *mold, mash, mop, mix, measure,* or *make.*

One Man Went to Mow

One man went to mow,

Went to mow a meadow.

One man and his dog

Went to mow a meadow.

Two men went to mow,

Went to mow a meadow.

Two men, one man and his dog

Went to mow a meadow.

Objectives

- Discuss the theme
- Use oral vocabulary words *celebration, job*
- Use complete simple sentences
- Recognize alliteration

Materials

- Read-Aloud Trade Book: *Alicia's Happy Day*
- Listening Library Audio CD

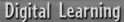

Digital Learning

 Rhyme on Listening Library Audio CD

ELL ENGLISH LANGUAGE LEARNERS

Beginning	Intermediate	Advanced
Confirm Understanding Review oral vocabulary using the **Trade Book** *Alicia's Happy Day.* Say, for example: *Show me the page where Alicia and the taxi driver wave to each other.* Repeat with other pages.	**Enhance Understanding** Ask children to describe what happens first and what happens last in the story. Guide children to answer in complete sentences and prompt them to add details.	**Story Characters** Pair children to play characters in the story. Have one partner play the role of Alicia and the other partner the role of a worker in the neighborhood.

Objectives

- Summarize a story
- Retell a story
- Respond to a story
- Develop fluency

Materials

- Read-Aloud Trade Book: *Alicia's Happy Day*
- Retelling Cards
- Activity Book, pp. 25–26
- Practice Book, p. 134

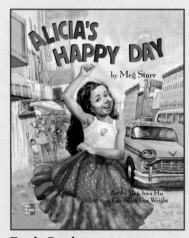

Trade Book

Digital Learning

Story on **Listening Library Audio CD**

ELL

Gesture and Talk Use gestures and other strategies to help make the text comprehensible.

pp. 2–3
Point to Alicia's smile. Say: *She is happy.* Have children point to each other's smiles and say: *He/She is happy.*

pp. 4–5
dance: Hum a tune and have children dance with you. As children dance, have them say: *We are dancing.*

Reread the Trade Book
Listening Comprehension

CONCEPTS ABOUT PRINT Display the cover and read the title aloud with children.

 STRATEGY Summarize

Remind children to summarize, or recall the important events from the beginning, middle, and end of the story, as they read it. *What do you remember about the story? What important things happened in it?*

 SKILL Retell

Explain to children that thinking about the characters, setting, and retelling main events from the story can help them remember and understand it. Display pages 2–3.

Think Aloud I remember that Alicia and her mother went outside and walked through their neighborhood. As I read, I'll remind myself of all that happens in each part of the story.

Read the **Trade Book** and use the prompts on the inside back cover.

pages 2–3

ILLUSTRATOR'S CRAFT
Think Aloud The illustrator painted the sun with twirling, swirling paint strokes. This shows that the day is twirly-swirly.

May you have a day that's twirly-swirly.

pages 4–5

 RETELL
Think Aloud Let me think about what has happened so far in the story. Alicia and her mother left the house to go somewhere. Alicia hears salsa music and starts to dance.

May you hear salsa and start to dance.

Develop Comprehension

pages 6–7

RETELL

- *Retell what is happening on these pages.* (Alicia sees flags flying.)

pages 8–9

SUMMARIZE

Think Aloud What important things have happened so far? Alicia and her mom are taking a walk. She hears music, sees flags, and has taxis stop for her.

pages 10–11

MAKE INFERENCES

- *Look at what the airplane is writing. What is Alicia **celebrating** today?* (It is Alicia's birthday. We can tell because the airplane is writing *Happy Birthday*.)

May the flags all fly for you.

Taxicabs all stop for you.

Airplanes write in the sky for you.

HAPPY BIRTHDAY

Comprehension

Summarize

- (pages 8–9) Let me think about what important things have happened so far. Alicia and her mother have left the house to go somewhere. Alicia hears salsa music and starts to dance.

Retell

- (pages 8–9) What has happened in the story? Alicia and her mom are taking a walk. She hears music, sees flags, and has taxis stop for her.

Story Words

(page 9) taxicabs   (page 14) pigeons

About the Author: Meg Starr

Meg Starr has been a day care teacher for more than twenty years. She wrote this book based on a salsa song, "Alicia's Happy Day," by Pepe Castillo.

**Trade Book
Inside Back Cover**

ELL

pp. 6–7
flags: Point to the flag and say the word. Ask children to point to the U.S. flag.

pp. 8–9
taxicab, stop: Point to the taxicab on pages 8–9 and ask children to repeat the word after you. Then ask children to line up and walk toward you. Put up your hand up and say: *Stop.* Play "Stop or Go" a few times and have children say *stop* when they stop moving.

pp. 10–11
sky: Draw a simple landscape on the board. Show the ground and the sky. Ask children to point to the sky. Have them write their names in the sky.

Text Evidence

Retell

Explain Remind children that when they answer a question, they must support their answer with text evidence.

Discuss Have children look at and listen to pages 12–17. Ask them to retell what happened in the middle of this story. (more good things happen) Have children use the illustrations to help them.

ELL

pp. 12–13
walk signs: Make a *walk* and a *don't walk* sign on paper. Hold up the *walk* sign and demonstrate walking. Contrast with *don't walk*. Then lead children in a walk around the classroom. Use the signs to direct the walk.

pp. 14–15
pigeon: Point to the pigeon on page 14. Say, *This is a pigeon,* and act out flapping your wings and flying. Have children repeat.

pp. 16–17
decorate: Draw a plain cake on the board. Say *cake*. Then add rosettes and candles to the cake and say: *I decorate the cake.* Ask children to help decorate the cake. *What are you doing?*

pp. 18–19
ribbon of peel: Point out the orange peel in the illustration. Explain that it resembles the shape of a ribbon that would appear on a present.

Develop Comprehension

pages 12–13

IDENTIFY CHARACTER

- *How do you think Alicia feels? Why do you think that?* (Possible answer: She feels happy. We can tell because she is smiling.)

pages 14–15

 MAIN IDEA AND DETAILS

- *What is the squirrel giving Alicia?* (an acorn) *What does the acorn have on it?* (a bow) *Why is the squirrel giving Alicia a present?* (It is her birthday.)

pages 16–17

RETELL

- *What is happening now?* (Children are drawing a birthday cake because it is Alicia's birthday.)

pages 18–19

SUMMARIZE

- *What is happening in the story?* (Possible answer: Alicia is walking in her neighborhood and people are working at their **jobs**, doing nice things for her because it is her birthday.)

pages 20–21

REREAD

Think Aloud There are some words I don't understand: *Helado de Coco.* The icey man is handing Alicia an ice cream. Maybe *coco* means "coconut." Maybe *helado* means "ice cream."

pages 22–23

CULTURAL PERSPECTIVES

■ *Alicia calls her mother and father Mammi and Poppi. She calls her aunt Titi. What special names do you call your parents and relatives?*

pages 24–25

SUMMARIZE

■ *What were the important events in the story?* (Alicia and her mother get ice cream, see a plane writing, and meet friends. They go to a party for Alicia. It is her birthday!)

page 26

AUTHOR'S PURPOSE

Think Aloud The author, Meg Starr, was inspired by the music for a song composed by Pepe Castillo, a salsa musician. She wrote this book to go along with Mr. Castillo's music.

Activity Book, pages 25–26
Practice Book, page 134

Retelling Rubric

4 Excellent
Retells the selection without prompting, in sequence, and using supporting details. Clearly describes the setting, main characters, and complete plot.

3 Good
Retells the selection with little guidance, in sequence, and using some details. Generally describes the setting, main characters, and plot.

2 Fair
Retells the selection with some guidance, mostly in sequence, and using limited details. Partially describes the setting, main characters, and plot.

1 Unsatisfactory
Retells the selection only when prompted, out of sequence, and using limited details. Does not describe the main characters or plot.

Respond to Literature

TALK ABOUT IT Ask children to talk about the words and illustrations that they liked. Have them refer to the **Trade Book** *Alicia's Happy Day* as they answer the questions.

- *What kind of music did Alicia want to hear?* (salsa) LOCATE

- *What were three wishes for Alicia's day?* (Possible answer: Three wishes were that flags would fly for her, airplanes would write sky messages for her, and her parents would hug her.) CONNECT

- *What was the main idea of this story?* (There were many good wishes for Alicia for her birthday.) COMBINE

Retell

Retelling Cards

GUIDED RETELLING
Remind children that as they listened to *Alicia's Happy Day*, they used the words and illustrations to understand the story. Now they will use the pictures on these cards to retell the story.

- Display **Retelling Card 1**. Based on children's abilities, use either the Guided, Modeled, or ELL prompts. The Modeled prompts contain support for English Language Learners based on levels of language acquisition.

- Repeat the procedure with the rest of the Retelling Cards, using the prompts to guide children's retelling.

- Discuss the story. *Who were some of the workers in Alicia's neighborhood? What **jobs** did they do? Where were they?*

- Have children act out their favorite parts of the story. Play salsa music. *How does the music remind you of the story? How is the music similar to other songs you listen to? How is it different?*

Fluency: Echo-Read

MODEL Reread pages 7–11, emphasizing the rhythm of the text. Then reread pages 12–17 and have children echo-read.

Quick Check

Can children summarize and retell to help understand a story?

Vocabulary

Sequence Words

Chant the following jingle:

First, *I say, "Good night."*

Next, *Mom says, "Sleep tight."*

Last, *I turn out the light.*

- Repeat each line and ask children to name the word that tells the order in which things happen.

- Have children follow a three-part set of directions: First, *stand up.* Next, *put your arms up.* Last, *touch your head.*

NAME SEQUENCE WORDS Give children three small classroom items, such as blocks, counting cubes, or markers. Have them take turns lining the items in a row and naming which is *first*, *next*, and *last*.

Story Words: *twirly-swirly, ribbon*

- Display and read pages 2–3 of *Alicia's Happy Day*. Ask children what they think *twirly-swirly* means. Explain that *twirl* and *swirl* mean to spin around in a circle. *I think a twirly-swirly day is one that makes you want to spin and dance. It might be a **celebration** day. Do you twirl and swirl when you celebrate? Why?*

- Display and read pages 18–19 of *Alicia's Happy Day*. Point out the picture of the orange peel and the written word *ribbon*. Explain that the orange peel looks like a ribbon. *A ribbon is a narrow piece of material. What can you tie with a ribbon?*

TIME TO MOVE!

Give children long pieces of ribbon. Say *swirl* and have children move just the ribbon in the air. Say *twirl* and have children move their bodies and the ribbons around. Ask them to name the item that is twirling or swirling. For example: *I twirl. The ribbon swirls.*

Objectives

- Identify and use words that name sequences
- Understand story words *twirly-swirly, ribbon*

Materials

- Read-Aloud Trade Book: *Alicia's Happy Day*

Digital Learning

 For children who need additional language support and oral vocabulary development, use the activities found at **www.macmillanmh.com**.

ELL

Reinforce Meaning Display the **Trade Book** *Alicia's Happy Day*. Ask children to show you the first, next, and last page of the story, as they say: *This is the first page. This is the next page. This is the last page.* Repeat with other books.

Objectives

- Blend /d/, /h/, /r/, /f/ sounds in words to form one-syllable words
- Identify initial /d/*d*, /h/*h*, /r/*r*, and /f/*f*
- Blend sounds in words with the *-ad* phonogram

Materials

- **Puppet**
- **Word-Building Cards**
- pocket chart

Phonemic Awareness

✔ Phoneme Blending

Model

Use the **Puppet** to model how to blend the sounds in the word *ran*.

Repeat the routine with *him*.

Happy is going to say the sounds in a word. Listen to Happy as he says each sound: /r/ /a/ /n/. Happy can blend these sounds together: /rrraaannn/, *ran*. Say the sounds with Happy: /r/ /a/ /n/, /rrraaannn/. Now say the word with Happy: *ran*.

Guided Practice/Practice

Say the sounds. Children blend the sounds to form words. Guide practice with the first word, using the same routine.

Happy is going to say the sounds in a word. Listen to Happy as he says each sound. You will repeat the sounds, then blend them.

/d/ /a/ /n/	/h/ /i/ /d/	/r/ /o/ /d/
/d/ /a/ /d/	/h/ /a/ /f/	/r/ /a/ /k/

Phonics

✔ Review

d h r f

Model

Display **Word-Building Card** *d*.

Repeat the routine for the letters *h, r, f*.

This is the letter *d*. The letter *d* stands for /d/. What is the letter? What sound does it stand for?

Say the word. Write the letter *d*.

Repeat with *hippo, rose, fire*.

Listen as I say a word: *dolphin. Dolphin* has /d/ at the beginning. The letter *d* stands for the /d/ sound at the beginning of *dolphin*. I'll write *d*.

Guided Practice/Practice

Say each word.

dog   fish   home   ride

Children write the letter that stands for the initial sound. Guide practice with the first word.

hat   dive   rope   face

Build Fluency: Sound-Spellings

 Display the following **Word-Building Cards**: *a, c, d, f, h, i, m, n, o, p, r, s, t.* Have children chorally say each sound. Repeat and vary the pace.

 # Blend with –*ad*

Model

Place Word-Building Card *h* in the pocket chart.

This is the letter *h*. The letter *h* stands for the /h/ sound. Say /h/.

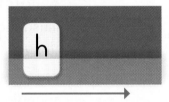

Place the letters *ad* in the pocket chart, leaving space after the *h*.

These are the letters *a* and *d*. The letters *a* and *d* stand for the sounds /a/ and /d/. Let's blend these two sounds together: /aaad/.

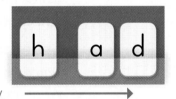

Place the letters *ad* closer to the letter *h*. Move your hand from left to right.

Repeat the routine with *mad*.

The beginning sound in the word is /h/, and the sound of the rest of the word is /ad/. Let's blend the beginning sound and the rest of the word together: /haaad/, *had*.

Guided Practice/Practice

Children blend the onset and rime in other words that end with -*ad*. Guide practice with the word *sad*, using the routine.

sad   had   pad

dad   mad   fad

What do you notice about the words *had, sad, fad, pad, dad, mad*? (They end with the letters *ad*; they end with the /ad/ sound; they rhyme.)

Objectives

- Read decodable words with /d/d, /r/r, /h/h
- Read the high-frequency words *for, you, are*
- Reread for fluency

Materials

- Decodable Reader: *Dad Can Pin It On*
- High-Frequency Word Cards: *a, for, is, are, you*

Decodable Text

For additional decodable passages, see pages 23–26 of the **Teacher's Resource Book**.

Decodable Reader

Read *Dad Can Pin It On*

REVIEW HIGH-FREQUENCY WORDS Display the **High-Frequency Word Cards** for **a**, **for**, **is**, **are**, and **you**. Review the words using the **Read/Spell/Write** routine.

Dad Can Pin It On

MODEL CONCEPTS ABOUT PRINT *I hold the book so the words on the cover are right side up. I read each sentence from left to right. I turn each page after I read it.*

PREDICT Ask children to say the title and describe the cover illustration. *Who are these people? What are they doing? What might this book be about?*

FIRST READ Turn to page 2. Have children point to each word, sounding out decodable words and saying the high-frequency words quickly. If children have difficulty, provide corrective feedback and continue to guide them page by page.

DEVELOP COMPREHENSION Ask the following: *What are Sam and Dad doing in the town?* (They are looking for a present for Mom.) *What happens when they get home?* (They give the present to Mom.)

SECOND READ Have partners reread the book together.

"It is a tan hat, Dad. Can it fit on Mom?"

2

"Not a tan hat, Sam."

3

"It is a fat cat, Dad. Mom can pat him!"

4

"Not a fat cat, Sam."

5

"Is it a red pin, Dad? It is a red pin for Mom."

6

"It is a pin, Sam! It is a red pin for me!"

7

"Dad, you can pin it on. Pin it on Mom!"

8

Decodable Reader

Writing

Interactive Writing: Sentences

REVIEW
Display and read aloud the lists that children created in the Shared Writing activity from the previous writing lesson.

WRITE
Today we will write sentences about Alicia's Happy Day.

Ask children to help you write the following sentence frames:

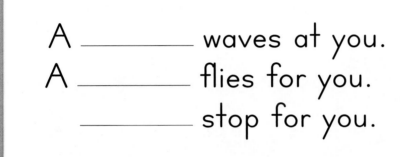

A ———— waves at you.
A ———— flies for you.
———— stop for you.

Read the sentences aloud as you track the print. Have children use the lists to suggest a word to complete the first sentence. Write the word in the frame. Ask children to help you by writing all of the letters they know. For example, have them write *ca* in *cabs*.

- Repeat with the second and third sentence frames.

- Read the completed sentences aloud with children as you track the print.

- Save the sentences to use in other writing activities this week.

- To extend the activity, have children dictate additional sentences by adding details by using the conjunction *because*: *Buses stop for you because it is your birthday.*

Write About It
Ask children to draw in their Writer's Notebooks a picture of something they see in their neighborhood. Have them write a label using the high-frequency words *are, for,* and *you.*

Objectives
- Write sentences
- Use letter knowledge to write letters in a word

Materials
- Shared Writing from Day 1

5-Day Writing

	Sentences
DAY 1	Shared: Lists
DAY 2	Interactive: Sentences
DAY 3	Independent: Prewrite and Draft Sentences
DAY 4	Independent: Revise and Edit Sentences
DAY 5	Independent: Publish and Present

ELL

Prewriting Planning Ask children to describe people and places they see in their neighborhoods. List responses and have children choose one to illustrate. Help them write a sentence to go with their drawings. Call attention to sentence punctuation.

Transitions That Teach

While children are packing up, have them tell about **jobs** people do.

DAY 3
At a Glance

WHOLE GROUP

Oral Language
- Build Robust Vocabulary
- Oral Vocabulary Cards: "The Elves and the Shoemakers"

✔ **Comprehension**
- Read "Is This the Job for You?"
- Text Features: Captions

✔ **High-Frequency Words**
- Review *are*, *for*, *you*

✔ **Phonemic Awareness**
- Phoneme Segmentation

✔ **Phonics**
- Cumulative Review
- Blend with *-at, -an*

Grammar
- Sentences

Writing
- Independent Writing: Prewrite and Draft Sentences

SMALL GROUP

- Differentiated Instruction, pages 1518–1543

Additional Vocabulary

To provide 15–20 minutes of additional vocabulary instruction, see Oral Vocabulary Cards 5-Day Plan. The pre- and posttests can be found in the **Teacher's Resource Book**, pages 224–225.

Oral Language

Talk About It ## Build Robust Vocabulary

BUILD BACKGROUND

Introduce the story "The Elves and the Shoemakers" using **Oral Vocabulary Card 1** and read the title aloud. *Some people do jobs that involve repairing or fixing things that are broken. Can you think of some jobs where the workers repair things?* Ask children to tell what they think is happening in each picture using complete sentences.

■ Read the story on the back of the cards. Pause at each oral vocabulary word and read the definition. Check children's understanding using the Use Illustrations, Compose Sentences, and Repeat Modeled Language prompts.

Oral Vocabulary Cards

Vocabulary Routine

Use the routine below to discuss the meaning of each word.

Define: When you **repair** something, you fix what is broken.
Example: Mom used glue to repair the broken picture frame.
Ask: What might you use to repair a broken toy?

Define: **Precise** means "very accurate and exact." Say the word with me.
Example: My friend gave me precise directions to her house.
Ask: When you cut something out, should you be precise or messy? Why?

Define: When you are **alert**, you pay attention to what is going on around you.
Example: The children stayed alert as they listened to the exciting story.
Ask: Why do you have to be alert when you cross the street?

SPIRAL REVIEW

■ Use the routine on Card 2 to review the words **job** and **celebration**.

■ Review last week's words: *admire, community, deliver, schedule, worker.*

Listen for Rhyme

IDENTIFY RHYME

Tell children that they will recite another rhyme. Play the rhyme and ask children to join in.

Discuss what the rhyme is about. *Have you ever gone to bed with your pants, socks, or shoes on? Why would someone do that?* Tell children that sometimes people who are very tired might fall asleep before they finish getting ready for bed. *Maybe John worked very hard and was not* **alert** *when he got ready for bed. What kind of job might John do that would make him feel very tired at the end of the day?*

Explain that the word *on* rhymes with *John* because they both end with the sounds /on/. Ask children to name other words that rhyme with *on*, such as *Ron* or *Don*. Replace *John* with one of the rhyming words. For example: *Diddle, diddle, dumpling, my son Ron.* Recite the rhyme with the new rhyming word.

Diddle, Diddle, Dumpling

Diddle, diddle, dumpling, my son John

Went to bed with his trousers on;

One shoe off and one shoe on;

Diddle, diddle, dumpling, my son John.

Objectives

- Discuss the theme
- Use oral vocabulary words: *alert, celebration, job, precise,* and *repair*
- Orally generate rhymes in response to spoken words

Materials

- Oral Vocabulary Cards: "The Elves and the Shoemakers"
- Listening Library Audio CD

Digital Learning

Rhyme on **Listening Library Audio CD**

Objectives

- Retell important facts
- Use photographs and captions to find information
- Identify the topic and details in expository text
- Discuss different community jobs
- Use a picture dictionary

Material

- Big Book of Explorations, Vol. 2: "Is This the Job for You?" pp. 9–12
- chart paper

Content Vocabulary

musician a person whose job is playing or singing music

architect a person whose job is working out the plans for bridges, houses, schools, and other buildings

Use a Picture Dictionary
Guide children to find each word in a picture dictionary.

Informational Text

Genre

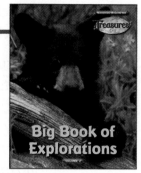

Big Book of Explorations

INFORMATIONAL TEXT: EXPOSITORY Tell children that this selection is **expository** text, a text that explains or gives information. Some expository text gives information using words and photographs. Tell children that sometimes photographs can give information more easily than words can.

READ "IS THIS THE JOB FOR YOU?"

- **Preview and Predict** Display the first page and read the title as you track the print. Point to the man on page 9. *This man is at work. He is doing a job in the community.* Turn the pages and point out the other photographs. *What will this photo essay be about? Which jobs will we learn about?*

- **Content Vocabulary** Introduce and discuss the vocabulary words.

- **Text Feature: Captions** *Captions tell readers more about what we see in photographs.* Point to the photo on page 9. *I can read the caption to find out what this man is doing. I can learn the name of his job. Read the caption. This man is a construction worker. A construction worker uses tools to build things. I can see that this construction worker is using tools to build a tall city building.*

CONTENT FOCUS

As you read page 10, point out that people earn money by doing their jobs. Ask children to use the information they learn from each photograph and caption to tell why each job is important to the community.

Point to the picture of the musicians. Explain that some musicians play instruments and some musicians sing. *What are these musicians doing?* Point to the photo of the architect. How are architects and construction workers similar? How are they different?

Read aloud page 11 and point to the veterinarian. *What is the name of this man's job?* (veterinarian) *What does a veterinarian do?* (takes care of animals) Point to the mail carrier. *What is the name of this woman's job?* (mail carrier) *How do mail carriers get around?* (Some drive; others walk.)

Help children identify the mixed-up jobs shown on page 12. Then have children tell which job they would like to do, explain why, and tell why that job is important to the community.

page 9

pages 10–11

page 12

Retell and Respond

- *Name the jobs we read about.*

- *Which jobs might you do if you liked to build things?*

- *What do veterinarians do? How do veterinarians help the community?*

- *What is the topic, or main idea, of this selection?*

Connect to Content

Social Studies: Which Job Is It?

- On chart paper, list the jobs discussed in the selection. Help children brainstorm other jobs that people do in the community. Add their ideas to the list. Ask children to suggest a picture to go with each job, and draw it on the chart. For example, draw a dog next to a veterinarian.

- Have children take turns choosing a job from the list. Tell them to give verbal clues about the job or to use pantomime and gestures until someone guesses it.

Objective

- Read the high-frequency words *are, for, you*

Materials

- High-Frequency Word Cards: *The, the, Are, are, for, you, Is, is*
- pocket chart
- Photo Cards: *baby, banana, box, carrots, vegetables*
- 2 index cards with: period mark, question mark
- large envelopes
- Activity Book, pp. 27–28
- Practice Book, pp. 135–136

High-Frequency Words

✔ *are, for, you*

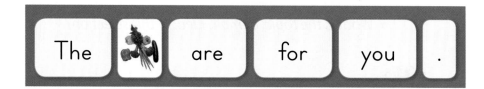

REVIEW Display the **High-Frequency Word Card** for **are**. Review the word using the **Read/Spell/Write** routine.

Repeat the routine for the words **for** and **you**.

APPLY Build sentences in the pocket chart using High-Frequency Word Cards and **Photo Cards**. Read each sentence aloud, then have children chorally read it as you track the print with your finger. Use the sentence below and the following: *Are the carrots for you? Is the box for you? Is the banana for the baby?*

| The | | are | for | you | . |

READ FOR FLUENCY Chorally read the Take-Home Book with children. Then have them reread the book to review high-frequency words and build fluency.

Quick Check

Can children read the words *are, for,* and *you*?

During **Small Group Instruction**

If No → **Approaching Level** Provide additional practice with high-frequency words, page 1528.

If Yes → **On Level** Children are ready to read the Take-Home Book.

Beyond Level Children are ready to read the Take-Home Book.

Activity Book, pages 27–28
Practice Book, pages 135–136

TIME TO MOVE!

Deliver the mail! Put paper, game chips, or Word-Building Cards in a few envelopes. Have a child give an envelope to a classmate and say: *These are for you.* The receiver opens the envelope and says: *These are for me.* Continue until each child has participated.

Phonemic Awareness

Phoneme Segmentation

Model

Use the **Puppet** to say the sounds in a word.

I will say a word, and Happy will say the sounds in the word. The word is *hid*. Listen to Happy say the sounds in *hid*: /h/ /i/ /d/. There are three sounds. Let's tap out the sounds in *hid* as we say them with Happy: /h/ /i/ /d/. What are the sounds? What is the word?

Repeat with *hat*.

Guided Practice/Practice

Children segment words into sounds as they tap them out. Guide practice with the first two words.

Happy will say a word. Say the sounds in the word as you tap them out. Then say the word.

did, /d/ /i/ /d/   *hip*, /h/ /i/ /p/

fin, /f/ /i/ /n/   *top*, /t/ /o/ /p/

rod, /r/ /o/ /d/   *can*, /k/ /a/ /n/

Objective

• Segment one-syllable words into two to three phonemes

Materials

• Puppet

Objectives

- Review sound-spellings for /k/c, /f/f, /n/n, /p/p, /t/t
- Blend sounds in words with the -an and -at phonograms

Materials

- Teaching Chart 1
- Word-Building Cards
- Word-Building Cards; Teacher's Resource Book, pp. 95–102
- pocket chart

Phonics

✓ Review

Model

Display "The Alphabet." Point to the letter *c*.	This is the letter *c*. It stands for /k/ at the beginning of *cat*. What is the letter? What sound does it stand for?
Repeat for /f/f, /n/n, /p/p, /t/t.	

Listen as I say a word: cap. Cap *begins with /k/. The letter* c *stands for the /k/ sound. I will hold up the* **Word-Building Card** *for* c. *Repeat for* find. *Have children identify the picture of the alphabet that begins with each sound.*

Teaching Chart 1

Guided Practice/Practice

Distribute copies of Word-Building Cards.	Listen as I say a word. Tell what sound is at the beginning of the word and what letter stands for that sound.

Say a word. Children hold up the letter that stands for the initial sound. Guide practice with the first word.

pet	not	talk
count	fun	next
poke	call	name
tell	pick	fix

Build Fluency: Sound-Spellings

Display the following Word-Building Cards: *a, c, d, f, h, i, m, n, o, p, r, s, t.* Have children chorally say each sound. Repeat and vary the pace.

Blend with *-at, -an*

Model

Place **Word-Building Card** *c* in the pocket chart.

This letter is *c*. It stands for /k/. Say /k/.

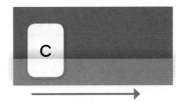

Place the letters *at* in the pocket chart, leaving space after the *c*. Point to the letters *at*.

These are the letters *a* and *t*. The letters *a* and *t* stand for /a/ and /t/. Let's blend these two sounds together: /aaat/.

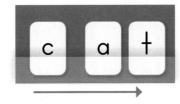

Place the letters *at* next to the letter *c*. Move your hand from left to right below the letters.

Repeat the routine with *pat*.

The beginning sound in the word is /k/, and the sound of the rest of the word is /at/. Let's blend the beginning sound and the rest of the word together: /kaaat/, *cat*.

Guided Practice/Practice

Children blend the onset and rime in other words that end with *-at* or *-an*. Guide practice with the words *sat* and *mat*, using the routine. Point out that by changing the first letter of each word, a new word is formed.

sat	mat	fat	hat	cat	pat
can	fan	man	pan	tan	ran

What do you notice about the words *cat, pat, sat, mat, fat,* and *hat*? (They end with the letters *at*; they end with the /at/ sounds; they rhyme. New words can be formed when letters are changed.)

What do you notice about the words *can, fan, man, pan, tan,* and *ran*? (They end with the letters *an*; they end with the /an/ sounds; they rhyme.)

ELL

Build Vocabulary Review the meaning of words in the Guided Practice. Model saying each word and ask children to repeat. Have them explain what each word means by pointing to pictures or real objects, acting out, or paraphrasing.

Objective

- Use complete simple sentences
- Understand and use prepositional phrases when speaking

Materials

- Big Book of Explorations, Vol. 2: "Is This the Job for You?" pp. 9–12
- Photo Cards: *ambulance, anchor, apple, baby, barn, box, bus, camera, comb, dime, dog, envelope, guitar, hammer, helicopter, house, jet, ladder, mop, nail, newspaper, paint, pen, phone, piano, pie, pizza, plate, rake, ring, rose, sandwich, saw, shirt, shoe, thermometer, train, vegetables, violin, watch, whistle, write, yarn, zoo*

ELL

Basic and Academic Vocabulary Display Photo Cards that show tools workers use in their jobs, such as *hammer, ladder, piano,* and *thermometer.* Pair English Language Learners with fluent speakers and have partners make up sentences about workers who use the pictured tools. For example: *A firefighter uses a ladder.* Write partners' sentences, read them chorally, and say: *Show me how this is a complete sentence.*

Grammar

Sentences

MODEL Remind children that a sentence tells a complete thought. Explain that a sentence has two parts: a naming part that tells *who* and a telling part that tells *what.*

■ Turn to pages 10–12 of the expository selection "Is This the Job for You?" and make up sentences about the photographs. For example: *The people play instruments in the band. The vet takes care of a sick dog.* Point out that these are sentences because they tell *who* and *what* people do at their **jobs**. Explain that *in the band* in the sentence *The people play instruments in the band* tells more about what or where something is happening.

■ Ask two children to make up a sentence about their jobs in the classroom. For example: *Shonice and Roberto pass out pencils.* Tell children that the naming part of the sentence is *Shonice and Roberto*; the telling part of the sentence is *pass out pencils.* Ask children to use complete sentences to tell about jobs other classmates have.

PRACTICE Show the **Photo Card** for *ambulance.* Model saying a sentence about a job related to the pictured item. *The card shows a picture of an ambulance. What kind of workers use ambulances? I know that a driver steers an ambulance to get to someone in need of medical help. Ambulances have sirens and move very fast. I can make a sentence about the ambulance driver:* The ambulance driver turned on the siren. *Does my sentence tell a complete thought? How do you know?*

■ Distribute Photo Cards and help children name their cards. Ask each child to tell a complete sentence about his or her card. If they have trouble, ask them to name the card. Have them describe how a worker might use the pictured item. Repeat the job title and what the worker would do with the pictured object, and then ask the child to create a sentence.

■ After each sentence, ask children to identify the naming part and the telling part. *Is this a complete sentence? Why?*

Writing

Independent Writing: Sentences

Display the sentences from the Interactive Writing activity.

BRAINSTORM

WRITING TRAIT: WORD CHOICE Explain that children will write about their own neighborhoods. First they need to think about words that they want to use.

Think Aloud Good writers carefully choose the right words to say what they want to say. When I think about my neighborhood, I think of the birds. They fly into the sky. I think the best word to describe how they fly is *soar*.

Ask children to think about what the people and things in their neighborhood do. List their ideas to use as a reference.

PREWRITE

Write the following sentence frame and read it aloud:

_____ for me.

Complete the sentence frame by writing the words *Birds soar*. Chorally read the completed sentence frame.

Ask children to select someone or something in their neighborhood to write about.

DRAFT

■ Have children write the sentence frame. Tell them to choose a descriptive or action word and something from the list to complete the sentence.

■ Have children illustrate their sentences.

■ Collect and save children's work to use tomorrow.

Write About It

Ask children to draw a picture of someone working in a neighborhood store. Have them label the picture.

Objectives

- Plan a first draft
- Begin to use writing trait: word choice
- Use complete simple sentences
- Use letter knowledge to write letters in a word

Materials

- Interactive Writing sentences from Day 2

5-Day Writing	
Sentences	
DAY 1	Shared: Lists
DAY 2	Interactive: Sentences
DAY 3	Independent: Prewrite and Draft Sentences
DAY 4	Independent: Revise and Edit Sentences
DAY 5	Independent: Publish and Present

ELL

Use New Language
Ask children to help you write a list of neighborhood stores that they go to with their families. Talk about the workers they meet there and list them next to the names of the stores. Use the listed words in sentences.

Transitions That Teach

While in line, have children tell about times they are very **alert**.

WHOLE GROUP

Oral Language
- Build Robust Vocabulary

Comprehension ✓
- Read Aloud: "Why the Moon Is in the Sky"

Vocabulary
- Words That Compare
- Story Words: *twirly-swirly, ribbon*

Phonemic Awareness ✓
- Phoneme Blending

Phonics ✓
- Cumulative Review
- Blend with *-ap, -am*
- Decodable Reader: *Dad Can Pin It On*

Writing
- Independent Writing: Revise and Edit Sentences

SMALL GROUP

- Differentiated Instruction, pages 1518–1543

Oral Language

 Talk About It

Build Robust Vocabulary

JOB NAMES

Discuss how names of workers are often clues to the kinds of work they do. *Some workers' names tell us the* **jobs** *they do. I am a teacher. What is my job? Does my job's name give you a clue?*

CREATE A CHART

Draw a two-column chart, or use **Teaching Chart G3**. Label the columns as shown. Read the titles together as you track the print.

Think Aloud I am a teacher, so I will write the word *teacher* under *Worker*. A teacher teaches in a school. So I will write the words *teaches in a school* under *What the Worker Does*.

Have children name other workers whose names end with *-er*. Ask children to tell what each worker does, using the name as a clue. *What* **precisely** *does the worker do? Why do they have to be* **alert**? Guide children to respond in complete sentences. Add their ideas to the chart as you read and track the print.

Worker	What the Worker Does
teacher	teaches in a school
builder	builds roads, bridges, or buildings
baker	bakes bread, cookies, cakes
writer	writes stories or articles
bus driver	drives people in a bus
drummer	plays drums in a band

ELL   ENGLISH LANGUAGE LEARNERS

Beginning	Intermediate	Advanced
Confirm Understanding Display **Photo Cards** of workers and identify them. For example: *This is a nurse. A nurse takes care of people who are sick. What does a nurse do?* (takes care of people who are sick) Continue with other cards.	**Enhance Understanding** Pair children and have partners tell each other riddles about the work they do. Provide an example: *I build homes and schools. Do you know what am I?* (You are a builder.)	**Express Opinions** Work with children to add other jobs to the chart. Then have children say which job they think is the best and why. Prompt them to elaborate on their responses.

Listen for Alliteration

IDENTIFY ALLITERATION

Remind children that sometimes, a group of words begin with the same sound. For example, in *A baby boy bounces the ball*, most of the words begin with the /b/ sound.

WORKER RHYME

Tell children that they will recite "One Man Went to Mow," the rhyme they learned about workers. Play the rhyme and have children join in.

Ask children to name and describe neighborhood workers they have learned about. *What kind of worker is described in the rhyme?* (gardener, landscaper) *Is this job something that is done at school or in the neighborhood?*

Explain that more workers join the man and dog in the rhyme. *How will adding two men to the job change the way the meadow is mowed?* (They will mow the meadow faster. They will take turns.)

Which words in "One Man Went to Mow" begin with the same sound? (*mow, meadow, man, men*) Let's think of more words that begin with the /m/ sound to add. For example, *Many men moved fast to mow the meadow.* Have children repeat this line, emphasizing the /m/ sound.

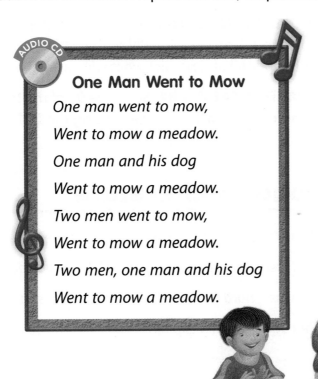

One Man Went to Mow

One man went to mow,

Went to mow a meadow.

One man and his dog

Went to mow a meadow.

Two men went to mow,

Went to mow a meadow.

Two men, one man and his dog

Went to mow a meadow.

Objectives

- Discuss the theme
- Associate jobs with the names of workers
- Contribute ideas for a chart
- Use oral vocabulary words *alert, celebration, job, precise,* and *repair*
- Identify alliteration

Materials

- Graphic Organizer; Teaching Chart G3

Oral Vocabulary

Have children use each word in a sentence about this week's stories.

alert   celebration
job   precise
repair

Review Work with children to review last week's words. *Describe things you can do in your* community. *Name someone you* admire *and explain why you* admire *them. Name some* workers *who* deliver *things. What would happen if a bus driver didn't follow her* schedule?

admire   community
deliver   schedule
worker

Digital Learning

Rhyme on **Listening Library Audio CD**

Objective

- Listen and respond to a folktale

Materials

- Read-Aloud Anthology: "Why the Moon Is in the Sky," pp. 93–96

ELL

Preview Vocabulary Draw or display a picture of a spider. Number the spider's legs and count them. Then explain that the main character in the folktale is a spider who has six sons. As children listen to the story, point out the number by which each son is referred to.

Readers Theater

BUILDING LISTENING AND SPEAKING SKILLS
Distribute copies of "The Three Little Pigs," Read-Aloud Anthology pages 169–184. Have children practice performing the play throughout the unit. Assign parts and have children present the play or perform it as a dramatic reading at the end of the unit.

Interactive
Read Aloud

Listening Comprehension

GENRE: LITERARY TEXT/FOLKTALE
Tell children that a **folktale** is a story that has been told over and over again for a very long time.

CULTURAL PERSPECTIVES
Explain that "Why the Moon Is in the Sky" is a folktale from Ghana, a country in West Africa. It was told by the Ashanti people to explain how the moon got in the sky. Tell children that there are many Ashanti folktales about a character named Anansi the Spider.

Read Aloud

READ "WHY THE MOON IS IN THE SKY"

- **MODEL ASKING QUESTIONS TO HELP SUMMARIZE** Use the Think Alouds provided at point of use in the folktale.

- **MODEL FLUENT READING** Read aloud the folktale with fluent expression. Stop occasionally so that children can summarize what has happened and predict what will happen next.

- **EXPAND VOCABULARY** See page 93 of the **Read-Aloud Anthology** to teach new words using the **Define/Example/Ask** routine.

Respond to Literature

TALK ABOUT IT Ask children to discuss the big idea of this folktale.

- *What were Anansi's six sons called? What **job** could each son do?*

- *Why was it hard for Anansi to choose which son helped the most?*

- *What does the story explain?*

Write About It

Ask children to draw their favorite character in the story and use descriptive and action words to write about what the character does.

Vocabulary

Words That Compare

REVIEW WORDS THAT COMPARE

I am going to read a story that uses words that compare. When you hear a word that compares two or more things, hold up your hand.

Read the following story:

> *Mark went to the store to buy clothes with his dad. They looked at the shirts. "Which one do you like?" asked his dad. Mark said, "I like the small red one." "I think the smaller blue one is better," said his dad. But only the smallest green one fit Mark. So they bought it. Then they looked at the mittens. "Which ones do you like?" asked his dad. Mark said, "I like the big red ones." "I think the bigger blue ones are better," said his dad. But only the biggest green ones fit Mark. So they bought them.*

Hold up pictures of the same item in different sizes. Encourage children to place the pictured items into categories of "big, bigger, biggest" or "small, smaller, smallest."

Story Words: *twirly-swirly, ribbon*

Display and read pages 2–3 of *Alicia's Happy Day*. Remind children that *twirl* and *swirl* mean to spin around in a circle. Tell children to think of things that might be described as twirly-swirly, such as leaves falling, people dancing at a **celebration**, or merry-go-rounds.

Display and read pages 14–15 of *Alicia's Happy Day*. Point out the ribbon on the acorn that the squirrel is giving Alicia on page 15. *Where have you seen ribbons?*

TIME TO MOVE!

Ask children to take a *big* step. Then have them take a *bigger* step, and then the *biggest* step they can. Then have children take a *small* step, a *smaller* step, and the *smallest* step they can. Have children say the step size as they make the movement.

Objectives

- Use words that compare
- Identify and sort pictures of objects into conceptual categories
- Review story words *twirly-swirly, ribbon*

Materials

- Read-Aloud Trade Book: *Alicia's Happy Day*
- pictures of the same item in different sizes

ELL

Reinforce Meaning Draw a big square, a bigger square, and the biggest square. Identify them by pointing to each and saying *big, bigger, biggest*. Then say each comparing word randomly and have children point to the correct square and repeat the word. Next, draw a small circle, a smaller circle, and the smallest circle and repeat the activity.

Objectives

- Blend sounds to form one-syllable words
- Review /a/a, /k/c, /d/d, /f/f, /h/h, /m/m, /n/n, /p/p, /r/r, /t/t
- Blend sounds in words with -ap, -am phonograms
- Review sound-spellings for /h/h, /d/d, /r/r, /n/n, /p/p, /m/m, /a/a

Materials

- Word-Building Cards
- Puppet
- Photo Cards: *alligator, car, dog, farm, horse, mouse, nose, penguin, rabbit, tiger*
- pocket chart
- Activity Book, pp. 29–30
- Practice Book, pp. 137–138

Phonemic Awareness

✔ Phoneme Blending

Model

Use the **Puppet** to model how to blend *ride*.

Repeat with *hid*.

Listen to Happy as he says the sounds in a word: /r/ /ī/ /d/. Listen to Happy again: /r/ /ī/ /d/. Now listen to Happy put those sounds together: *ride*.

Say the sounds with Happy: /r/ /ī/ /d/. Now say the word: *ride*.

Guided Practice/Practice

Repeat the routine with these words. Guide practice with the first word.

/s/ /i/ /k/, *sick*	/h/ /ō/ /m/, *home*
/p/ /a/ /s/, *pass*	/s/ /a/ /d/, *sad*
/m/ /ē/ /t/, *meet*	/d/ /o/ /t/, *dot*

Phonics

✔ Review

Model

Place **Word-Building Cards** *a, c, d, f, h, m, n, p, r, t* in the pocket chart.

Let's say the names of these letters together.

Show the **Photo Card** for *penguin*.

Repeat with *horse*.

This is a picture of a *penguin*. The word begins with /p/. The letter *p* stands for /p/. I will place the penguin next to *p*.

Guided Practice/Practice

Display the Photo Cards one at a time. Have children say the picture name and match it with the initial letter. Guide practice with *tiger*.

Say the picture name. What letter stands for the beginning sound? Place the picture next to the letter.

Build Fluency: Sound-Spellings

SPIRAL REVIEW Display the following **Word-Building Cards**: *a, c, d, f, h, i, m, n, o, p, r, s, t*. Have children chorally say each sound. Repeat and vary the pace.

✔ Blend with *-ap, -am*

Model

Place Word-Building Card *m* in the pocket chart.

This is the letter *m*. It stands for the /m/ sound. Say /m/.

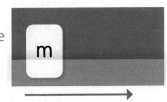

Place the letters *ap* in the pocket chart, leaving space after the *m*. Point to the letters *ap*.

These are the letters *a* and *p*. The letters *a* and *p* stand for /a/ and /p/. Let's blend these two sounds together: /aaap/.

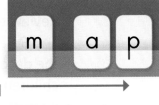

Place the letters *ap* next to the letter *m*. Move your hand below the letters.

Repeat the routine with *sap*.

Listen as I blend the beginning /m/ sound and the rest of the word /ap/: /mmmaaap/, *map*. Now you say it: /mmmaaap/, *map*.

Guided Practice/Practice

Children blend the onset and rime in other words that end with *-ap* and *-am*. Guide practice with the words *nap* and *Sam*, using the routine.

nap   cap   tap   rap
Sam   ham   Pam   dam

What is the same about the words *rap, cap, nap, tap*? (They end with the letters *-ap*; they rhyme.)

What is the same about the words *Sam, ham, Pam, dam*? (They end with the letters *-am*, and they rhyme.)

Corrective Feedback

Blending: Sound Error Model the sound that children missed, then have them repeat the sound. For example, for the word *map*, say: *My turn.* Tap under the letter *p* in the word *map* and say: *Sound? What's the sound?* Then return to the beginning of the word. Say: *Let's start over.* Blend the word with children again.

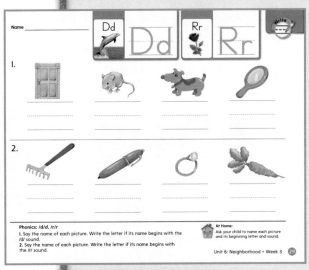

Activity Book, pages 29–30
Practice Book, pages 137–138

Objectives

- Read decodable words with /d/d, /r/r, /h/h
- Read the high-frequency words *for, you, are*
- Reread for fluency

Materials

- Decodable Reader: *Dad Can Pin It On*
- High-Frequency Word Cards: *a, for, is, are, you*
- Sound-Spelling Cards: *Dolphin, Hippo, Rose*

Decodable Text

For additional decodable passages, see pages 23–26 of the **Teacher's Resource Book**.

Decodable Reader

Read *Dad Can Pin It On*

REVIEW Review this week's high-frequency words and phonics skills using the word lists on the inside back cover of *Dad Can Pin It On*.

Dad Can Pin It On

Review the high-frequency words **for**, **is**, **are**, **you**, and **a** using the **Read/Spell/Write** routine. Then have children chorally read the high-frequency word list.

Review the phonics skills /d/d, /h/h, and /r/r using the *Dolphin, Hippo,* and *Rose* **Sound-Spelling Cards**. Then have children chorally read the decodable word list. Model blending as needed and take note of children who struggle while reading these words. Provide additional instruction and practice during Small Group time.

MODEL CONCEPTS ABOUT PRINT Guide children to follow along. *Open the book by turning the cover to see the title page. Then turn each page as you read it, starting with the first page and ending with the last page. Now read the book.*

REREAD FOR FLUENCY Have children reread the book with a partner. Circulate and listen in, providing corrective feedback as needed. Then have children reread the book independently.

"It is a tan hat, Dad. Can it fit on Mom?"
2

"Not a tan hat, Sam."
3

"It is a fat cat, Dad. Mom can pat him!"
4

"Not a fat cat, Sam."
5

"Is it a red pin, Dad? It is a red pin for Mom."
6

"It is a pin, Sam! It is a red pin for me!"
7

"Dad, you can pin it on. Pin it on Mom!"
8

Decodable Reader

Writing

Independent Writing: Sentences

REVISE AND EDIT

Distribute children's sentences from Day 3. Have children reread them and check for the following:

- Does my sentence tell about something or someone I see in my neighborhood?

- Did I add any details to best say what I wanted?

- Did I begin my sentence with a capital letter and end it with a period?

- Did I draw a picture of someone or something in my neighborhood?

PARTNERS

Circulate and help children as they review and self-correct their writing. Guide them to use their letter-sound knowledge to check spelling. Tell children to write their name at the top of their writing. Have children share their sentences with a partner.

Daniel

People smile for me.

Write About It

Ask children to draw and label a picture of a favorite part of their neighborhood.

Objectives

- Revise and edit sentences
- Use letter knowledge to write letters in a word
- Revise drafts by adding details
- Capitalize the first letter in a sentence

Materials

- children's writing from Day 3
- Writer's Checklist; Teacher's Resource Book, p. 205

5-Day Writing

Sentences	
DAY 1	Shared: Lists
DAY 2	Interactive: Sentences
DAY 3	Independent: Prewrite and Draft Sentences
DAY 4	Independent: Revise and Edit Sentences
DAY 5	Independent: Publish and Present

ELL

Prewriting Planning Ask children about places they like in their neighborhood, such as a park. Then help them complete the sentence *I like the _____ because _____.* Have children draw pictures to illustrate their sentences.

Transitions That Teach

Have children talk about the **precise** way they should be lined up.

Oral Language
- Build Robust Vocabulary

✔ **Comprehension**
- Strategy: Summarize
- Skill: Retell
- Read Across Texts

✔ **Vocabulary**
- Review High-Frequency Words
- Build Fluency
- Review Sequence Words

✔ **Phonemic Awareness**
- Phoneme Segmentation

✔ **Phonics**
- Build Fluency
- Read Words
- Dictation

Writing
- Independent Writing: Publish and Present

- Differentiated Instruction, pages 1518–1543

Review and Assess
Oral Language
Build Robust Vocabulary

REVIEW WORDS

Review this week's oral vocabulary words with children. Explain that all of the words will be used to discuss an anniversary party. Tell children that an *anniversary* is the recognition of a special date each year. For example, many people celebrate the anniversary of their marriage.

Use the following questions to check children's understanding:

- How might people **celebrate** their wedding anniversary?
- What might **alert** someone to a surprise party?
- How would a cook be **precise** when making an anniversary cake?
- What tools would people use to **repair** a party dress?
- What **jobs** do people do to prepare for a party?

REVIEW RHYMES ABOUT WORKING

Recite the rhyme "Diddle, Diddle, Dumpling" and ask children to join you. Have children describe jobs using complete sentences that would make them so tired they would fall asleep with their clothes on.

Then recite the rhyme "One Man Went to Mow" with children. Discuss the motions made while mowing. *Why would mowing a meadow make you tired?* Have children create actions to go with the rhyme and recite it again.

Review and Assess
Comprehension

 STRATEGY Summarize

REFLECT ON THE STRATEGY Tell children that thinking about the most important parts of the beginning, middle, and end of the story will help them understand and remember it.

 SKILL Retell

Direct children to review *Alicia's Happy Day* and "Why the Moon Is in the Sky" to help them retell the main events from each selection.

- In *Alicia's Happy Day, why was this day a happy* **celebration** *for Alicia? What people did Alicia meet? What did they say or do?*

- *How do Anansi's six sons help him when he is in trouble? What did Anansi do after that?*

Reading Across Texts

Create a Venn diagram like the one shown to compare the fiction story *Alicia's Happy Day* and the expository photo essay "Is This the Job for You?" Discuss the workers and different jobs shown in the selections.

Alicia's Happy Day
fiction story: did not really happen

people act like real people

illustrations

many different workers
people who care for others
people who work indoors and outdoors

Is This the Job for You?
expository selection

real people and things

photographs

Guide children to draw pictures or write sentences to compare the two selections. Have them add their work to their Writing Portfolios. Tell children to pick a fiction or expository selection to read for pleasure.

Objectives
- Review the strategy and skill
- Retell a main event from a story heard
- Compare and contrast characters, stories, and genres
- Listen and share information

Materials
- Read-Aloud Trade Book: *Alicia's Happy Day*
- Big Book of Explorations, Vol. 2: "Is This the Job for You?"
- Read-Aloud Anthology: "Why the Moon Is in the Sky," pp. 93–96
- Activity Book, p. 31

Activity Book, page 31

Objectives

- Review high-frequency words *are, for, you, is, play, have*
- Review sequence words
- Build fluency

Materials

- High-Frequency Word Cards; Teacher's Resource Book, pp. 103–110
- High-Frequency Word Cards: *are, for, you, have, is, play*
- sequence words written on index cards: *first, next, last*

Fluency

Connected Text Have children reread this week's **Decodable Reader** with a partner. Circulate, listen in, and note those children who need additional instruction and practice reading this week's decodable and sight words.

Decodable Reader
Dad Can Pin It On

Review and Assess
Vocabulary

 ## High-Frequency Words

Distribute copies of the following **High-Frequency Word Cards** to children: **are**, **for**, **you**, **is**, **play**, and **have**. Say: *When you hear the word on your card, stand and hold up your Word Card.*

- *Joe and I like to* play *with* you.
- You are *my friend.*
- *This* is *a surprise* for you.
- *I* have *a present* for you.
- *These books* are *good.*

Build Fluency: Word Automaticity

Display the High-Frequency Word Cards. Point quickly to each card, at random, and have children read the word as fast as they can.

are	for	have

Sequence Words

Make up sets of sequence word cards: *first, next,* and *last*. Divide the class into groups of three and give each group a set of cards. Help children read the cards. Then have each group line up according to their card. Have children switch cards and then reorder themselves.

Rapid Naming Display a set of the sequence word cards and have children name them quickly.

TIME TO MOVE!

Hide the High-Frequency Word Cards for *are, for,* and *you* around the room. Choose three children to find them. Say: *First, [name of child] will find the card* are. *Next, [name of second child] will find the card* for. *Last, [name of third child] will find the card* you. Give children hints to the cards' locations.

Review and Assess
Phonemic Awareness

Phoneme Segmentation

Guided Practice

Use the **Puppet**.

Repeat with *fun*.

> Happy will say a word. We will say the sounds that make up the word. Listen to Happy say the word: *rip. Rip* has three sounds: /r/ /i/ /p/. Say the word with me: *rip.* Now say the three sounds: /r/ /i/ /p/.

Practice

Use the Puppet to say the words. Children segment words into sounds. Guide practice with the first word.

> Happy will say a word. Say each sound in the word. Then say the word again.
>
> hop, /h/ /o/ /p/   coat, /k/ /ō/ /t/
>
> mad, /m/ /a/ /d/   in, /i/ /n/
>
> hide, /h/ /ī/ /d/   sick, /s/ /i/ /k/

Objective

• Segment words into phonemes

Materials

• Puppet

Objectives

- Use letter-sound relationships to decode words in text
- Write simple one-syllable words

Materials

- Word-Building Cards
- 6 index cards with: *The, cap, is, for, you,* period mark
- 6 index cards with: *Are, you, on, the, mat,* question mark
- Sound Box
- WorkBoard Sound Boxes; Teacher's Resource Book, p. 136
- Activity Book, p. 32

Activity Book, page 32

Review and Assess
Phonics

Build Fluency: Sound-Spellings

Rapid Naming Display the following **Word-Building Cards:** *a, c, d, f, h, i, m, n, o, p, r, s, t.* Have children chorally say each sound as quickly as they can.

✓ Read Words

Apply

Distribute the first set of cards. Have children stand in sequence.	Let's read the sentence together. The cap is for you.
Repeat, using the other set of cards.	Let's read the sentence together. Are you on the mat?

✓ Dictation

Dictate sounds for children to spell.	Listen as I say a sound. Repeat the sound, then write the letter that stands for the sound. /d/ /a/ /t/ /i/ /f/ /k/ /o/ /r/ /h/ /n/
Then dictate words for children to spell. Model for children how to use the **Sound Boxes** to segment the sounds in the words. Have them repeat.	Now let's write some words. I will say a word. I want you to repeat the word, then think about how many sounds are in the word. Use your Sound Boxes to count the sounds. Then write one letter for each sound you hear.
Write the letters and words on the board for children to self-correct.	hip hop pad sad dot rot rap hat ram rat fan can

Review and Assess
Writing

Independent Writing: Sentences

PUBLISH
Tell children that you will gather their pictures and sentences to create a class display in a section of the Big Question Board.

- Brainstorm ideas for a title, such as "In the Neighborhood."

- Create a banner for the display. Write the title on it.

- Add children's illustrated sentences to the display.

PRESENT
Ask children to take turns reading their sentences to the class and discussing what the picture shows. Have them discuss the **job** they wrote about. Guide them to speak in complete sentences.

LISTENING, SPEAKING, AND VIEWING
- Remind children to speak clearly and to be good listeners when a classmate is talking. Guide them to listen to each other, interact and respond appropriately, recognize when it is appropriate to speak, and ask appropriate questions.

PARTNERS

- Keep the neighborhood display up for everyone to view and enjoy. Have children write their own name at the top of their work and add a copy of it to their Writing Portfolios. Tell them to select favorite work samples to share with you and family members.

5-Day Writing

Sentences	
DAY 1	Shared: Lists
DAY 2	Interactive: Sentences
DAY 3	Independent: Prewrite and Draft Sentences
DAY 4	Independent: Revise and Edit Sentences
DAY 5	Independent: Publish and Present

Ricky

The pretzel man cooks for me.

Write About It
Ask children to draw a job they like to do at school and label it.

Transitions That Teach
While waiting for dismissal, have children tell about something that they **repair** when it is broken.

ON YOUR OWN

Draw a Celebration

Have children draw pictures to show a special celebration. Ask them to display and discuss their pictures.

ELL

Partners When partners make up sentences with the high-frequency words, pair English Language learners with children who are more proficient. Write their sentences, read them together, and point to the high-frequency words.

Approaching Level

Oral Language

Objective Preteach oral vocabulary: *job, celebration*
Materials • none

THEME WORDS: *job, celebration*

- Tell children the meanings for **job** and **celebration**. *A job is the work you do. A cab driver's* job *is to drive people from place to place. A celebration is a joyful gathering for a special occasion. We bought balloons for my sister's birthday* celebration.

- Discuss the words with children. *What neighborhood* job *would you like to do? What events or holidays do we* celebrate?

- Have children use the following sentence frames to generate complete oral sentences using the vocabulary words: _____ *is an important job because* _____. *The last celebration I went to was* _____.

High-Frequency Words

Objective Review high-frequency words
Materials • **High-Frequency Word Cards:** *are, for, you*

REVIEW WORDS: *are, for, you*

- Display the **High-Frequency Word Card** for **are**.

- **Read** Point to and say the word *are. This is the word* are. *We use it to say:* You are, we are, they are. *You are my friend.*

- **Spell** *The word* are *is spelled* a-r-e. Have children read and spell *are*.

- **Write** Finally, have children write the word *are*.

- Repeat the **Read/Spell/Write** routine for the words *for* and *you*.

PARTNERS

- Have children work with a partner to make up sentences using the words *are, for,* and *you*. Ask them to talk about things they might give each other at a celebration.

HIGH-FREQUENCY WORDS REVIEW

Tier 2

Display the High-Frequency Word Cards for words previously taught, one card at a time, and have children chorally read and spell the word. Mix and repeat. Note words children need to review.

Approaching Level

Phonemic Awareness

Objective Categorize initial sounds
Materials • **Puppet** • **Photo Cards:** *deer, doll, hand, horse, rake, rock*

✔ **PHONEME CATEGORIZATION**

Model

■ Have the **Puppet** name a **Photo Card** and then say another word that begins with the same sound. *This is a horse. Horse begins with /h/. I can think of another word that begins with /h/. House begins with /h/.*

■ Repeat with the Photo Cards *doll* and *rock*.

Guided Practice/Practice

■ Have the Puppet name the other Photo Cards. Have children say the initial sound and another word with that same initial sound.

Phonics

Objective Recognize words that begin with /h/h, /d/d, and /r/r
Materials • **Sound-Spelling Cards:** *Hippo, Dolphin, Rose* • **Word-Building Cards**
• **Photo Cards:** *hand, hammer, hat, horse, deer, doctor, dog, doll, door, rabbit, ring, rock, rose*

✔ **RETEACH /h/h, /d/d, /r/r**

Model

■ Display the Photo Card for *hand* and the *Hippo* **Sound-Spelling Card**. *This letter is* h. *It stands for the /h/ sound at the beginning of* hand. *I place an* h *card on the hand because* hand *begins with /h/. Say /h/. Trace the* h *on your* **Word-Building Card** *as you say /h/.* Repeat the routine for *d* and *r*.

Guided Practice/Practice

■ Display the Photo Cards. *This is the picture of a hammer. What sound do you hear at the beginning of* hammer? *What letter stands for /h/? Place an* h *on the hammer because* hammer *begins with /h/.* Repeat with remaining Photo Cards.

■ Have children trace letters *h, d, r,* on their Word-Building Cards.

■ Point out children and objects in the classroom with names that begin with initial /h/, /d/, and /r/ (*hall, desk, rack*).

Tier 2

SOUND-SPELLINGS REVIEW

Display Word-Building Cards *m, a, s, p, t, i, n, c, o, f, h, d, r,* one at a time. Have children chorally say the sound. Repeat and vary the pace.

Puppet

I Play!

Have children draw a picture of someone playing in the classroom or neighborhood. Ask them to write a sentence describing the picture, using the sentence frame:

I play _____.

I play scientist.

ELL

Extra Practice Provide additional practice in recognizing and naming letters for children whose native languages do not use the symbols of the Latin alphabet.

On Level

High-Frequency Words

Objective Review high-frequency words *for, you, are, is, play*

Materials • **High-Frequency Word Cards:** *for, you, are, is, play*

REVIEW

- Display the **High-Frequency Word Card** for **play**.
- **Read** Point to and say the word *play. This is the word* play. *It describes what you and I do for fun. We play games together.*
- **Spell** *The word* play *is spelled* p-l-a-y. Have children read and spell *play*.
- **Write** Finally, have children write the word *play*.
- Repeat with **for**, **you**, **are**, and **is**. Then have partners make up sentences using the words. Ask them to talk about how they play together.

Phonemic Awareness/Phonics

Objective Identify and blend with /a/a, /d/d, /h/h, /p/p, /f/f

Materials • **Word-Building Cards** • pocket chart

PHONEME BLENDING

Model

- Tell children you are thinking of some things in a toy store. *Listen as I say the sounds of the words: /d/ /o/ /l/. I will blend the sounds: /dooolll/,* doll. *Say the sounds with me: /d/ /o/ /l/, /dooolll/,* doll. *Now say the word with me:* doll. Repeat with other toys.

Practice

- Have children think of stuffed animals found in a toy store. Ask them to say the sounds in the animal's name and then blend the sounds. Have children figure out the names of the items.

REVIEW /a/a, /d/d, /h/h, /p/p, /f/f

Model

- Display **Word-Building Card** a. *The name of this letter is* a. *This letter stands for the /a/ sound we hear at the beginning of* apple. *What is the sound? I'll hold up the* a *card because* apple *begins with /a/.* Repeat with d, h, p, and f.
- Distribute small Word-Building Cards to children. Say: *acrobat, hippo, fig, parrot, doll, apple, rake, pen, ham, feather, dime.* Children hold up their small Word-Building Cards and say the initial sound of the word you name. Guide practice with the first two words.

Beyond Level

High-Frequency Words/Vocabulary

Objective Reinforce high-frequency words *said, she*
Materials • none

✔ ACCELERATE

- Write *said* and *she* on the board.

- **Read** Point to and say the word *said. This is the word* said. *We use it to say who talked. The librarian said I could take two books.*

- **Spell** *The word* said *is spelled* s-a-i-d. Have children read and spell *said.*

- **Write** Finally, have children write the word *said.* Repeat with *she.*

- Have children work with a partner to make up oral sentences using *said* and *she.* Ask them to talk about what a girl or woman said.

EXPAND ORAL VOCABULARY

- **Synonyms** Review the meaning of the oral vocabulary word *alert* with children. Then explain that a *synonym* is a word that means the same thing as another word.

- Say: *A synonym for the word* alert *is* attentive. Attentive *lifeguards watch swimmers in a pool so they will be ready if someone needs help.*

- Have children take turns using the new word *attentive* in a sentence. Then tell children that they will work with a partner to discuss when it is good to be attentive.

Phonics

Objective Read words with *d, h,* and *r*
Materials • **Sound-Spelling Cards:** *Dolphin, Hippo, Rose* • **Word-Building Cards**
• pocket chart

✔ ENRICH

- Show the *Dolphin* **Sound-Spelling Card**. Tell children that the /d/ sound is spelled with *d. Dolphin begins with the /d/ sound. What other words begin with /d/?* Repeat with *Hh* and *Rr.*

- Have children blend more complex words with *d, h, r.* Write the following words on the board for children to read: *deck, habit, hall, honk, dish, rash, had, hill, radish, hams, fish, mash.*

- Display **Word-Building Cards** *a, e, i, m, n, d, h, r, s, t, w.* Have partners make as many words with the letters as they can. Ask them to list their words. Have children share their lists.

ON YOUR OWN

Write Rhyme and Chimes

Have children write and illustrate the Rhyme and Chime they created in the High-Frequency Words lesson.

ELL

Partners When partners make up sentences with high-frequency words, pair English Language Learners with children who are more proficient. Write their sentences, read them together, and point to the high-frequency words.

ELL ENGLISH LANGUAGE LEARNERS

Oral Language Warm-Up

Content Objective Learn theme vocabulary
Language Objective Repeat and act out a rhyme to demonstrate understanding
Materials • **Listening Library Audio CD** • **Visual Vocabulary Resources**

BUILD BACKGROUND KNOWLEDGE

All Language Levels

One Man Went to Mow
One man went to mow,
Went to mow a meadow.
One man and his dog
Went to mow a meadow.

Two men went to mow,
Went to mow a meadow.
Two men, one man and his dog
Went to mow a meadow.

■ Continue developing vocabulary around the unit theme "Neighborhood" using "One Man Went to Mow." Pantomime mowing and say that a meadow has lots of grass. Teach the word *grass* using one of the **Visual Vocabulary Resources**.

■ Point out that *cut the grass* and *mow a meadow* are almost the same. Have children repeat the phrase *mow a meadow* three times. Explain that many people in a neighborhood have jobs taking care of plants and yards.

■ Play "One Man Went to Mow" on the **Audio CD**. Act out each line as you chant the rhyme; for example, pantomime mowing.

■ Then teach children the pantomime gestures. Emphasize the words *one, went to mow, mow a meadow,* and *two*.

■ Ask children to tell what they know about outdoor jobs. Build on their responses to model speaking in complete sentences.

Academic Language

Language Objective Use academic language in classroom conversations

All Language Levels

■ This week's academic words are **boldfaced** throughout the lesson. Define the word in context and provide a clear example from the selection. Ask children to generate an example.

Cognates

Help children identify similarities and differences in pronunciation and spelling between English and Spanish cognates.

Cognates

alert	*alerta*
celebration	*celebración*
precise	*preciso*
repair	*reparar*

Academic Language Used in Whole Group Instruction

Oral Vocabulary Words	Vocabulary and Grammar Concepts	Strategy and Skill Words
alert celebration job precise repair	sequence words sentences	summarize retell story events sentences

ELL ENGLISH LANGUAGE LEARNERS

Vocabulary

Language Objective Demonstrate understanding and use of key words by discussing workers in the neighborhood

Materials • **Visual Vocabulary Resources**

PRETEACH KEY VOCABULARY

All Language Levels

Use the **Visual Vocabulary Resources** to preteach the weekly oral vocabulary words *alert, celebration, job, precise,* and *repair.* Focus on one or two words per day. Use the detailed routine on the cards.

- Define the word in English and provide the example given.

- Define the word in Spanish, if appropriate, and indicate if the word is a cognate.

- Display the picture and explain how it illustrates or demonstrates the word.

- Then engage children in structured partner-talk about the image, using the key word.

- Ask children to chorally say the word three times.

- Point out any known sound-spellings or focus on a key aspect of phonemic awareness related to the word.

PRETEACH FUNCTION WORDS AND PHRASES

All Language Levels

Use the Visual Vocabulary Resources to preteach the function phrases *to you* (give to you) and *for you* (to do something for you). Focus on one phrase per day. Use the detailed routine on the cards.

- Define the phrase in English and, if appropriate, in Spanish. Point out if the phrase is a cognate.

- Refer to the picture and engage children in talk about the phrase. For example, children will partner-talk using sentence frames, or they will listen to sentences and replace a word or phrase with the new function phrase.

- Ask children to chorally repeat the phrase three times.

TEACH BASIC WORDS

Beginning/Intermediate

Use the Visual Vocabulary Resources to teach the basic words *store, taxicab, walk sign, park bench,* and *vendors.* Teach these words about "city sights" using the routine provided on the card.

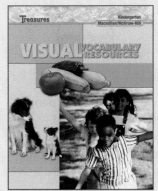

Visual Vocabulary Resources

ON YOUR OWN
Draw and Write

Have children draw people celebrating a special occasion. Ask them to write a sentence about it.

Approaching Level

Oral Language

Objective Reinforce oral vocabulary
Materials • none

THEME WORDS: *job, celebration*

■ Say: *We've talked about different **jobs** that people in the community do. We've also discussed different occasions for **celebrations**, such as a birthday or a holiday.*

■ *What are some jobs people do in our school?*

■ *What is a celebration you enjoy? Who do you celebrate with?*

■ *Who helps prepare for a celebration? What jobs are done to prepare for a celebration? Would you like to have one of these jobs? Why or why not?* Tell children to respond in complete sentences.

High-Frequency Words

Objective Reteach high-frequency words
Materials • **High-Frequency Word Cards:** *are, for, you*
• **Sound-Spelling WorkBoards**

RETEACH WORDS: *are, for, you*

Tier 2

■ Distribute a **WorkBoard** to each child. Then display the **High-Frequency Word Card** for **are**.

■ Use the **Read/Spell/Write** routine to reteach the word. Point to and say the word. *This is the word* are. *We use it to say:* You are, we are, they are. *You* are *working hard in school.* Are *is spelled* a-r-e. Have children read and spell *are*. Then have them write the word on their WorkBoards. Repeat the routine for the words **for** and **you**.

■ Have children work with a partner to make up sentences using the words *are, for,* and *you*. Ask them to talk about things they give each other at a celebration.

CUMULATIVE REVIEW

Display the High-Frequency Word Cards for words previously taught, one card at a time. Have children chorally read and spell the words. Mix and repeat. Note words children need to review.

ELL

Partners When pairing children to make up sentences, pair English Language Learners with children who are more proficient. Write their sentences, read them together, and point out the high-frequency words.

Approaching Level

Phonemic Awareness

Objective Blend sounds to form words
Materials • **Puppet**

Tier 2

PHONEME BLENDING

Model

■ Hold up the **Puppet**. *Happy is going to say the sounds in a word: /h/ /o/ /g/. Happy can blend these sounds together: /hooog/. Now you say the sounds: /h/ /o/ /g/. Say the word with Happy:* hog.

Guided Practice/Practice

■ Have the Puppet say /h/ /i/ /t/. Ask children to repeat the sounds. *Now you blend the sounds and say the word with Happy: /hiiit/,* hit. Repeat with the following:

/h/ /o/ /t/	/h/ /a/ /m/	/r/ /o/ /d/	/d/ /i/ /p/
/h/ /i/ /d/	/f/ /i/ /n/	/f/ /a/ /n/	/d/ /a/ /n/
/n/ /o/ /d/	/k/ /a/ /n/	/r/ /a/ /t/	/r/ /i/ /d/

Phonics

Objective Reinforce letter-sound correspondence for /r/r, /d/d, /h/h, /f/f, /o/o, /k/c
Materials • **Sound-Spelling Cards:** *Rose, Dolphin, Hippo, Fire, Octopus, Camel*
• **Sound-Spelling WorkBoards** • **Word-Building Cards**

RECOGNIZE /r/r, /d/d, /h/h, /f/f, /o/o, /k/c

Model

■ Display the *Rose* **Sound-Spelling Card**. *The letter* r *stands for the /r/ sound, as in* rose. *What is this letter? What sound does it stand for?* Repeat for *d, h, f, o,* and *c.*

■ Trace *r, d, h, f, o,* and *c* on the **Word-Building Cards**. *I will say a sentence. We will trace* r *on the cards when we hear /r/.* Use sentences such as: *Rita reads red books.* Repeat for *d, h, f, o,* and *c.*

Guided Practice/Practice

■ Distribute a **WorkBoard** to each child. Say: *hog, ox, camera, octagon, dog, doll, ribbon, deer, fan, cat, fat, car, rose, ham, hat.* Have children write the initial letter of each word on their WorkBoard. Guide them with the first two words.

CUMULATIVE REVIEW

Display Word-Building Cards *m, a, s, p, t, i, n, c, o, f, h, d,* and *r,* one at a time. Point to the letters in a random order. Have children chorally say the sound. Repeat and vary the pace.

Puppet

Corrective Feedback

Sound Error Model the sound that children missed, then have them repeat the sound. For example, for the word *hog,* say: *My turn.* Tap under the letter *o* in the word *hog* and say: *Sound? What's the sound?* Then return to the beginning of the word. Say: *Let's start over.* Blend the word with children again.

Sound-Spelling WorkBoard

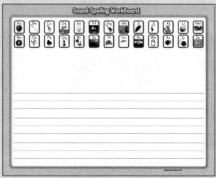

Sound-Spelling WorkBoard

On Level

Phonics

Objective   Blend with *-ad* to form words

Materials   • **Word-Building Cards**   • pocket chart
                 • **Sound-Spelling WorkBoards**

REVIEW *-ad*

- **Blend Words** Place **Word-Building Cards** *p, a,* and *d* in the pocket chart. Point to each letter for children to identify. Move your hand from left to right below the letters as you blend the word. *Listen as I blend the three sounds together: /paaad/, pad. What's the word?* Repeat the routine for *had* and *fad*.

- Have children write *pad* several times on their **WorkBoards** as they say /p/ /a/ /d/, /paaad/, *pad*. Have them repeat with *had* and *fad*.

Beyond Level

Phonics

Objective   Read words with *d, h,* and *r*

Materials   • **Word-Building Cards**   • pocket chart

ACCELERATE

- Display Word-Building Cards *r, e, s, t* in a pocket chart. Point to each letter as you say each sound. *The word* rest *has four sounds: /r/ /e/ /s/ /t/. Say the sounds with me: /r/ /e/ /s/ /t/. Listen as I blend the sounds: /rrreeessst/. When two consonants are together at the end of a word, we usually say the sounds for both consonants: /r/ /e/ /ssst/. Say it with me: /ssst/. Let's blend all of the sounds together: /rrreeessst/.* Repeat with *lift.*

- Help children read words with final blends. Write the following words on the board: *desk, dust, fist, just, mask, fast, crisp, grasp, task, wasp, rust, gift.* Model blending as needed.

Corrective Feedback

Blending Error Model the sound that children missed, then have them repeat the sound. For example, for the word *rest*, say: *My turn.* Tap under the letters *st* in the word *rest* and say: *Sounds? What are the sounds?* Then return to the beginning of the word. Say: *Let's start over.* Blend the word with children again.

ELL ENGLISH LANGUAGE LEARNERS

Access to Core Content

Content Objective Develop listening comprehension

Language Objective Discuss text using key words and sentence frames

Materials • **ELL Resource Book**, pp. 172–177

PRETEACH TRADE BOOK

All Language Levels

Use the Interactive Question-Response Guide on **ELL Resource Book** pages 172–177 to introduce children to *Alicia's Happy Day*. Preteach half of the selection on Day 1 and half on Day 2.

- Use the prompts provided in the guide to develop meaning and vocabulary. Use the partner-talk and whole-class responses to engage children and increase student talk.

- When completed, revisit the selection and prompt children to talk about the photographs. Provide sentence starters as needed and build on children's responses to develop language.

ELL Resource Book

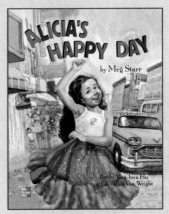

Trade Book

Beginning	Intermediate	Advanced
Use Visuals During the Interactive Reading, select several pictures. Describe them and have children summarize what you said.	**Summarize** During the Interactive Reading, select a few lines of text. After you read them and explain them, have children summarize the text.	**Expand** During the Interactive Reading, select a larger portion of text. After you read it and explain it, have children summarize the text.

Approaching Level

High-Frequency Words

Objective Recognize high-frequency words *are, for, you, play, is*

Materials
- **High-Frequency Word Cards:** *are, for, you, play, is*
- **Word-Building Cards**

REVIEW WORDS: *are, for, you, play, is*

- Display the **High-Frequency Word Card** for **are**. Say the word and have children repeat it. Point to each letter and have children name it.

- Distribute **Word-Building Cards** for *a, r, e* to each child. Model putting the letters together to form *are*. Then have children form *are*.

- Repeat the above routines with the words **for**, **you**, **play**, and **is**.

- Ask a question with the word *play*: *Which toys do you play with the most?* Have children use *play* to answer the question. Continue with the other words.

CUMULATIVE REVIEW

Display the High-Frequency Word Cards for words previously taught, one card at a time. Have children chorally read and spell the words. Mix and repeat. Note words children need to review.

Phonemic Awareness

Objective Blend sounds to form words

Materials
- **Puppet**
- **Photo Cards:** *dog, doll, hand, hat, rake, rock, rose*

PHONEME BLENDING

Tier 2

Model
- Have the **Puppet** segment the word *fin*: /f/ /i/ /n/. Then blend the sounds and say the word. Repeat with *fan*.

- Display the **Photo Card** for *hat*. Have the Puppet segment the word *hat* into sounds: /h/ /a/ /t/. Blend the sounds and say the word: /haaat/, *hat*. Repeat with the rest of the Photo Cards.

Guided Practice/Practice
- Have three children stand in a row. Ask the first child to say the sound /h/. Have the next child say /a/. Guide the child to extend the sound /aaa/. Have the third child say /t/. Have all three blend the sounds to say the word /haaat/, *hat*.

- Repeat with each picture name on the Photo Cards. Provide guidance as needed.

ELL

Extra Practice During the Cumulative Review, pair children at different levels of proficiency and have partners take turns reading and spelling the high-frequency words to each other.

Puppet

Approaching Level

Phonics

Objectives   Review blending words with *-at* and *-an;* build fluency
Materials   • **Word-Building Cards**   • pocket chart

REVIEW SKILLS

Tier
2

Model

■ Place **Word-Building Card** *h* in the pocket chart. *The name of this letter is* h. *This letter stands for the /h/ sound. Say /h/. What is the letter? What is the sound?*

■ Place *a* next to *h*. *The name of this letter is* a. *This letter stands for the /a/ sound. Say /a/. What is the letter? What is the sound?* Repeat with letter *t*.

■ Move your hand from left to right below the letters *hat*. *Listen as I blend the three sounds together: /haaat/,* hat. *What's the word? Let's blend the word together: /h/ /a/ /t/, /haaat/,* hat. Change the *h* to *f* and repeat the routine to blend the sounds in *fat*.

Guided Practice/Practice

■ Give *f, a, n* cards to children. Ask each child to form *fan* and say the sounds for the letters on his or her cards. Have children blend the sounds to say the word *fan*. Repeat with *fat, Dan, tan*.

Build Fluency

■ Have children blend *hat, fat, fan, Dan, tan* as quickly as they can.

Decodable Reader

Objective   Preteach Decodable Reader *Dad Can Pin It On*
Materials   • **Decodable Reader:** *Dad Can Pin It On*

PRETEACH *Dad Can Pin It On*

■ Display the cover of the book and read the title. Open to the title page and point out the title. *Let's read the title on the title page together.* Have children sound out each word as you run your finger under it. *Look at the picture. What is the boy doing? What do you think is in the box?*

■ Page through the book. Ask children what they see in each picture. Ask children to find the words *for* and *you*.

■ Read the book chorally with children. Have children point to each word or rebus as they read it. Provide corrective feedback as needed.

■ Ask children to use *for* to talk about the pictures. *The pin is for Mom.*

■ After reading, ask children to recall what happened in the story.

Decodable Reader

ON YOUR OWN

Thank-You Cards

Review the different gifts that Dad and Sam were considering for Mom. Have children write a thank-you card that Mom may have written to Sam and Dad.

On Level

Decodable Reader

Objective Reread *Dad Can Pin It On* to develop fluency
Materials • **Decodable Reader:** *Dad Can Pin It On*

REREAD FOR FLUENCY

- Ask children to page through the illustrations in *Dad Can Pin It On*. Have them use their own words to identify and describe the characters and to retell what the book was about.

- Have children reread a page or two of *Dad Can Pin It On*. Work with them to read with accuracy and expression. Model reading a page. Point out how your voice went up at the end of a question: "Can it fit on Mom?" *At the end of a question, your voice naturally goes up.*

- Provide time to listen as children read their page(s). Comment on their accuracy and expression and provide corrective feedback by modeling proper fluency.

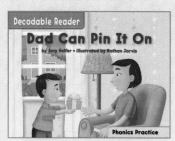

Decodable Reader

Beyond Level

Decodable Reader

Objective Reread *Dad Can Pin It On* to reinforce fluency
Materials • **Decodable Reader:** *Dad Can Pin It On*

REREAD FOR FLUENCY

- Ask children to look at the illustrations in *Dad Can Pin It On* and use their own words retell what the book was about.

- Have partners reread *Dad Can Pin It On*. Listen as children read. Comment on their accuracy and expression. Model fluency to provide corrective feedback.

INNOVATE

- Remind children that Dad put a pin on Mom. Mention that another gift that can be pinned on is a paper flower corsage. Have children draw paper flowers to put on a friend. Have them paste their flower on card stock and write "I can pin it on."

ELL — ENGLISH LANGUAGE LEARNERS

Access to Core Content

Content Objective Develop listening comprehension
Language Objective Discuss text using key words and sentence frames
Materials • **ELL Resource Book**, pp. 178–179

PRETEACH BIG BOOK OF EXPLORATIONS

All Language Levels

Use the Interactive Question-Response Guide on **ELL Resource Book** pages 178–179 to preview the **Big Book of Explorations** selection "Is This the Job for You?" Preteach half of the selection on Day 3 and half on Day 4.

Grammar

Content Objective Identify complete sentences
Language Objective Speak in complete sentences, using sentence frames
Materials • **Trade Book:** *Alicia's Happy Day* • **Photo Cards**

SENTENCES

All Language Levels

- Review sentences. Tell children that a sentence tells a complete thought. It has a naming part and a telling part.

- Remind children of the story *Alicia's Happy Day*. Say this sentence from the story: *Airplanes write in the sky for you.*

- Point out the naming part *Airplanes*. Explain that the naming part tells who or what the sentence is about. The sentence is about airplanes. Ask: *What is the telling part? What do the airplanes do?* (write in the sky for you) Provide a telling part: *jumps rope with me.* Have children provide a naming part. Ask: *Who jumps rope with me?*

PEER DISCUSSION STARTERS

All Language Levels

- Distribute **Photo Cards** of people, such as *baby, astronaut, queen,* and *girl.*

- Pair children and have them complete sentence frames such as: *The girl _____.* Ask them to expand on their sentences by providing as many details as they can. For example: *The girl visits her grandmother.* Circulate, listen in, and take note of each child's language use and proficiency.

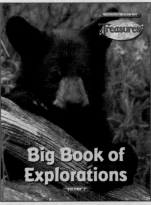

Big Book of Explorations

Puppet

Corrective Feedback

Blending Error Model the sound that children missed, then have them repeat the sound. For example, for the word *hop*, say: *My turn.* Tap under the letter *p* in the word *hop* and say: *Sound? What's the sound?* Then return to the beginning of the word. Say: *Let's start over.* Blend the word with children again.

ELL

Extra Practice Provide additional practice in recognizing and naming letters for children whose native languages do not use the symbols of the Latin alphabet.

Approaching Level

Phonemic Awareness

Objective	Blend sounds to form words
Materials	• **Puppet**

PHONEME BLENDING

Tier 2

Model
- Hold up the **Puppet**. *Listen as Happy says the sounds in the word* hop: /h/ /o/ /p/. *Now Happy will blend the sounds:* /hooop/, hop. *Happy put* /h/, /o/, *and* /p/ *together to say the word* hop. *Listen to the next word.* Repeat blending with the words *tap* and *rod*.

Guided Practice/Practice
- Have children put sounds together to say words. Guide practice with the first word. Use the Puppet to say the following sounds:

/k/ /a/ /t/ *(cat)*	/r/ /i/ /p/ *(rip)*	/t/ /o/ /p/ *(top)*
/d/ /a/ /n/ *(Dan)*	/f/ /a/ /t/ *(fat)*	/h/ /i/ /p/ *(hip)*
/p/ /i/ /n/ *(pin)*	/m/ /o/ /p/ *(mop)*	/r/ /a/ /p/ *(rap)*

Phonics

Objective	Blend sounds to form words with -ap, -an, -am, -at, -ad
Materials	• **Word-Building Cards** • pocket chart

REVIEW SKILLS

Tier 2

Model
- Place **Word-Building Cards** *m*, *a*, and *n* in the pocket chart. *The name of this letter is* m. *The letter* m *stands for the* /m/ *sound. Say* /m/. *The name of this letter is* a. *The letter* a *stands for the* /a/ *sound. Say* /a/. *The name of this letter is* n. *The letter* n *stands for the* /n/ *sound. Say* /n/.

- Point under the word and say the sound each letter stands for as you point to it: /m/ /a/ /n/. *Now I blend the three sounds together:* /mmmaaannn/, man.

Guided Practice/Practice
- Keep the Word-Building Cards in the pocket chart. Have children take turns pointing under the cards, saying the letter sounds, and blending the word: /m/ /a/ /n/, /mmmaaannn/, man. Repeat with *tap, pan, ham, hat, sat, mad, map,* and *sad*.

Approaching Level

Leveled Reader Lesson 1

Objective Read *We Work for You* to apply skills and strategies
Materials • **Leveled Reader:** *We Work for You*

BEFORE READING

- **Preview and Predict** Read the title and the name of the author. *Who do you see on the cover? What are they doing?* Turn to the title page and point out that it also has the title and the name of the author. *What do you think the book is about?*

- **Model Concepts About Print** Demonstrate book handling as children follow along with their books. *I hold the book so that the cover faces me and the words are right side up. I open the book by turning the cover. Then I turn each page as I read it, starting on the first page and ending on the last page at the back of the book.*

- **Review High-Frequency Words** Write **are**, **for**, **you**, **can**, **we**, and **the**, and read each word aloud. Guide children as they name the letters in each word. Have children find each word in the book and point to the word as they read it.

- **Page Through the Book** Name unfamiliar terms and identify the rebus pictures.

- **Set a Purpose for Reading** *Let's find out what workers do for us.*

DURING READING

- Remind children to use the rebuses and illustrations to gain information and to look for the high-frequency words *are, for, you, can, we,* and *the.*

- Show children how to monitor comprehension and self-correct if a word doesn't sound right or doesn't make sense in the sentence. *On page 3, I see a word that's easy to read. It's* dig. *I see that word within the bigger word,* diggers, *on page 2. If I can read* dig, *I can figure out* diggers. *This happens on the other pages, too. The smaller word on the right-hand page helps me read the longer word on the left-hand page.*

- Monitor children's reading and provide help as needed.

AFTER READING

- Ask children to point out words that they had trouble reading and to share strategies they used to help figure them out.

- Ask children to retell the story and to share personal responses. *Do you know anyone who does the job that the bears do? How are they similar to the bears? How are they different?*

Leveled Reader

Digital Learning

Use the **Leveled Reader Audio CD** for fluency building *after* children read the book with your support during Small Group time.

ON YOUR OWN

Use Illustrations

Describe or show children a comic strip. Have them retell *We Work for You* by drawing a comic strip for each thing that happens in the story in order.

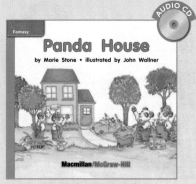

Leveled Reader

ELL

Retell Use the Interactive Question-Response Guide Technique to help English Language Learners understand *Panda House*. As you read, make meaning clear by pointing to pictures, demonstrating word meaning, paraphrasing text, and asking children questions.

ON YOUR OWN

Build an Animal House

Help children fold a piece of paper into quarters. Ask them to choose an animal and to think about the house that animal would build. What would the animal do first, second, third, and last? Have them draw the first thing the animal would do in the first box. Continue with the rest of the boxes. Help children write a caption in each box.

On Level

Leveled Reader Library

Leveled Reader Lesson 1

Objective Read *Panda House* to apply skills and strategies
Materials   • **Leveled Reader:** *Panda House*

BEFORE READING

- **Preview and Predict** Read the title and the name of the author: *What animals do you see on the cover? What are the animals doing? Where are the animals? What season is it? What will this story be about?* Open and page through the book. Name unfamiliar items.

- **Model Concepts About Print** Demonstrate book handling. *I hold the book so that the cover faces me and the words are right side up. I open the book by turning the front cover. Then I turn each page as I read it.*

- **Review High-Frequency Words** Write **for**, **you**, **are**, and **we** on chart paper. Have children find each word in the book and point under the word as they read it.

- **Set a Purpose for Reading** *Let's find out what the pandas build.*

DURING READING

- Have children turn to page 2 and begin whisper-reading the first two pages.

- Remind children to look for the high-frequency words and to use the illustrations to check meaning.

- Monitor children's reading and provide help. Stop during the reading and ask open-ended questions to facilitate discussion, such as: *What happens in the beginning of the story? What happens in the middle of the story? Who are the characters in this story? What is the setting?* Build on children's responses to develop deeper understanding of the text.

AFTER READING

- Ask children to point out words they had trouble reading and to share strategies they used to figure them out. Reinforce good behaviors, such as: *Darren, I noticed that you used the illustrations to help you figure out difficult words, such as* building.

- **Retell** Ask children to retell the story. Help them make a personal connection. *Would you like the pandas to help you in your home? Why or why not? What would you have them do?*

Beyond Level

Leveled Reader Lesson 1

Objective Read *Bunny Town Helpers* to apply skills and strategies
Materials • **Leveled Reader:** *Bunny Town Helpers*

Leveled Reader

BEFORE READING

- **Preview and Predict** Read the title and the name of the author on the front cover. *What animals do you see? Where are they? What are they wearing? What are they doing? What do you think the book is about?* Turn to the title page and point out that it also has the title and the name of the author. Page through the book with children and pause to name unfamiliar items.

- **Introduce Story Words** Point to the word *library* on page 8. Read the sentence. Have children use the word *library* to figure out the word *librarian*. Repeat with *bakers* and *bakery* on page 10.

- **Set a Purpose for Reading** *Let's find out who the helpers are.*

DURING READING

- Remind children that when they come to an unfamiliar word, they can look for familiar chunks in the word, break the word into syllables and sound out each part, or think about what the word might mean. If the word does not sound right or make sense in the sentence, children can self-correct.

- Monitor children's reading and provide help as needed.

AFTER READING

- Ask children to point out words they had trouble reading and to share the strategies they used.

- Tell children to retell the story and to share personal responses. *Who has a job you would like? What is the job? Why do you think you would like it? What would you need to do this job?*

- **Analyze** *The author does not tell everything that each helper does. For example, you read that the teacher teaches reading and writing. What else do teachers do? What else does each of the other helpers do?*

- Have children work in pairs to choose a profession from *Bunny Town Helpers*. Have them research the profession in a children's encyclopedia and list the main responsibilities.

- **Model** Have children use their lists to write an advertisement for the profession they chose. Write on the board, for example: *Soccer coach wanted! Soccer coaches explain the rules. They demonstrate soccer skills. They help children play their best.*

ON YOUR OWN

Write About a Job

Have children draw a job they wish they had and write a sentence about it.

I want to plant gardens.

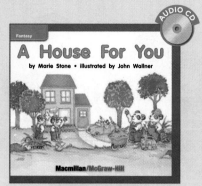

Leveled Reader

Vocabulary

Preteach Vocabulary Use the routine in the **Visual Vocabulary Resources**, pages 370–371, to preteach the ELL Vocabulary listed on the inside front cover of the Leveled Reader.

ELL ENGLISH LANGUAGE LEARNERS

Leveled Reader

Content Objective Read to apply skills and strategies
Language Objective Retell information using complete sentences
Materials • **Leveled Reader:** *A House For You*

BEFORE READING

All Language Levels

- **Preview** Read the title *A House For You*. Ask: *What's the title? Say it again.* Repeat with the author's name. Point to the cover illustration and say: *I see some bears. They are building a house.* Point to the bears and the house as you name them. *Now turn to a partner and tell about this picture.*

- **Page Through the Book** Use simple language to tell about the illustration on each page. Immediately follow up with questions, such as: *What are the bears doing now? Show me how they dig.*

- **Review Skills** Use the inside front cover to review the phonics skill and high-frequency words.

- **Set a Purpose** Say: *Let's read to find out who this house is for.*

DURING READING

All Language Levels

- Have children whisper-read each page, or use the differentiated suggestions below. Circulate, listen in, and provide corrective feedback, such as modeling how to decode words.

- **Retell** Stop after every two pages and ask children to state what they have learned so far. Reinforce language by restating children's comments when they have difficulty using story-specific words. Provide differentiated sentence frames to support children's responses and engage children in partner-talk where appropriate.

Beginning	Intermediate	Advanced
Echo-Read Have children echo-read after you.	**Choral-Read** Have children choral-read with you.	**Choral-Read** Have children choral-read.
Check Comprehension Point to pictures and ask questions such as: *Do you see the paint? Point to the paint.*	**Check Comprehension** Ask questions/prompts such as: *Describe what you see in this picture. What are the bears doing?*	**Check Comprehension** Ask: *What different jobs did the bears do to build the house? Who will live in the house?*

ELL ENGLISH LANGUAGE LEARNERS

AFTER READING

All Language Levels

Book Talk Children will work with peers of varying language abilities to discuss their books for this week. Display the four **Leveled Readers** read this week: *Bunny Town Helpers* (Beyond Level), *Panda House* (On Level), *We Work for You* (Approaching Level), and *A House For You* (English Language Learners).

Ask the questions and provide the prompts below. Call on children who read each book to answer the questions or respond to the prompt. If appropriate, ask children to find the pages in the book that illustrate their answers.

> • What kind of building was in your book?
>
> • Name some workers in your book.
>
> • What do the workers do?
>
> • How are these workers like workers you know? How are they different?
>
> • What is your favorite part of the book? Tell about it.

Develop Listening and Speaking Skills Tell children to remember the following:

■ Share information in cooperative learning interactions. Remind children to work with their partners to retell the story and complete any activities. Ask: *What happened next in the story?*

■ Employ self corrective techniques and monitor their own and other children' language production. Children should ask themselves: *What parts of this passage were confusing to me? Can my classmates help me clarify a word or sentence that I don't understand?*

■ Use high-frequency English words to describe people, places, and objects.

■ Narrate, describe, and explain with specificity and detail. Ask: *Where did the story take place? Can you describe the setting? What else did you notice?*

■ Express opinions, ideas, and feelings on a variety of social and academic topics. Ask: *What do you think about the characters in the story?*

Puppet

Approaching Level

Phonemic Awareness

Objective Segment words into phonemes
Materials • **Puppet**

✓ **PHONEME SEGMENTATION**

Tier 2

Model

- Hold up the **Puppet**. *Happy will say the sounds in* rat. *Listen: /r/ /a/ /t/,* rat. *There are three sounds in* rat: */r/ /a/ /t/. Say the word with me:* rat. *Now say the three sounds: /r/ /a/ /t/.* Repeat with *fun.*

Guided Practice/Practice

- *Happy will say a word. You will say each sound in the word and then say the word.*

rim, /r/ /i/ /m/	hid, /h/ /i/ /d/	dim, /d/ /i/ /m/	coat, /k/ /ō/ /t/
rock, /r/ /o/ /k/	hop, /h/ /o/ /p/	did, /d/ /i/ d/	sick, /s/ /i/ /k/
rid, /r/ /i/ /d/	dot, /d/ /o/ /t/	mad, /m/ /a/ d/	in, /i/ /n/

Phonics

Objective Reinforce blending with -ap, -an, -am, -at, -ad and build fluency
Materials • **Word-Building Cards** • pocket chart
• **Sound-Spelling WorkBoards**

✓ **BUILD FLUENCY**

Tier 2

Model

- Place **Word-Building Cards** *f, a, n* in the pocket chart. Blend the sounds to say the word: /f/ /a/ /n/, /fffaaannn/: *fan.* Replace the beginning or ending letter to make other words, such as *man, ran, pan, pad, pat, Pam.*

- Repeat the routine with children using the words *hat* and *map.*

Guided Practice/Practice

- Guide children to use the Word-Building Cards to build words with -ap, -an, -am, -at, and -ad. Have children blend the sounds to say the words. Guide practice by building *man* and *pan.*

Build Fluency

- Display the Word-Building Card for *d.* Have children name the letter as quickly as they can. Then ask them to write the letter *d* on their **WorkBoards** several times as they say /d/. Repeat for *c, f, h, m, n, p, r, s, t.*

ELL

Extra Practice Provide additional practice in recognizing and naming letters for children whose native languages do not use the symbols of the Latin alphabet.

Approaching Level

Leveled Reader Lesson 2

Objective Reread *We Work for You* to reinforce fluency and retelling

Materials • **Leveled Reader:** *We Work for You*

FOCUS ON FLUENCY

- Tell children that you will read one page of the book and they will read that page right after you. They will follow along in their books and work to read at the same speed and with the same expression that you use.

SKILL RETELL

- *Who is the story about? What is one kind of work the bears do? What are the other kinds of work? What do you call the job that they do? Where do they work? Would you like to do this job? Why or why not?*

REREAD PREVIOUSLY READ BOOKS

- Distribute copies of the past six **Leveled Readers**. Tell children that rereading the books will help them develop their skills and enjoy language.

- Circulate and listen in as children read. Stop them periodically and ask them how they are figuring out words or checking their understanding. Tell children to read other previously read Leveled Readers during independent reading time.

High-Frequency Words

Objective Review high-frequency words *are, for, you, play,* and *is*

Materials • **High-Frequency Word Cards; Teacher's Resource Book,** pp. 103–110
• **High-Frequency Word Cards:** *are, for, you, play, is*

BUILD WORD AUTOMATICITY: *are, for, you, play, is*

- Distribute copies of the word **are**. Say the word and have children repeat it. Have children name the letters in the word. Repeat with the words **for, you, play,** and **is.**

- **Build Fluency** Use the High-Frequency Word Cards to review previously taught words. Show each word and have children chorally read it. Shuffle the cards and repeat, guiding children to read more rapidly.

Leveled Reader

Act Out the Story

Divide children into three groups. Have each group prepare to act out what happens in the beginning, middle, or end of the story. Then have groups perform story events in the order they happened.

Meet Grade-Level Expectations

As an alternative to this day's lesson, guide children through a reading of the On Level Leveled Reader. See page 1534. Since both books contain the same vocabulary, phonics, and comprehension skills, the scaffolding you provided will help most children gain access to this more challenging text.

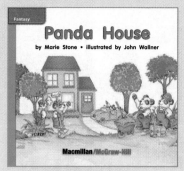

Leveled Reader

Building with Blocks

Have pairs of children use blocks to build structures of their choice. Then have the children draw a picture of what they built. Help them write a caption for their picture.

We are building a house.

On Level

Leveled Reader Lesson 2

Objective   Reread to apply skills and strategies to retell a story
Materials   • **Leveled Reader:** *Panda House*

BEFORE READING

■ Ask children to page through *Panda House* and recall what the book is about. Reinforce vocabulary by repeating children's sentences using more sophisticated language. For example: *The pandas did all of the work. They built a beautiful house.*

DURING READING

■ Have children join you in a choral-reading of the story. Model reading with expression. *When I read page 8, I see that the sentence ends with an exclamation point. I read that sentence with extra emotion. It is a happy ending. The bears are finished, and the family can move in.* Ask children to use the same kind of expression when they read. Discuss how reading a variety of texts, with expression, can help them enjoy the language.

■ Assign each child a page. Have children practice by whisper-reading. *Follow along as other children read, and be ready to read when it is your turn. Remember, use lots of expression.*

AFTER READING

■ Have children retell the selection in their own words. *What happened at the beginning of the story? What happened in the middle of the story? What happened at the end of the story?*

■ *What did the pandas do to build their house? Could this story really happen? Why or why not?*

■ Have children make connections to their own experiences. *Have you ever built something? Who helped you? What materials did you use?*

Beyond Level

Leveled Reader Lesson 2

Objective   Reread to apply skills and strategies to retell a story
Materials   • **Leveled Reader:** *Bunny Town Helpers*

BEFORE READING

- Ask children to page through *Bunny Town Helpers* and retell what happened. *What happened in the beginning? What happened in the middle? What happened at the end?*

DURING READING

- Assign each child a page of the book to read aloud. Have children practice by whisper-reading. *Follow along as each child reads, and be ready to come in when it is your turn. Remember, use lots of expression.* Have children ask questions about the text.

AFTER READING

- Explain that summarizing is telling the most important ideas in the story. Model the strategy: *Dot and Hal wanted to know who the town helpers were, so Dad brought them into town. They met town helpers. Dot and Hal helped the town by planting flowers.* Guide children in creating their own summaries of the story.

Expand Vocabulary

Objective   Identify and use words with multiple meanings
Materials   • **Leveled Reader:** *Bunny Town Helpers*

ENRICH: MULTIPLE-MEANING WORDS

Gifted & Talented

- Point out that some words have more than one meaning. Have children find the word *rolls* on page 10 in *Bunny Town Helpers*. Ask them to point to the rolls in the picture. Explain that a roll is a small, round piece of bread. Explain that the word *rolls* also describes an action. Ask a volunteer to roll a small ball on the floor and then describe the action: *Tyrell rolls the ball.*

- Point to the word *plant* on page 16 and explain that *plant* describes an action. Explain that the word *plant* also describes flowers, trees, and other things that grow in the ground.

- Start a 3-column chart. Label one column *Things* and the other *Actions*. Write the two meanings for *rolls* and *plant* on the chart.

- Have children brainstorm other multiple-meaning words, such as *rock, phone, stamp,* and *pass*. Record responses on the chart. Have children use the words speaking in complete sentences.

Leveled Reader

ON YOUR OWN

Make a List

Have children draw a worker they know. Ask them to picture the worker doing his or her job. Have them list things the worker needs to do the job.

ELL

Partners When children draw pictures of workers they know and list their tools, pair English Language Learners with children who are more proficient. Prompt pairs to name the tools and provide help as needed to list the tools.

ELL ENGLISH LANGUAGE LEARNERS

Fluency

Content Objectives Reread the Decodable Reader to develop fluency; develop speaking skills

Language Objective Tell a partner what a selection is about

Materials • **Decodable Reader:** *Dad Can Pin It On*

REREAD FOR FLUENCY

Beginning

- Review the high-frequency words **are**, **for**, **you**, **is**, and **play** using the **Read/Spell/Write** routine.

Intermediate/Advanced

- Use each word in a sentence that illustrates its use, such as: *These crayons are for you*. Hand a box of crayons to a child.

- Then provide sentence starters for children to complete. Where appropriate, act out responses. For example: *This pencil is for you.*

All Language Levels

- Guide children through a choral-reading of *Dad Can Pin It On*. Point to the question mark on page 2 of *Dad Can Pin It On*. Tell children that when a sentence ends in a question mark, our voice goes up at the end. Model reading the question and have children chorally repeat.

DEVELOP SPEAKING/LISTENING SKILLS

All Language Levels

- Have children reread *Dad Can Pin It On* to a partner. Remind them to listen carefully and follow along in their book as their partner is reading. Work with children to read with appropriate speed and expression.

- Ask children to tell their partner about the pictures on each page. Then have the other partner describe the pictures. Circulate, listen in, and provide additional language as needed.

Beginning	Intermediate	Advanced
Confirm Understanding Point to the pictures for partners to identify. Ask: What do you see? Restate the correct answer in a complete sentence.	**Express Opinions** Ask partners to tell you which is their favorite picture in the book. Prompt them to explain why it is their favorite picture.	**Compare and Contrast** Have partners compare two different pictures and describe them. Prompt them to explain how they are alike and different.

ELL ENGLISH LANGUAGE LEARNERS

High-Frequency Words

Content Objective Spell high-frequency words correctly
Language Objective Write in complete sentences, using sentence frames
Materials • **Sound-Spelling WorkBoards** • **Sound-Spelling Cards** • **Photo Cards**

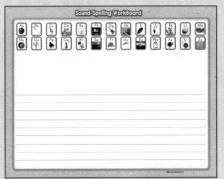

Sound-Spelling WorkBoard

Beginning/Intermediate

- Write the high-frequency words **are**, **for**, and **you** on the board. Have children copy the words on their **WorkBoards**. Then help children make up a sentence for each word. Provide the sentence starters *My hands are _____. This _____ is for you.*

Advanced

- Children should first orally state each sentence. Correct as needed. Then they can draw a picture to complete the sentence. For children who are ready, help them spell words using their growing knowledge of English sound-spelling relationships. Model how to segment the word children are trying to spell and attach a spelling to each sound. Use the **Sound-Spelling Cards** to reinforce the spellings for each English sound.

Writing

All Language Levels

- Say the word *hip* and ask children to write it. Point to your hip as you say *hip*. Then use the word in context: *I shut the door with my hip.* Have them write the word five times as they say *hip*. Demonstrate correct letter formation, as needed. Repeat with *rat* and *den*.

- Then display a set of **Photo Cards**. Select at least five cards whose picture names begin with /d/ (*deer, doctor, dog, doll, dolphin*), with /h/ (*hammer, hand, hat, horse, hippo*), and with /r/ (*rose, rock, rope, rabbit, rake*).

- Say the name of each card, stretching or reiterating the initial sound to emphasize it. You may also need to model correct mouth formation when forming the sound. Use the articulation pictures and prompts on the back of the small Sound-Spelling Cards for support. Tell children to write the first letter in each picture name on their WorkBoards.

Phonemic Awareness/ Phonics

For English Language Learners who need more practice with this week's phonemic awareness and phonics skills, see the Approaching Level lessons. Focus on minimal contrasts, articulation, and those sounds that do not transfer from the child's first language to English. For a complete listing of transfer sounds, see pages T10–T31.

Weekly Assessment

Use your Quick Check observations and the assessment opportunities identified below to evaluate children's progress in key skill areas.

Skills	Quick Check Observations	Pencil and Paper Assessment
PHONEMIC AWARENESS/ PHONICS /h/h, /d/d, /r/r **d r**	1477, 1514	Activity Book, pp. 24, 29–30, 32 Practice Book, pp. 137–138
HIGH-FREQUENCY WORDS *for, you, are* **are you**	1498	Activity Book, pp. 24, 27–28 Practice Book, pp. 135–136
COMPREHENSION Retell	1488	Activity Book, pp. 25–26, 31 Practice Book, p. 134

Quick Check Rubric

Skills	1	2	3
PHONEMIC AWARENESS/ PHONICS	Does not connect the sounds /h/, /d/, /r/ with the letters *Hh, Dd, Rr* and has difficulty blending the CVC words *hat, ham, hit, hip, had, dad, mad, dot, rat, Ron.*	Usually connects the sounds /h/, /d/, /r/ with the letters *Hh, Dd, Rr* and blends the CVC words *hat, ham, hit, hip, had, dad, mad, dot, rat, Ron* with only occasional support.	Consistently connects the sounds /h/, /d/, /r/ with the letters *Hh, Dd, Rr* and blends the CVC words *hat, ham, hit, hip, had, dad, mad, dot, rat, Ron.*
HIGH-FREQUENCY WORDS	Does not identify the high-frequency words.	Usually recognizes the high-frequency words with accuracy, but not speed.	Consistently recognizes the high-frequency words with speed and accuracy.
COMPREHENSION	Does not retell the story using the pictures and text.	Usually retells the story using the pictures and text.	Consistently retells the story using the pictures and text.

DIBELS LINK

PROGRESS MONITORING
Use your DIBELS results to inform instruction.
IF...
Initial Sound Fluency (ISF)   0–24

THEN...
Evaluate for Intervention

TPRI LINK

PROGRESS MONITORING
Use your TPRI scores to inform instruction.
IF...
Phonemic Awareness   Still Developing
Graphophonemic Knowledge   Still Developing
Listening Comprehension   Still Developing

THEN...
Evaluate for Intervention

Diagnose		Prescribe
Review the assessment answers with children. Have them correct their errors. Then provide additional instruction as needed.		
PHONEMIC AWARENESS/ PHONICS /h/h, /d/d, /r/r	**IF...** **Quick Check Rubric:** Children consistently score 1 or **Pencil and Paper Assessment:** Children get 0–2 items correct	**THEN...** Reteach Phonemic Awareness and Phonics Skills using the **Phonemic Awareness and Phonics Intervention Teacher's Edition**. Use the Build Fluency lesson in upcoming weeks to provide children practice reading words with /h/h, /d/d, and /r/r.
HIGH-FREQUENCY WORDS *for, you, are*	**Quick Check Rubric:** Children consistently score 1 or **Pencil and Paper Assessment:** Children get 0–2 items correct	Reteach High-Frequency Words using the **Phonics Intervention Teacher's Edition**. Use the High-Frequency Words lesson in upcoming weeks to provide children practice reading the words *for*, *you*, and *are*.
COMPREHENSION Skill: Retell	**Quick Check Rubric:** Children consistently score 1 or **Pencil and Paper Assessment:** Children get 0–2 items correct	Reteach Comprehension Skill using the **Comprehension Intervention Teacher's Edition**.

Response to Intervention

To place children in **Tier 2** or **Tier 3** Intervention use the *Diagnostic Assessment*.

- Phonemic Awareness
- Phonics
- Vocabulary
- Comprehension
- Fluency

Teacher Notes

Use this page to record lessons that work well or need to be adapted for future reference.

Lessons that work well

Lessons that need adjustments

Use this page to record lessons that work well or need to be adapted for future reference.

Lessons that work well

Lessons that need adjustments

Unit 6 Computer Literacy

Objectives

- Open a document
- Type text into a document
- Save a document

Materials

- www.macmillanmh.com

Vocabulary

home keys on the keyboard they are A, S, D, F for the left hand and J, K, L for the right hand

key to type text into a document

text displayed, printed words, sentences, and paragraphs

document (file) a page or pages created on a computer

save to store a document in a computer's memory or on a disk

Computer Literacy
Focus on Keyboard and Internet Skills and Media Literacy
www.macmillanmh.com

Remind children never to pull on the cables around the computer.

Computer Literacy
Computer Basics

ACCESS PRIOR KNOWLEDGE

Discuss with children. Encourage them to take turns speaking:

- *How can a keyboard help you with your work on a computer?*

EXPLAIN

- Tell children about the different keys on a keyboard. Share with them how good typists use **home keys** to type.
- Discuss with children how keyboards enable us to **key text** into a document.

MODEL

- Point out the keyboard to children. Show them that the keys are not in alphabetical order. Show them how to place their fingers on the home keys. Model how to keep your fingers on the home keys while typing.
- Show children how to open a word processing **document**.
- Demonstrate how to key text into the document.

Technology Makes a Difference

Explain that

▶ The computer does not automatically remember what we key into a document.

▶ In order to have the computer remember what we tell it, we must **save** the document.

▶ We can save a document by using the drop-down File menu or the disk icon. Have children locate both of these in a word processing program.

▶ Have children practice saving a document.

Media Literacy
Magazine Madness

ACCESS PRIOR KNOWLEDGE

Discuss with children:

- What are some other things we can read besides books? (newspapers, journals, Web sites, comic books, magazines, poems)

- Why do you think people like to read magazines? (Magazines are short, focus on one subject, and have good variety.)

- *What magazines does your school library media center subscribe to?*

EXPLAIN

Introduce the lesson vocabulary by discussing each word and its definition with children.

- **Magazines** are published on regular schedule–usually once a week or once a month.

- People like magazines because of their **variety** A magazine can include several different types and styles of writing.

- Magazines contain different types of **articles**. Articles are short written reports about news events.

- There are many different **categories** of magazines, including automobile magazines, computer magazines, sports magazines, health and fitness magazines, and news magazines.

MODEL

- Bring a variety of age-appropriate magazines to the classroom for children to examine. You will need one magazine for each group of four children. Ask children to examine the cover and make predictions about the articles they might find inside the magazine.

- In their groups, have children brainstorm ideas for a new magazine. It could be a magazine about a favorite hobby, a place in the community, or a group of people. Encourage children to work together, following the rules for discussion, including taking turns and speaking one at a time.

- Provide children with art materials and have them create a cover for their magazine. Explain that their cover should include the name of the magazine, pictures or illustrations, and words or phrases about what will be inside.

Objectives

- Identify different forms of media
- Understand the role of magazines in media
- Create a cover for a new magazine

Materials

- examples of magazines
- art supplies

LOG ON ▶ FIND OUT

Media Literacy Activities
Lessons that help children identify and explore different uses of writing and photographs in magazines

Theme Project Wrap-Up
Research/Organizing and Presenting Ideas

After children complete their projects, they can have a Neighborhood Day and present their findings.

 Step 3 **Review and Evaluate**

How do I share what I have learned?

The following checklists and Scoring Rubric will help you and children assess their projects.

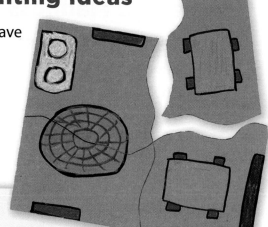

Teacher's Checklist

Assess the Research Process

Plan the Project
- ✔ Chose appropriate sources to answer research questions.
- ✔ Used a variety of sources to gather evidence.
- ✔ Used descriptive words to describe various neighborhoods.

Do the Project
- ✔ Logically organized material.
- ✔ Used pictures and writing to document information.
- ✔ Presented main ideas from research.

Assess the Presentation

Speaking
- ✔ Shared information and ideas.
- ✔ Spoke clearly and to the point.
- ✔ Demonstrated courteous responses to audience.

Representing
- ✔ Used visuals to enhance information.
- ✔ Used visuals appropriate for the topic.
- ✔ Made sure everyone could see the visuals.

Assess the Listener

Listening
- ✔ Set a purpose for listening.
- ✔ Listened attentively to the speaker without interrupting.

Children's Checklist

Research Process
- ✔ Where did you find the best project ideas?
- ✔ Did you use more than one resource to find information?

Presenting
Speaking
- ✔ Did you speak in a loud, clear voice?
- ✔ Did you speak in complete sentences?

Representing
- ✔ Were your visuals and writing easy to understand?
- ✔ Did you pass around your visuals so everyone could see them?
- ✔ Was your report too short or too long?

SCORING RUBRIC FOR THEME PROJECT

4 Excellent	3 Good	2 Fair	1 Unsatisfactory
The child	The child	The child	The child
• presents the main idea with supporting details; • may make sophisticated observations; • presents accurate, well-produced visuals that enhance the topic.	• clearly fulfills all the steps of the project; • provides adequate details; • makes several relevant observations.	• attempts to present some of the required steps; • demonstrates some difficulty with research; • may make somewhat unclear observations.	• does not appear to grasp the task in its entirety; • has great difficulty with organizational skills; • presents unnecessary or inaccurate information.

 Home-School Connection

Neighborhood Day provides an excellent opportunity for home and community involvement.

■ Ask family members, other children, and members of the community to children's presentations.

■ Have children write thank-you notes to those who attended the presentations. Guide them to respect the age, gender, and culture of the recipient.

Big Question Wrap-Up

Review the Big Question for this unit with children. Discuss what they have learned about their neighborhoods. Have children respond to the following questions: *What do you like best about your neighborhood? What is one thing you could do to make your neighborhood better?* Remind children to take turns when speaking.

Administer the Test

Unit 6 TEST

TESTED SKILLS AND STRATEGIES

COMPREHENSION STRATEGIES AND SKILLS

• Strategy: Summarize

• Skills: Identify main idea and details, retell

HIGH-FREQUENCY WORDS

• *are, for, you*

PHONEMIC AWARENESS

• Phoneme blending

• Phoneme isolation (/h/, /d/, /r/)

• Phoneme segmentation

PHONICS

• *h, d, r*

• Review *-at, -an* phonograms

CONCEPT WORDS

• Sequence words

Use Multiple Assessments for Instructional Planning

To create instructional profiles for your children, look for patterns in the results from any of the following assessments.

Running Records

Use the instructional reading level determined by the Running Record calculations for regrouping decisions.

Benchmark Assessments

Administer tests three times a year as an additional measure of both children's progress and the effectiveness of the instructional program.

Analyze the Data

Use information from a variety of informal and formal assessments, as well as your own judgment, to assist in your instructional planning. Children who consistently score at the lowest end of each range should be evaluated for Intervention. Use the **Diagnostic Assessment** for guidelines in the **Intervention Teacher's Editions**.

Diagnose		Prescribe
ASSESSMENTS	**IF...**	**THEN...**
UNIT TEST	0–15 Correct	Reteach skills using the **Intervention Teacher's Editions**.
RUNNING RECORDS	Rebus	Reteach skills using the **Intervention Teacher's Editions**.

For users of DIBELS

Use the results from the DIBELS Progress Monitoring tests to confirm instructional decisions.

DIBELS LINK

PROGRESS MONITORING
Use your DIBELS results to inform instruction.
IF...
Initial Sound Fluency (**ISF**)   0–7
Phoneme Segmentation Fluency (**PSF**)   Start midyear

THEN...
Evaluate for Intervention

For users of TPRI

Use the scores from the TPRI as a progress monitoring tool to confirm instructional decisions.

TPRI LINK

PROGRESS MONITORING
Use your TPRI scores to inform instruction.
IF...

Phonemic Awareness	Still Developing
Graphophonemic Knowledge	Still Developing
Listening Comprehension	Still Developing

THEN...
Evaluate for Intervention

Response to Intervention

To place chlidren in Tier 2 or Tier 3 Intervention use the *Diagnostic Assessment*.

- Phonemic Awareness
- Phonics
- Vocabulary
- Comprehension
- Fluency

Instructional Routines

Professional Development

- Read the routine prior to using *Treasures*. Use the Routine QuickNotes as a reminder of key routine steps throughout Unit 1, or as needed.

- View the online classroom video clip through **TeacherWorks Plus**. Watch master teachers use these routines.

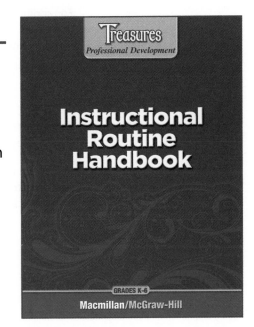

1. **Phonological Awareness/ Phonemic Awareness**
   Rhyme
   Oddity Tasks
   Sound Categorization
   Oral Blending
   Oral Segmentation
   Manipulation

2. **Phonics**
   Blending
   Introducing Sound-Spelling Cards
   Letter Recognition
   Building Words
   Building Fluency
   Reading Decodables
   Multisyllabic Words Routine

3. **Fluency**
   Strategies

4. **Vocabulary**
   Define/Example/Ask Routine
   Strategies

5. **High-Frequency Words**
   Read/Spell/Write Routine
   Reading Pre-decodables

6. **Spelling**
   Dictation

7. **Comprehension**
   Strategies
   Skills
   Reading Big Books
   Reading Student Book

8. **Writing**
   Conferences
   Revision Assignments
   Writing Process
   Using Rubrics
   Using Anchor Papers
   Writers' Express Sequence

9. **Research Process**
   Big Question Board

10. **Classroom Management**
    Workstation Flip Charts
    Contracts
    Centers
    Small Groups

11. **Listening/Speaking/Viewing**

12. **Assessment**

Additional Readings

By the Authors and Illustrators

For additional information on authors, illustrators, and selection content, go to www.macmillanmh.com.

Rickert, Janet Elizabeth. *Russ and the Apple Tree.* **Woodbine, 1999.** Russ wants a swing set in his backyard instead of an apple tree. However, the day comes when he and his father pick apples, and Russ discovers a surprise.

Related to the Theme

Use these and other classroom or library resources to provide additional read alouds to build academic language.

Beck, Scott. *Little House, Little Town.* **Abrams, 2004.** Small town life is depicted cheerfully as the people in the neighborhood go about their daily activities; accompanied by appealing illustrations.

Crews, Nina. *The Neighborhood Mother Goose.* **Greenwillow, 2004.** Forty-one familiar Mother Goose rhymes are presented on a background of colorfully photographed neighborhood scenes with children.

Keats, Ezra Jack. *Hi, Cat!* **Viking, 1999.** Archie meets a stray cat, on his way to play with his friends, who becomes his pet by the time he gets home.

Treays, Rebecca. *My Street.* **Educational Development Corporation, 1999.** A young girl goes on an adventure and explores the street she lives on.

Tresselt, Alvin. *Wake Up! City.* **HarperCollins, 1990.** This describes all the things that happen in a city as it wakes up to a new morning.

Willems, Mo. *Knuffle Bunny.* **Hyperion Books, 2004.** Trixie is enjoying her time with her daddy as they go to the laundromat, until she realizes on the way home that she doesn't have her favorite stuffed animal.

WEEK 2	WEEK 3
Gomi, Taro. *Spring Is Here.* **Chronicle Books, 1999.** The themes of growth and renewal are explored through the illustrations of a young calf as he grows with each passing season.	**Mellage, Nanette.** *Coming Home: A Story of Josh Gibson, Baseball's Greatest Home Run Hitter.* **Troll, 2002.** The story of one of the greatest hitters in baseball comes to life. Cornelius Van Wright's watercolor illustrations add an evocative and tender sensibility to the story.
Ajmera, Maya. *Be My Neighbor.* **Charlesbridge, 2004.** This shows the functions of a community and the variety of neighborhoods throughout the world.	**Banks, Kate.** *The Night Worker.* **Farrar Straus Giroux, 2000.** Alex looks forward to the night he can go to work with his father, who is an engineer and wears a hard hat.
Caseley, Judith. *On the Town.* **Greenwillow, 2002.** For a homework assignment, Charlie and his mother explore their town and write down what they see.	**Heo, Yumi.** *One Afternoon.* **Orchard Books, 1998.** Young Minho and his mother do their errands around town, as he absorbs all the sights and sounds of their city.
Enderle, Judith Ross, and Gordon, Stephanie Jacob. *Something's Happening on Calabash Street.* **Chronicle Books, 2000.** Each person on Calabash Street is bringing a different ethnic food to the street fair.	**Kalman, Bobbie.** *Community Helpers from A to Z.* **Crabtree Publishing, 1997.** Careers from *A* to *Z* are explained in this photo-essay, which shows people working at their jobs.
Fleischman, Paul, and Hawkes, Kevin. *Sidewalk Circus.* **Candlewick Press, 2004.** A young girl watches from a bus stop as the circus performers prepare the acts that will soon appear in town.	**Rockwell, Anne.** *At the Firehouse.* **HarperCollins, 2003.** Captain Jack describes what takes place at the firehouse to Jason and his friend, Camilla, using dalmatians as the characters in this colorfully illustrated story.
Sis, Peter. *Madlenka.* **Frances Foster, 2000.** Madlenka goes around the block in her multicultural neighborhood showing her loose tooth to friends and vendors; feeling as if she is taking a trip around the world.	**Rockwell, Anne.** *Career Day.* **HarperCollins, 2000.** Children introduce the different careers that members of their family have, such as a judge, a nurse, a veterinarian, and a construction worker.
Slate, Joseph. *Miss Bindergarten Takes a Field Trip with Kindergarten.* **Puffin, 2001.** Miss Bindergarten takes her class on a field trip around their town to visit the post office, library, and fire station. They meet the people who work in each place.	**Zimmerman, Andrea.** *Dig!* **Harcourt, 2004.** Mr. Rally has several jobs that need his attention around town. He tends to his tasks with his digging machine and the help of his dog, Lightning.

Theme Bibliography

Selection Honors, Prizes, and Awards

Bus Stops

by *Taro Gomi*

Author: *Taro Gomi*, winner of Parents' Choice Silver Honor Award (1995) for *Who Ate It?*

Alicia's Happy Day

by *Meg Starr*

Illustrated by *Ying-Hwa Hu & Cornelius Van Wright*

Illustrators: *Ying-Hwa Hu and Cornelius Van Wright*, winners of the Carter G. Woodson Book Award (2002) from National Council for Social Studies for *Coming Home: A Story of Josh Gibson, Baseball's Greatest Home Run Hitter*

Resources

Audio Bookshelf
44 Ocean View Drive
Middletown, RI 02842
800-234-1713
www.audiobookshelf.com

Discovery Communications
4540 Preslyn Drive
Raleigh, NC 27616
888-892-3484

Dorling Kindersley
375 Hudson Street
New York, NY 10014
Tel: 800-631-8571
Fax: 201-256-0000
http://us.dk.com

Great Plains National Instructional Television Library
GPN Educational Media
1407 Fleet Street
Baltimore, MD 21231
800-228-4630
http://shopgpn.com

Innovative Educators
P.O. Box 520
Montezuma, GA 31063
888-252-KIDS
Fax: 888-536-8553
www.innovative-educators.com

Library Video Co.
P.O. Box 580
Wynnewood, PA 19096
800-843-3620
www.libraryvideo.com

Listening Library
400 Hahn Road
Westminster, MD 21157
800-243-4504

Live Oak Media
P.O. Box 652
Pine Plains, NY 12567
800-788-1121
www.liveoakmedia.com

Macmillan/McGraw-Hill
220 East Danieldale Road
DeSoto, TX 75115-9960
Tel: 800-442-9685
Fax: 972-228-1982
www.macmillanmh.com

MCA Video
MCA Records/Universal Studios
100 Universal City Plaza
Universal City, CA 91608
818-777-1000

Microsoft Corp.
One Microsoft Way
Redmond, WA 98052
800-426-9000
www.microsoft.com

National Geographic Society
1145 17th Street N.W.
Washington, DC 20036
800-647-5463
www.nationalgeographic.com

Recorded Books
270 Skipjack Road
Prince Frederick, MD 20678
800-636-3399
www.recordedbooks.com

Sunburst Communications
Sunburst Technology
1550 Executive Drive
Elgin, IL 60123
888-492-8817
www.sunburst.com

SVE & Churchill Media
6465 North Avondale Avenue
Chicago, IL 60631
800-253-2788

Tom Snyder Productions
100 Talcott Avenue
Watertown, MA 02472
800-342-0236
www.tomsnyder.com

Weston Woods
143 Main Street
Norwalk, CT 06851
800-243-5020
www.teacher.scholastic.com/products/westonwoods/

Web Sites

Go to www.macmillanmh.com.
Use the zip code finder to locate other resources in your area.

The Academy of Natural Sciences
http://www.ansp.org/

Acadia National Park
http://www.nps.gov/acad

Agriculture in the Classroom
http://www.agclassroom.org/

Arches National Park
http://www.nps.gov/arch

Asian American History Resources Online - CET
http://www.cetel.org/res.html

Association of Zoos and Aquariums
http://www.aza.org/

Bronx Zoo
http://www.bronxzoo.com/

Cincinnati Zoo
http://www.cincinnatizoo.org/

Colonial Williamsburg
http://www.history.org/

Denali National Park and Preserve
http://www.nps.gov/dena

Ellis Island
http://www.ellisisland.org/

Glacier National Park
http://www.nps.gov/glac

Grand Canyon National Park
http://www.nps.gov/grca

Grand Teton National Park
http://www.nps.gov/grte

High Museum of Art, Atlanta
http://www.high.org/

International Civil Rights Center and Museum
http://www.sitinmovement.org/

Japanese American National Museum
http://www.janm.org/

K12Station – Library of K–12 Education Links
http://www.k12station.com/k12link_library.html

Kids.gov
http://www.kids.gov/

KidsHealth in the Classroom
http://classroom.kidshealth.org/

Meteorology
http://www.wxdude.com/

The Metropolitan Museum of Art, New York
http://www.metmuseum.org/

Minneapolis Institute of Arts
http://www.artsmia.org/

Minnesota Zoo
http://www.mnzoo.com/

MoMA | The Museum of Modern Art
http://www.moma.org/

Monterey Bay Aquarium
www.montereybayaquarium.org

Mount Rushmore National Memorial
http://www.nps.gov/moru

Museum of Fine Arts, Boston
http://www.mfa.org/

Museum of Science, Boston
http://www.mos.org/

Museum of Science and Industry, Chicago
http://www.msichicago.org/

NASA
http://www.nasa.gov/

NASA Kids' Club
http://www.nasa.gov/audience/forkids/kidsclub/flash/index.html

National Air and Space Museum
http://www.nasm.si.edu/

National Civil Rights Museum
http://www.civilrightsmuseum.org/home.htm

National Museum of African American History and Culture
http://nmaahc.si.edu/

National Museum of American History
http://americanhistory.si.edu/

National Museum of the American Indian
http://www.nmai.si.edu/

National Museum of Women in the Arts
http://www.nmwa.org/

National Music Museum
http://www.usd.edu/smm/

National Park Service
http://www.nps.gov/

National Weather Service Education Resources
http://www.nws.noaa.gov/om/edures.shtml

National Women's History Museum
http://www.nwhm.org/

National Zoo
http://nationalzoo.si.edu/

Native American Facts for Kids: Resources on American Indians for Children and Teachers
http://www.native-languages.org/kids.htm

New England Aquarium
http://www.neaq.org/index.php

New York Aquarium
http://www.nyaquarium.com/

Newseum
http://www.newseum.org/

Omaha's Henry Doorly Zoo
http://www.omahazoo.com/

Philadelphia Museum of Art
http://www.philamuseum.org/

Philadelphia Zoo
http://www2.philadelphiazoo.org/

Plimoth Plantation
http://www.plimoth.org/

Redwood National and State Parks
http://www.nps.gov/redw

Rocky Mountain National Park
http://www.nps.gov/romo

Saint Louis Art Museum
http://www.slam.org/

San Diego Zoo
http://www.sandiegozoo.com/

San Francisco Museum of Modern Art
http://www.sfmoma.org/

Shedd Aquarium
http://www.sheddaquarium.org/

Smithsonian Education
http://www.smithsonianeducation.org/

Smithsonian: Science and Technology
http://www.si.edu/Encyclopedia_SI/science_and_technology/

Space Center Houston
http://www.spacecenter.org/

Tennessee Aquarium
http://www.tennis.org/

United States Holocaust Memorial Museum
http://www.ushmm.org/

University of California Museum of Paleontology
http://www.ucmp.berkeley.edu/

The White House Historical Association
http://www.whitehousehistory.org/

Yellowstone National Park
http://www.nps.gov/yell

Yosemite National Park
http://www.nps.gov/yose

Zion National Park
http://www.nps.gov/zion

High-Frequency Words

High-Frequency Words	UNIT/WEEK
I	Start Smart Week 1
can	Start Smart Week 2
we	Unit 1 Week 1
the	Unit 1 Week 2
like	Unit 2 Week 1
a	Unit 2 Week 2
see	Unit 3 Week 1
go	Unit 3 Week 2
to	Unit 4 Week 1
have	Unit 4 Week 2
is	Unit 5 Week 1
play	Unit 5 Week 2
are	Unit 6 Week 1
for	Unit 6 Week 2
you	Unit 6 Week 2
this	Unit 7 Week 1
do	Unit 7 Week 1
and	Unit 7 Week 2
what	Unit 7 Week 2
little	Unit 8 Week 1
said	Unit 8 Week 1
here	Unit 8 Week 2
was	Unit 8 Week 2
she	Unit 9 Week 1
he	Unit 9 Week 1
has	Unit 9 Week 2
look	Unit 9 Week 2
with	Unit 10 Week 1
my	Unit 10 Week 1
me	Unit 10 Week 2
where	Unit 10 Week 2

Oral Vocabulary

Week		Theme Words	Oral Vocabulary Card Words	
1	**Russ and the Firehouse**	neighborhood equipment	borrow organize frequently	neighborhood equipment
2	**Bus Stops**	community worker	admire deliver schedule	community worker
3	**Alicia's Happy Day**	job celebration	repair precise alert	job celebration

Language Transfers:

The Interaction Between English and Students' Primary Languages

Dr. Jana Echevarria
California State University, Long Beach

Dr. Donald Bear
University of Nevada, Reno

It is important for teachers to understand why English Language Learners (ELLs) use alternative pronunciations for some English words. Many English sounds do not exist or transfer to other languages, so English Language Learners may lack the auditory acuity to "hear" these English sounds and have difficulty pronouncing them. These students are not accustomed to positioning their mouth in a way the sound requires. The charts that appear on the following pages show that there is variation among languages, with some languages having more sounds in common and thus greater transfer to English than others.

For example, an English speaker may be able to pronounce the /r/ in the Spanish word *pero* ("but"), but not the /rr/ trill in *perro* ("dog"). The English speaker may also lack the auditory acuity to detect and the ability to replicate the tonal sounds of some Chinese words. Similarly, a Vietnamese speaker may have difficulty pronouncing /th/ in words such as *thin* or *thanks*.

Further, English Language Learners make grammatical errors due to interference from their native languages. In Spanish, the adjective follows the noun, so often English Language Learners say "the girl pretty" instead of "the pretty girl." While English changes the verb form with a change of subject (*I walk. She walks.*), some Asian languages keep the verb form constant across subjects. Adding /s/ to the third person may be difficult for some English Language Learners. Students may know the grammatical rule, but applying it consistently may be difficult, especially in spoken English.

When working with English Language Learners, you should also be aware of sociocultural factors that affect pronunciation. Students may retain an accent because it marks their social identity. Speakers of other languages may feel at a social distance from members of the dominant English-speaking culture.

English Language Learners improve their pronunciation in a nonthreatening atmosphere in which participation is encouraged. Opportunities to interact with native English speakers provide easy access to language models and give English Language Learners practice using English. However, students should not be forced to participate. Pressure to perform—or to perform in a certain way—can inhibit participation. In any classroom, teacher sensitivity to pronunciation differences contributes to a more productive learning environment.

Phonics, word recognition, and spelling are influenced by what students know about the sounds, word structure, and spelling in their primary languages. For example, beginning readers who speak Spanish and are familiar with its spelling will often spell short *o* with an *a*, a letter that in Spanish makes the short *o* sound. Similarly, English Language Learners who are unaccustomed to English consonant digraphs and blends (e.g., /ch/ and *s*-blends) spell /ch/ as *sh* because /sh/ is the sound they know that is closest to /ch/. Students learn about the way pronunciation influences their reading and spelling, beginning with large contrasts among sounds, then they study the finer discriminations. As vocabulary advances, the meaning of words leads students to the sound contrasts. For example, *shoe* and *chew* may sound alike initially, but meaning indicates otherwise. Students' reading and discussions of what they read advances their word knowledge as well as their knowledge in all language and literacy systems, including phonics, pronunciation, grammar, and vocabulary.

Phonics Transfers:
Sound Transfers

This chart indicates areas where a positive transfer of sounds and symbols occurs for English Language Learners from their native languages into English. This symbol (✔) identifies a positive transfer. "Approximate" indicates that the sound is similar.

Sound Transfers	Spanish	Cantonese	Vietnamese	Hmong	Korean	Khmer
Consonants						
/b/ as in bat	✔	approximate	approximate	approximate	approximate	✔
/k/ as in cake, kitten, peck	✔	✔	✔	✔	✔	✔
/d/ as in dog	✔	approximate	approximate	✔	approximate	✔
/f/ as in farm	✔	✔	✔	✔		
/g/ as in girl	✔	approximate	✔	approximate	approximate	
/h/ as in ham	✔	✔	✔	✔	✔	approximate
/j/ as in jet, page, ledge		approximate	approximate		approximate	
/l/ as in lion	✔	✔	✔	✔	✔	
/m/ as in mat	✔	✔	✔	✔	✔	✔
/n/ as in night	✔	✔	✔	✔	✔	✔
/p/ as in pen	✔	✔	✔	approximate	✔	✔
/kw/ as in queen	✔	approximate	✔		✔	✔
/r/ as in rope	approximate					✔
/s/ as in sink, city	✔	✔	✔	✔	✔	approximate
/t/ as in ton	✔	✔	approximate	approximate	✔	✔
/v/ as in vine	✔		✔	✔		
/w/ as in wind	✔	✔			✔	✔
/ks/ as in six	✔				✔	✔
/y/ as in yak	✔	✔		✔	✔	✔
/z/ as in zebra			✔			
Digraphs						
/ch/ as in cheek, patch	✔	approximate		✔	✔	✔
/sh/ as in shadow			✔	✔	✔	
/hw/ as in whistle					✔	✔
/th/ as in path	approximate		approximate			
/TH/ as in that	approximate					
/ng/ as in sting	✔	✔	✔	✔	✔	approximate

Sound Transfers	Spanish	Cantonese	Vietnamese	Hmong	Korean	Khmer
Short Vowels						
/a/ as in cat	approximate		approximate	✔	✔	
/e/ as in net	✔	approximate	approximate		✔	
/i/ as in kid	approximate	approximate			✔	
/o/ as in spot	approximate	approximate	approximate	approximate	approximate	✔
/u/ as in cup	approximate	approximate	✔		✔	✔
Long Vowels						
/ā/ as in lake, nail, bay	✔	approximate	approximate	approximate	✔	✔
/ē/ as in bee, meat, cranky	✔	approximate	✔	✔	✔	✔
/ī/ as in kite, tie, light, dry	✔	approximate	✔	✔	✔	✔
/ō/ as in home, road, row	✔	approximate	approximate		✔	
/ū/ as in dune, fruit, blue	✔	approximate	✔	✔	✔	✔
/yü/ as in mule, cue	✔	approximate			✔	
r-Controlled Vowels						
/är/ as in far	approximate	approximate				
/ôr/ as in corn	approximate	approximate				
/ûr/ as in stern, bird, suburb	approximate	approximate				
/âr/ as in air, bear						
/îr/ as in deer, ear						
Variant Vowels						
/oi/ as in boil, toy	✔	approximate	approximate		✔	✔
/ou/ as in loud, down	✔	approximate	✔	approximate	✔	✔
/ô/ as in law	approximate	✔	✔	approximate	approximate	✔
/ o̊ / as in laundry	approximate	approximate	✔	approximate	approximate	✔
/ôl/ as in salt, call	approximate	approximate			approximate	✔
/ü/ as in moon, drew	✔	approximate	approximate	✔	✔	✔
/u̇/ as in look		approximate	approximate		approximate	✔
/ə/ as in askew			approximate		✔	

Phonics Transfers:
Sound-Symbol Match

Sound-Symbol Match	Spanish	Cantonese	Vietnamese	Hmong	Korean	Khmer
Consonants						
/b/ as in bat	✔		✔			
/k/ as in cake	✔		✔			
/k/ as in kitten	✔		✔	✔		
/k/ as in peck						
/d/ as in dog	✔		✔	✔		
/f/ as in farm	✔			✔		
/g/ as in girl	✔		✔			
/h/ as in ham			✔	✔		
/j/ as in jet, page, ledge						
/l/ as in lion	✔		✔	✔		
/m/ as in mat	✔		✔	✔		
/n/ as in night	✔		✔	✔		
/p/ as in pen	✔		✔	✔		
/kw/ as in queen			✔			
/r/ as in rope	approximate					
/s/ as in sink, city	✔		✔			
/t/ as in ton	✔		✔	✔		
/v/ as in vine	✔		✔	✔		
/w/ as in wind	✔					
/ks/ as in six	✔					
/y/ as in yak	✔			✔		
/z/ as in zebra						
Digraphs						
/ch/ as in cheek, patch	✔					
/sh/ as in shadow						
/hw/ as in whistle						
/th/ as in path			✔			
/TH/ as in that						
/ng/ as in sting	✔		✔			
Short Vowels						
/a/ as in cat			✔	✔		
/e/ as in net	✔		✔			
/i/ as in kid						
/o/ as in spot			✔	✔		
/u/ as in cup						

Sound-Symbol Match	Spanish	Cantonese	Vietnamese	Hmong	Korean	Khmer
Long Vowels						
/ā/ as in lake						
/ā/ as in nail						
/ā/ as in bay						
/ē/ as in bee						
/ē/ as in meat						
/ē/ as in cranky						
/ī/ as in kite, tie, light, dry						
/ō/ as in home, road, row						
/ū/ as in dune			✔	✔		
/ū/ as in fruit, blue						
/yū/ as in mule, cue						
r-Controlled Vowels						
/är/ as in far	✔					
/ôr/ as in corn	✔					
/ûr/ as in stern	✔					
/ûr/ as in bird, suburb						
/âr/ as in air, bear						
/îr/ as in deer, ear						
Variant Vowels						
/oi/ as in boil	✔		✔			
/oi/ as in toy	✔					
/ou/ as in loud						
/ou/ as in down						
/ô/ as in law						
/ô/ as in laundry						
/ôl/ as in salt	✔					
/ôl/ as in call						
/ü/ as in moon, drew						
/ů/ as in look						
/ə/ as in askew						

How to Use the Phonics Transfer Charts

To read and speak fluently in English, English Language Learners need to master a wide range of phonemic awareness, phonics, and word study skills. The Phonics Transfer Charts are designed to help you anticipate and understand possible student errors in pronouncing or perceiving English sounds.

1. **Highlight Transferrable Skills** If the phonics skill transfers from the student's primary language to English, state that during the lesson. In most lessons an English Language Learner feature will indicate which sounds do and do not transfer in specific languages.

2. **Preteach Non-Transferrable Skills** Prior to teaching a phonics lesson, check the chart to determine if the sound and/or spelling transfers from the student's primary language into English. If it does not, preteach the sound and spelling during Small Group time. Focus on articulation, using the backs of the small **Sound-Spelling Cards**, and the minimal contrast activities provided.

3. **Provide Additional Practice and Time** If the skill does NOT transfer from the student's primary language into English, the student will require more time and practice mastering the sound and spellings. Continue to review the phonics skill during Small Group time in upcoming weeks until the student has mastered it. Use the additional resources, such as the extra decodable stories in the **Teacher's Resource Book**, to provide oral and silent reading practice.

Teaching Supports for Students Transitioning from Spanish to English

The **Sound-Spelling Cards** have been created to assist you in working with English Language Learners. For example:

1. The dotted border on many of the cards indicates that the sound transfers from Spanish to English. On these cards, the same image is used in both English and Spanish (e.g., *camel/camello*). Therefore, students learning the sound in Spanish can easily transfer that knowledge to English.

2. Students whose primary language is not English will need additional articulation support to pronounce and perceive non-transferrable English sounds. Use the articulation photos on the backs of the Sound-Spelling Cards and the student-friendly descriptions of how to form these sounds during phonics lessons.

Sound-Spelling Cards

Transfer Skill Support

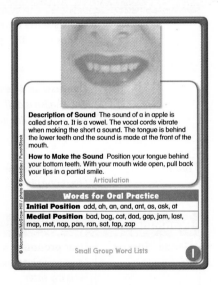

Description of Sound The sound of a in apple is called short a. It is a vowel. The vocal cords vibrate when making the short a sound. The tongue is behind the lower teeth and the sound is made at the front of the mouth.

How to Make the Sound Position your tongue behind your bottom teeth. With your mouth wide open, pull back your lips in a partial smile.

Articulation

Words for Oral Practice
Initial Position add, ah, an, and, ant, as, ask, at
Medial Position bad, bag, cat, dad, gap, jam, last, map, mat, nap, pan, ran, sat, tap, zap

Small Group Word Lists

Articulation Support

Grammar Transfers:
Grammatical Form

This chart can be used to address common mistakes that some English Language Learners make when they transfer grammatical forms from their native languages into English.

Grammatical Form	Transfer Mistakes in English	Native Language	Cause of Difficulty
Nouns			
Plural Marker -s	**Forgets plural marker -s** *I have 3 sister.*	Cantonese, Haitian Creole, Hmong, Korean, Vietnamese, Khmer	Native language does not use a plural marker.
Countable and Uncountable Nouns	**Confuses countable and uncountable nouns** *the homeworks* or *the informations*	Haitian Creole, Spanish	Countable and uncountable nouns are different in English and native language.
Possessives	**Uses prepositions to describe possessives** *the book of my brother* as opposed to *my brother's book*	Haitian Creole, Hmong, Spanish, Vietnamese	Possession is often described using a prepositional phrase.
	Avoids using 's *dog my father* as opposed to *my father's dog*	Haitian Creole, Vietnamese, Khmer	A noun follows the object in the native language.
Articles			
	Consistently omits articles *He has book. They want dog not cat.*	Cantonese, Haitian Creole, Hmong, Korean, Vietnamese, Khmer	There is no article in the native language or no difference between *the* and *a*.
	Overuses articles *The English is difficult. The soccer is popular in the Europe.*	Haitian Creole, Hmong, Spanish	Some languages use articles that are omitted in English.
a/an	**Mistakes *one* for *a/an*** *She is one nurse.*	Haitian Creole, Hmong, Vietnamese	The native language either does not use articles or uses articles differently.
Pronouns			
Gender-Specific Pronouns	**Uses pronouns with the inappropriate gender** *He is my sister.*	Cantonese, Haitian Creole, Hmong, Korean, Spanish, Khmer	The third person pronoun in the native language is gender free, or the personal pronoun is omitted.
	Uses inappropriate gender, particularly with neutral nouns *The day is sunny. She is beautiful.*	Spanish	Nouns have feminine or masculine gender in the native language, and the gender may be carried over into English.

Grammatical Form	Transfer Mistakes in English	Native Language	Cause of Difficulty
Pronouns			
Object Pronouns	**Confuses subject and object pronouns** _Her talks to me._	Cantonese, Hmong, Khmer	The same pronoun form is used for subject and object in the native language.
	Omits object pronouns _That girl is very rude, so nobody likes._	Korean, Vietnamese	The native language does not use direct objects.
Pronoun and Number Agreement	**Uses the wrong number for pronouns** _I saw many red birds. It was pretty._	Cantonese, Korean	The native language does not require number agreement.
Subject Pronouns	**Omits subject pronouns** _Mom isn't home. Is at work._	Korean, Spanish	Subject pronouns may be dropped because in the native language the verb ending gives information about the number and/or gender.
Pronouns in Clauses	**Omits pronouns in clauses** _If don't do homework, they will not learn._	Cantonese, Vietnamese	The native language does not need a subject in the subordinate clause.
Pronouns and Nouns	**Overuses pronouns with nouns** _This school, it very good._	Hmong, Vietnamese	This is popular in speech in some languages. The speaker mentions a topic, then makes a comment about it.
	Avoids pronouns and repeats nouns _Carla visits her sister every Sunday, and Carla makes a meal._	Korean, Vietnamese	In the native language, the speaker repeats nouns and does not use pronouns.
Pronoun _one_	**Omits the pronoun _one_** _I saw two dogs, and I like the small._	Spanish	Adjectives can stand alone in the native language, but English requires a noun or _one_.
Possessive Forms	**Confuses possessive forms** _The book is my._	Cantonese, Hmong, Vietnamese	Cantonese and Hmong speakers tend to omit the final _n_ sound, which may create confusion between _my_ and _mine_.

Grammar Transfers:
Grammatical Form

Grammatical Form	Transfer Mistakes in English	Native Language	Cause of Difficulty
Verbs			
Present Tense	**Omits -s in present tense, third person agreement** *He like pizza.*	Cantonese, Haitian Creole, Hmong, Korean, Vietnamese, Khmer	Subject-verb agreement is not used in the native language.
Irregular Verbs	**Has problems with irregular subject-verb agreement** *Tom and Sue has a new car.*	Cantonese, Hmong, Korean, Khmer	Verbs' forms do not change to show the number of the subject in the native language.
Inflectional Endings	**Omits tense markers** *I study English yesterday.*	Cantonese, Haitian Creole, Hmong, Korean, Vietnamese, Khmer	The native language does not use inflectional endings to change verb tense.
Present and Future Tenses	**Incorrectly uses the present tense for the future tense** *I go next week.*	Cantonese, Korean	The native language may use the present tense to imply the future tense.
Negative Statements	**Omits helping verbs in negative statements** *Sue no coming to school.*	Cantonese, Korean, Spanish	The native language does not use helping verbs in negative statements.
Present-Perfect Tense	**Avoids the present-perfect tense** *Marcos live here for three months.*	Haitian Creole, Vietnamese	The native language does not use the present-perfect verb form.
Past-Continuous Tense	**Uses the past-continuous tense for recurring action in the past** *When I was young, I was talking a lot.*	Korean, Spanish	In the native language, the past-continuous tense is used but in English the expression *used to* or the simple past tense is used.
Main Verb	**Omits the main verb** *Talk in class not good.*	Cantonese	Cantonese does not require an infinitive marker when using a verb as a noun. Speakers may confuse the infinitive for the main verb.
Main Verbs in Clauses	**Uses two or more main verbs in one clause without any connectors** *I took a book went studied at the library.*	Hmong	In Hmong, verbs can be used consecutively without conjunctions or punctuation.
Linking Verbs	**Omits the linking verb** *He hungry.*	Cantonese, Haitian Creole, Hmong, Vietnamese, Khmer	In some languages, *be* is implied in the adjective form. In other languages, the concept is expressed with a verb.
Helping Verb in Passive Voice	**Omits the helping verb in the passive voice** *The homework done.*	Cantonese, Vietnamese	In Cantonese and Vietnamese, the passive voice does not require a helping verb.

Grammatical Form	Transfer Mistakes in English	Native Language	Cause of Difficulty
Verbs			
Passive Voice	**Avoids the passive voice** *They speak English here.* *One speaks English here.* *English is spoken here.*	Haitian Creole	The passive voice does not exist in the native language.
Transitive Verbs	**Confuses transitive and intransitive verbs** *The child broke.* *The child broke <u>the plate</u>.*	Cantonese, Korean, Spanish	Verbs that require a direct object differ between English and the native language.
Phrasal Verbs	**Confuses related phrasal verbs** *I ate at the apple.* *I ate up the apple.*	Korean, Spanish	Phrasal verbs are not used in the native language, and there is often confusion over their meaning.
Have and *be*	**Uses *have* instead of *be*** *I have thirst.* *He has right.*	Spanish	Spanish and English have different uses for *have* and *be*.
Adjectives			
Word Order	**Places adjectives after nouns** *I saw a car red.*	Haitian Creole, Hmong, Spanish, Vietnamese, Khmer	Nouns often precede adjectives in the native language.
	Consistently places adjectives after nouns *This is a lesson new.*	Cantonese, Korean	Adjectives always follow nouns in the native language.
-er and *-est* Endings	**Avoids *-er* and *-est* endings** *I am more old than you.*	Hmong, Korean, Spanish, Khmer	The native language shows comparative and superlative forms with separate words.
-ing and *-ed* Endings	**Confuses *-ing* and *-ed* forms** *Math is bored.*	Cantonese, Korean, Spanish, Khmer	Adjectives in the native language do not have active and passive meanings.
Adverbs			
Adjectives and Adverbs	**Uses an adjective where an adverb is needed** *Talk quiet.*	Haitian Creole, Hmong, Khmer	Adjectives and adverb forms are interchangeable in the native language.
Word Order	**Places adverbs before verbs** *He quickly ran.* *He ran quickly.*	Cantonese, Korean	Adverbs usually come before verbs in the native language, and this tendency is carried over into English.
Prepositions			
	Omits prepositions *I like come school.*	Cantonese	Cantonese does not use prepositions the way that English does.

Grammar Transfers

How to Use the Grammar Transfer Charts

The grammar of many languages differs widely from English. For example, a student's primary language may use a different word order than English, may not use parts of speech in the same way, or may use different verb tenses. The Grammar Transfer Charts are designed to help you anticipate and understand possible student errors in speaking and writing standard English. With all grammar exercises, the emphasis is on oral communication, both as a speaker and listener.

1. **Highlight Transferrable Skills** If the grammar skill transfers from the student's primary language to English, state that during the lesson. In many lessons an English Language Learner feature will indicate which skills do and do not transfer.

2. **Preteach Non-Transferrable Skills** Prior to teaching a grammar lesson, check the chart to determine if the skill transfers from the student's primary language into English. If it does not, preteach the skill during Small Group time. Provide sentence frames and ample structured opportunities to use the skill in spoken English. Students need to talk, talk, and talk some more to master these skills.

3. **Provide Additional Practice and Time** If the skill does NOT transfer from the student's primary language into English, the student will require more time and practice mastering it. Continue to review the skill during Small Group time. Use the additional resources, such as the grammar lessons in the **Intervention Kit** (K–3) or review lessons, in upcoming weeks.

4. **Use Contrastive Analysis** Tell students when a skill does not transfer and include contrastive analysis work to make the student aware of how to correct their speaking and writing for standard English. For example, when a student uses an incorrect grammatical form, write the student sentence on a **WorkBoard**. Then write the correct English form underneath. Explain the difference between the student's primary language and English. Have the student correct several other sentences using this skill, such as sentences in their Writer's Notebooks.

5. **Increase Writing and Speaking Opportunities** Increase the amount of structured writing and speaking opportunities for students needing work on specific grammatical forms. Sentence starters and paragraph frames, such as those found in the lessons, are ideal for both written and oral exercises.

6. **Focus on Meaning** Always focus on the meanings of sentences in all exercises. As they improve and fine-tune their English speaking and writing skills, work with students on basic comprehension of spoken and written English.

To help students move to the next level of language acquisition and master English grammatical forms, recast their responses during classroom discussions or provide additional language for them to use as they respond further. Provide leveled-language sentence frames orally or in writing for students to use as they respond to questions and prompts. Below are samples.

English Language Learner Response Chart

Beginning (will respond by pointing or saying one word answers)	**Sample Frames** (simple, short sentences) *I see a _____.* *This is a _____.* *I like the _____.*
Early Intermediate (will respond with phrases or simple sentences)	**Sample Frames** (simple sentences with adjectives and adverbs added, and compound subjects or predicates) *I see a _____ _____.* *The _____ animal is _____.* *There are _____ and _____.*
Intermediate (will respond with simple sentences and limited academic language)	**Sample Frames** (harder sentences with simple phrases in consistent patterns; some academic language included) *The animal's prey is _____ because _____.* *The main idea is _____ because _____.* *He roamed the park so that _____.*
Early Advanced (will begin to use more sophisticated sentences and some academic language)	**Sample Frames** (complex sentences with increased academic language, beginning phrases and clauses, and multiple-meaning words) *When the violent storm hit, _____.* *As a result of the revolution, the army_____.* *Since most endangered animals are _____, they _____.*
Advanced (will have mastered some more complex sentence structures and is increasing the amount of academic language used)	Use the questions and prompts provided in the lessons for the whole group. Provide additional support learning and using academic language. These words are boldfaced throughout the lessons and sentence starters are often provided.

Cognates

Cognates are words in two languages that look alike and have the same or similar meaning (e.g., *school/escuela, telephone/teléfono*) and can be helpful resources for English Language Learners. This list identifies some Spanish cognates for the academic language used during the lessons.

Students must also be aware of false cognates—words that look similar in two languages, but have different meanings, such as *soap* in English and *sopa* (meaning *soup*) in Spanish.

accent	*acento*	**context**	*contexto*
action	*acción*	**contrast**	*contrastar*
action verb	*verbo de acción*	**definition**	*definición*
adjective	*adjetivo*	**demonstrative**	*demostrativo*
adverb	*adverbio*	**denotation**	*denotación*
alphabetical order	*orden alfabético*	**description**	*descripción*
analogy	*analogía*	**dialogue**	*diálogo*
analyze	*analizar*	**dictionary**	*diccionario*
antecedent	*antecedente*	**direct**	*directo*
antonym	*antónimo*	**effect**	*efecto*
apostrophe	*apóstrofe*	**evaluate**	*evaluar*
article	*artículo*	**event**	*evento*
author	*autor*	**example**	*ejemplo*
cause	*causa*	**exclamation**	*exclamación*
classify	*clasificar*	**family**	*familia*
combine	*combinar*	**fantasy**	*fantasía*
compare	*comparar*	**figurative**	*figurativo*
complex	*complejo*	**fragment**	*fragmento*
comprehension	*comprensión*	**future**	*futuro*
conclusion	*conclusión*	**generalization**	*generalización*
confirm	*confirmar*	**generalize**	*generalizar*
conjunction	*conjunción*	**glossary**	*glosario*
connotation	*connotación*	**Greek**	*Griego*
consonant	*consonante*	**homophone**	*homófono*

idea	*idea*	**prefix**	*prefijo*
identify	*identificar*	**preposition**	*preposición*
illustration	*ilustración*	**prepositional**	*preposicional*
indirect	*indirecto*	**present**	*presente*
introduction	*introducción*	**problem**	*problema*
irregular	*irregular*	**pronunciation**	*pronunciación*
language	*lenguaje*	**punctuation**	*puntuación*
Latin	*Latín*	**reality**	*realidad*
myth	*mito*	**relationship**	*relación*
negative	*negativo*	**sequence**	*secuencia*
object	*objeto*	**singular**	*singular*
opinion	*opinión*	**solution**	*solución*
order	*orden*	**structure**	*estructura*
origin	*orígen*	**subject**	*sujeto*
paragraph	*párrafo*	**suffix**	*sufijo*
part	*parte*	**syllable**	*sílaba*
perspective	*perspectiva*	**synonym**	*sinónimo*
persuasion	*persuación*	**technique**	*técnica*
phrase	*frase*	**text**	*texto*
plural	*plural*	**theme**	*tema*
possessive adjective	*adjetivo posesivo*	**verb**	*verbo*
predicate	*predicado*	**visualize**	*visualizar*
prediction	*predicción*	**vowel**	*vocal*

ELL ENGLISH LANGUAGE LEARNERS

The **English Language Learners** in your classroom have a variety of backgrounds. An increasing proportion of English Language Learners are born in the United States. Some of these students are just starting school in the primary grades; others are long-term English Language Learners, with underdeveloped academic skills. Some students come from their native countries with a strong educational foundation. The academic skills of these newly arrived students are well developed and parallel the skills of their native English-speaking peers. Other English Learners immigrate to the United States with little academic experience.

These English Learners are not "blank slates." Their oral language proficiency and literacy in their first languages can be used to facilitate literacy development in English. Systematic, explicit, and appropriately scaffolded instruction and sufficient time help English Learners attain English proficiency and meet high standards in core academic subjects.

Beginning

This level of language proficiency is often referred to as the "silent" stage, in which students' receptive skills are engaged. It is important that teachers and peers respect a language learner's initial silence or allow the student to respond in his or her native language. It is often difficult for teachers to identify the level of cognitive development at this stage, due to the limited proficiency in the second language. It is important to realize that these beginning students have a wide range of abilities in their first language. They are able to transfer knowledge and skills from their first language as they develop English and learn grade-level content. Beginning students include those with limited formal schooling: young students just starting school, as well as older students. Other beginning students have had schooling in their native language and are academically parallel to nativeEnglish-speaking peers.

The Beginning Student...

- recognizes English phonemes that correspond to phonemes produced in primary language;
- is able to apply transferable grammar concepts and skills from the primary language;
- initially demonstrates more receptive than productive English skills;
- produces English vocabulary to communicate basic needs in social and academic settings;
- responds by pointing to, nodding, gesturing, acting out, and manipulating objects/pictures;
- speaks in one-or two-word responses as language develops;
- draws pictures and writes letters and sounds being learned.

Early Intermediate

At this level, students are considered more advanced beginning English Learners. They are developing early production skills, but their receptive skills are much more advanced than their speaking ability. At this stage it is critical that the students continue to listen to model speakers.

The Early Intermediate Student...

- recognizes English phonemes that correspond to phonemes produced in primary language;
- is able to apply transferable grammar concepts and skills from the primary language;
- understands more spoken English than the beginning student;
- speaks in one- or two-word utterances;
- may respond with phrases or sentences;
- produces English vocabulary words and phrases to communicate basic needs in social and academic settings;
- begins to ask questions, role-play, and retell;
- begins to use routine expressions;
- demonstrates an internalization of English grammar and usage by recognizing and correcting some errors when speaking and reading aloud;
- increases correct usage of written and oral language conventions.

Intermediate

Students at this level begin to tailor their English language skills to meet communication and learning demands with increasing accuracy. They possess vocabulary and knowledge of grammatical structures that allow them to more fully participate in classroom activities and discussions. They are generally more comfortable producing both spoken and written language.

The Intermediate Student...

- pronounces most English phonemes correctly while reading aloud;
- can identify more details of information that has been presented orally or in writing;
- uses more complex vocabulary and sentences to communicate needs and express ideas;
- uses specific vocabulary learned, including academic language;
- participates more fully in discussions with peers and adults;
- reads and comprehends a wider range of reading materials;
- writes brief narratives and expository texts;
- demonstrates an internalization of English grammar and usage by recognizing and correcting errors when speaking and reading aloud.

Early Advanced

Students at this language proficiency level possess vocabulary and grammar structures that approach those of an English-proficient speaker. These students demonstrate consistent general comprehension of grade-level content that is presented.

The Early Advanced Student...

- applies knowledge of common English morphemes in oral and silent reading;
- understands increasingly more nonliteral social and academic language;
- responds using extensive vocabulary;
- participates in and initiates more extended social conversations with peers and adults;
- communicates orally and in writing with fewer grammatical errors;
- reads with good comprehension a wide range of narrative and expository texts;
- writes using more standard forms of English on various content-area topics;
- becomes more creative and analytical when writing.

Advanced

The student at this language proficiency level communicates effectively with peers and adults in both social and academic situations. Students can understand grade-level text but still need some English language development support, such as preteaching concepts and skills. While the English language proficiency of these students is advanced, some linguistic support for accessing content is still necessary.

The Advanced Student...

- understands increasingly more nonliteral social and academic language;
- responds using extensive vocabulary;
- communicates orally and in writing with infrequent errors;
- creates more complex narratives and expository writing in all content areas.

English Language Learner Profiles
Facilitating Language Growth

Beginning

Student's Behaviors	Teacher's Behaviors	Questioning Techniques
■ Points to or provides other nonverbal responses ■ Actively listens ■ Responds to commands ■ Understands more than he or she can produce	■ Gestures ■ Focuses on conveying meanings and vocabulary development ■ Does not force students to speak ■ Shows visuals and real objects ■ Writes words for students to see ■ Pairs students with more proficient learners ■ Provides speaking and writing frames and models	■ Point to the _____. ■ Find the _____. ■ Put the _____ next to the _____. ■ Do you have the _____? ■ Is this the _____? ■ Who wants the _____?

Early Intermediate

Student's Behaviors	Teacher's Behaviors	Questioning Techniques
■ Speaks in one- or two-word utterances ■ Uses short phrases and simple sentences ■ Listens with greater understanding	■ Asks questions that can be answered by yes/no ■ Asks either/or questions ■ Asks higher-order questions with one-word answers ■ Models correct responses ■ Ensures supportive, low-anxiety environment ■ Does not overtly call attention to grammar errors ■ Asks short "wh" questions	■ Yes/no (Did you like the story?) ■ Either/or (Is this a pencil or a crayon?) ■ One-word responses (Why did the dog hide?) ■ General questions that encourage lists of words (What did you see in the book bag?) ■ Two-word responses (Where did I put the pen?)

Intermediate

Student's Behaviors	Teacher's Behaviors	Questioning Techniques
■ Demonstrates comprehension in a variety of ways ■ Speaks in short phrases or sentences ■ Begins to use language more freely	■ Provides frequent comprehension checks ■ Asks open-ended questions that stimulate language production	■ Why? ■ How? ■ How is this like that? ■ Tell me about _____. ■ Talk about _____. ■ Describe _____. ■ What is in your book bag?

Early Advanced

Student's Behaviors	Teacher's Behaviors	Questioning Techniques
■ Participates in reading and writing activities to acquire information ■ Demonstrates increased levels of accuracy and correctness and is able to express thoughts and feelings ■ Produces language with varied grammatical structures and academic language ■ May experience difficulties in abstract, cognitively demanding subjects	■ Fosters conceptual development and expanded literacy through content ■ Continues to make lessons comprehensible and interactive ■ Teaches thinking and study skills ■ Continues to be alert to individual differences in language and culture	■ What would you recommend/why? ■ How do you think this story will end? ■ What is this story about? ■ What is your favorite part of the story? ■ Describe/compare _____. How are these similar/different? ■ What would happen if _____? ■ Why do you think that? Yes, tell me more about _____.

Fostering Classroom Discussions

Strategies for English Language Learners

One of the most effective ways in which to increase the oral language proficiency of your English Language Learners is to give students many opportunities to do a lot of talking in the classroom. Providing the opportunities and welcoming all levels of participation will motivate students to take part in the class discussions. You can employ a few basic teaching strategies that will encourage the participation of all language proficiency levels of English Language Learners in whole class and small group discussions.

☑ WAIT/DIFFERENT RESPONSES

- Be sure to give students enough time to answer the question.
- Let students know that they can respond in different ways depending on their levels of proficiency. Students can
  - answer in their native language;
  - ask a more proficient ELL speaker to repeat the answer in English;
  - answer with nonverbal cues (pointing to related objects, drawing, or acting out).

> **Teacher:** Where is Charlotte?
>
> **ELL Response:** (Student points to the web in the corner of the barn.)
>
> **Teacher:** Yes. Charlotte is sitting in her web. Let's all point to Charlotte.

☑ REPEAT

- Give positive confirmation to the answers that each English Language Learner offers. If the response is correct, repeat what the student has said in a clear, loud voice and at a slower pace. This validation will motivate other ELLs to participate.

> **Teacher:** How would you describe the faces of the bobcats?
>
> **ELL Response:** They look scared.
>
> **Teacher:** That's right, Silvia. They are scared. Everyone show me your scared face.

☑ REVISE FOR FORM

- Repeating an answer allows you to model the proper form for a response. You can model how to answer in full sentences and use academic language.
- When you repeat the answer, correct any grammar or pronunciation errors.

> **Teacher:** Who are the main characters in the story *Zathura*?
>
> **ELL Response:** Danny and Walter is.
>
> **Teacher:** Yes. Danny and Walter <u>are</u> the main characters. Remember to use the verb <u>are</u> when you are telling about more than one person. Let's repeat the sentence.
>
> **All:** Danny and Walter <u>are</u> the main characters.

☑ REVISE FOR MEANING

■ Repeating an answer offers an opportunity to clarify the meaning of a response.

> **Teacher:** Where did the golden feather come from?
>
> **ELL Response:** The bird.
>
> **Teacher:** That's right. The golden feather came from the Firebird.

☑ ELABORATE

■ If students give a one-word answer or a nonverbal cue, elaborate on the answer to model fluent speaking and grammatical patterns.

■ Provide more examples or repeat the answer using proper academic language.

> **Teacher:** Why is the girls' mother standing with her hands on her hips?
>
> **ELL Response:** She is mad.
>
> **Teacher:** Can you tell me more? Why is she mad?
>
> **ELL Response:** Because the girls are late.
>
> **Teacher:** Ok. What do you think the girls will do?
>
> **ELL Response:** They will promise not to be late again.
>
> **Teacher:** Anyone else have an idea?

☑ ELICIT

■ Prompt students to give a more comprehensive response by asking additional questions or guiding them to get to an answer.

> **Teacher:** Listen as I read the caption under the photograph. What information does the caption tell us?
>
> **ELL Response:** It tells about the butterfly.
>
> **Teacher:** What did you find out about the butterfly?
>
> **ELL Response:** It drinks nectar.
>
> **Teacher:** Yes. The butterfly drinks nectar from the flower.

Making the Most of Classroom Conversations

Use all the speaking and listening opportunities in your classroom to observe students' oral language proficiency.

■ Response to oral presentations

■ Responding to text aloud

■ Following directions

■ Group projects

■ Small Group work

■ Informal, social peer discussions

■ One-on-one conferences

The **English Language Learner Resource Book** provides Speaking and Listening Checklists to help you monitor students' oral language proficiency growth.

Treasures
Support for Students with Dyslexia

Characteristics of Dyslexia

A student with dyslexia is a student who continually struggles with reading and spelling but displays an ability to learn when there are no print materials involved. Even though the student receives the same classroom instruction as most other students, he continues to have difficulties with reading and spelling.

Students identified with dyslexia often have difficulties in the following areas

- reading words in isolation
- decoding nonsense words accurately
- oral reading (slow and inaccurate)
- learning to spell

The difficulties in these areas are usually the result of student's struggles with:

- phonological awareness: segmenting, blending, and manipulating words
- naming letters and pronouncing their sounds.
- phonological memory
- rapid naming of the letters of the alphabet or familiar objects

Effective Instruction

To address the needs of a student with dyslexia, instruction should be delivered in small groups. The instruction should be explicit, intensive, employ multisensory methods, as needed, and be individualized. It should include instruction on:

- phonemic awareness that has students detect, segment, blend and manipulate sounds
- phonics, emphasizing the sound/symbol relationships for decoding and encoding words
- morphology, semantics and syntax
- fluency with patterns of language
- strategies for decoding, encoding, word recognition, fluency and comprehension

Resources:
The International Dyslexia Association Website: www.interdys.org
The Dyslexia Handbook: Procedures Concerning Dyslexia and Related Disorders (Revised 2007) Texas Education Agency, Austin, TX, Publication Number: GE8721001

Treasures Reading and Language Arts Program

Treasures is a scientifically-based core program that offers sequential, explicit, and effective instruction in phonological awareness, phonics, morphology, fluency, vocabulary, and reading comprehension. Students are given many opportunities to practice and review these skills to help prevent reading difficulties before they begin.

INTERVENTION

Weekly Small Group Lessons
Intervention Teacher's Editions

Tier 2 Instruction is provided in weekly small group lessons in the **Treasures** Teacher's Editions. These lessons provide targeted instruction in priority skills taught in the week. **Tier 2 Intervention Teacher's Editions** provide additional instruction for struggling students in the areas of phonemic awareness, phonics, vocabulary, fluency, and comprehension, grammar and writing.

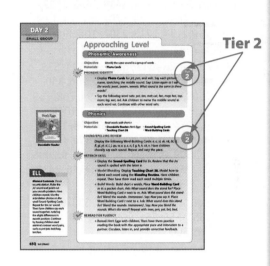

INTERVENTION

Reading Triumphs
Intervention Program

Reading Triumphs provides intensive instruction. Explicit, sequential lessons delivered through clear instructional routines for all the key components of reading are embedded in the program. The "no assumption instruction" allows for both teacher and student success.

A

Key 1 = Unit 1

Key 1 = Unit 1

G

Genre

Key 1 = Unit 1

H

I

J

Key 1 = Unit 1

R

S

W

Key 1 = Unit 1

Acknowledgments

"Alicia's Happy Day" by Meg Starr, illustrated by Ying-hwa Hu & Cornelius Van Wright. Text copyright © 2002 by Meg Starr. Illustrations copyright © 2002 by Ying-hwa Hu & Cornelius Van Wright. Published by arrangement with Star Bright Books.

"Bus Stops" by Taro Gomi. Copyright © 1987 by Taro Gomi. English text copyright © 1988 by Chronicle Books, LLC. First published in Japan by Kaisei-sha Publishing Co., Ltd., Tokyo. English translation rights arranged through Japan Foreign Rights Center. Published by arrangement with Chronicle Books, LLC, San Francisco, California, USA. All rights reserved.

"Russ and the Firehouse" by Janet Elizabeth Rickert, photographs by Pete McGahan. Copyright © 2000 by Janet Elizabeth Rickert. Published by arrangement with Woodbine House, Inc.

"The Park" from CRICKETY CRICKET! by James S. Tippitt. Reprinted by permission of HarperCollins Publishers.

"Won't You Be My Neighbor? (It's A Beautiful Day In This Neighborhood) from MISTER ROGERS' NEIGHBORHOOD. Words and Music by Fred Rogers. Copyright © 1967 Fred M. Rogers. Copyright renewed. International Copyright Secured.

Book Covers

BE MY NEIGHBOR. Reprinted by permission of Charlesbridge Publishing.

CAREER DAY. Reprinted by permission of HarperCollins Publishers.

COMMUNITY HELPERS FROM A TO Z. Reprinted by permission of Crabtree Publishing Company.

HI, CAT! Reprinted by Simon & Schuster Children's Publishing Division.

MISS BINDERGARTEN TAKES A FIELD TRIP. Reprinted by permission of Penguin Putnam Books for Young Readers.

MY STREET. Reprinted by permission of EDC Publishing.

ON THE TOWN. Reprinted by permission of HarperCollins Publishers.

ONE AFTERNOON. Reprinted by permission of Orchard Books, a division of Scholastic, Inc.

WAKE UP, CITY! Reprinted by permission of HarperCollins Publishers.

Photography Credits

All Photographs are by Ken Cavanagh or Ken Karp for Macmillan/McGraw-Hill (MMH) except as noted below:

xiii: Veer. 1301: Brad Perks Lightscapes/Alamy. 1308: Seizo TERASAKI. 1385: Medioimages/PunchStock. 1392: Seizo TERASAKI. 1469: Rich Reid/National Geographic/AGE Fotostock. 1476: Seizo TERASAKI. 1553: Pixtal/PunchStock.

Use this page to record lessons that work well or need to be adapted for future reference.

Lessons that work well.

Lessons that need adjustments.

Use this page to record lessons that work well or need to be adapted for future reference.

Lessons that work well.

Lessons that need adjustments.

Use this page to record lessons that work well or need to be adapted for future reference.

Lessons that work well.

Lessons that need adjustments.